SOCIAL PROBLEMS IN INDIA

SOCIAL PROBLEMS IN INDIA

N.G. Pendse
Sukanta Sarkar

ISBN : 978-93-5128-106-1

Price : ₹ 900

First Published, 2015

Published by

Kalpaz Publications
C-30, Satyawati Nagar
Delhi-110052, Ph. : 9212142040
E-mail: kalpaz@hotmail.com

Laser Typesetting : Future Computer, Delhi
Printed at : G. Print Process, Delhi

Cataloging in Publication Data—DK
Courtesy: D.K. Agencies (P) Ltd. <docinfo@dkagencies.com>

Sarkar, Sukanta, author.
Social problems in India / Sukanta Sarkar.
pages cm
Includes bibliographical references (pages).
ISBN 9789351281061

1. Social problems—India. I. Title.

DDC 361.10954 23

Contents

Preface

Human society is a group of people involved in persistent interpersonal relationships, or a large social grouping sharing the same geographical or social territory. More broadly, a society may be illustrated as an economic, social, or industrial infrastructure, made up of varied collection of individuals. Members of a society may be from different ethnic groups. Society, in general, addresses the fact that an individual has limited means rather as an autonomous unit. Human societies are organised most often according to their primary means of subsistence. Societies may also be structured politically. Societies are social groups that differ according to subsistence strategies, the ways that humans use technology their needs for. The main form of food production in such societies is the daily collection of wild plants and the hunting of wild animals. Hunter move around constantly in search of food. Fruits and vegetables grown in garden plots cleared from the jungle or forest provide the main source of food in a horticultural society. Agrarian societies use agricultural technological advances to cultivate crops over a large area. As access to electronic information resources increased at the beginning of the 21st century, special attention was extended from the information on society to the societal knowledge. People of many nations united by common political and cultural traditions, beliefs, or values sometimes are also said to form a society.

In this connection, we want to place on record our deep appreciation to Professor Ajay Pathak, Vice-chancellor, ICFAI University, Tripura, Agartala for providing valuable inputs. We desire to express our heartiest thanks to Professor B.K.Panda, Department of Economics, Berhampur University, Odisha who despite his busy schedule and hectic academic engagements, all the time has encouraged and supported us. We are also beholden to Professor Md. Atuar Rahman, Department of Agriculture, International University of Business Agriculture and Technology, Dhaka,

Bangladesh whose erudition and scholarly tidbits for preparing are still afresh in our mind. We also thank Dr Pradeep Kumar Pandey, Centre for Judicial Studies, Dibrugarh University, Assam; Dr Rakesh Joshi, Department of Economics, Saurashtra University, Gujarat; Dr D. Pulla Rao, Department of Economics, Andhra University; Dr Vibhuti Patel, Professor-cum-Director, Centre for Study of Social Exclusion and Inclusive Policy, SNDT Women's University, Mumbai; Dr Wakar Amin, Department of Social Work, University of Kashmir, J & K.; Dr Shazia Manzoor, Assistant professor, Department of Social Work, University of Kashmir, J & K; Dr Pallab Kanti Ghoshal, Department of Commerce, Netaji Subhas College, Udaipur, for their valuable suggestions and moral support.

We are heartily grateful to Professor R. Prasad, Professor Ashish Kumar Shivastava and Professor L.S. Nigam, Pandit Ravishankar Shukla University, Raipur, Chhatisgarh who have always encouraged us to carry on this constructive work. Further, we express our heartily thanks to each and every person who directly/indirectly helped us in preparing this work.

It is hoped that this book will be very useful to society in general and students of sociology in particular. Comments and suggestions are most welcome.

Professor N.G. Pendse
Dr Sukanta Sarkar

Abbreviations

ADJ	:	Additional District Judge
AEC	:	African Economic Community
AIDS	:	Acquired Immune Deficiency Syndrome
ATT	:	Arms Trade Treaty
ATTF	:	All Tripura Tiger Force
AUWSP	:	Accelerated Urban Water Supply Programme
CACP	:	Commission on Agricultural Cost and Price
CBDT	:	Central Board of Direct Taxes
CBN	:	Central Bureau of Narcotics
CBSI	:	Caribbean Basin Security Initiative
CCPA	:	Child Care and Protection Act
CPARG	:	Canadian Pediatric AIDS Research Group
CRC	:	Convention on the Rights of the Child
CVC	:	Central Vigilance Commission
DLF	:	Darfur Liberation Front
DoE	:	Department of Education
DROC	:	Democratic Republic of Congo
DUP	:	Democratic Unionist Party
ECOWAS	:	Economic Community of West African States
FGM	:	Female Genital Mutilation
GIRoA	:	Government of the Islamic Republic of Afghanistan
GWOT	:	Global War on Terrorism
HCR	:	Head Count Ratio
HPI	:	Human Poverty Index
HUDCO	:	Housing and Urban Development Corporation Limited
HYV	:	High Yield Variety
ICMPD	:	International Centre for Migration Policy Development
IDSMT	:	Integrated Development of Small & Medium Towns
IDUs	:	Injecting Drug Users
IGR	:	Income Gap Ratio
IHL	:	International Humanitarian Law
ILO	:	International Labour Organisation
IRDP	:	Integrated Rural Development Programme
ISACS	:	International Small Arms Control Standards
ISI	:	Inter-Services Intelligence
JEI-K	:	Jamaat-e-Islami (Kashmir)

JeM	:	Jaish-e-Mohammed
JEM	:	Justice and Equality Movement
JKLF	:	Jammu and Kashmir Liberation Front
JNNURM	:	Jawaharlal Nehru National Urban Renewal Mission
MCC	:	Maoist Communist Centre
MCPS	:	Monopoly Cotton Procurement Scheme
MIDS	:	Madras Institute of Development Studies
MoU	:	Memorandum of Understanding
MoUD	:	Ministry of Urban Development
NACO	:	National AIDS Control Organisation
NACP	:	National AIDS Control Programme
NCLP	:	National Child Labour Project
NCRB	:	National Crime Records Bureau
NCRL	:	National Commission on Rural Labour
NEP	:	New Economic/Industrial Policy
NHRC	:	National Human Rights Commission
NLFT	:	National Liberation Front of Tripura
NSSO	:	National Sample Survey Organisation
OAU	:	Organisation of African Unity
PFDS	:	Pooled Finance Development Scheme
PMRY	:	Prime Minister's Rozgar (Employment) Scheme
POA	:	Programme of Action
PPP	:	Purchasing-Power Parity
PWG	:	Peoples' War Group
SACS	:	State AIDS Control Societies
SADC	:	Southern African Development Community
NAF	:	National Alliance Forces
SALW	:	Small Arms and Light Weapons
SC	:	Supreme Court
SEEUY	:	Self-Employment Scheme for Educated Unemployed Youth
SIT	:	Special Investigation Team
SLA	:	Sudan Liberation Army
SLM/A	:	Sudan Liberation Movement/Army
SLM	:	Sudan Liberation Movement
SPLA	:	Sudan People's Liberation Army
TFWP	:	Temporary Foreign Worker Program
TI	:	Transparency International's
TRYSEM	:	Training of Rural Youth for Self-Employment
ULBs	:	Urban Local Bodies
ULFA	:	United Liberation Front of Asom
UN	:	United Nations
NUITA	:	National Union for the Total Independence of Angola
UNODA	:	United Nations Office for Disarmament Affairs
UNODC	:	UN Office on Drugs and Crime
VZV	:	Varicella zoster Virus
WHO	:	World Health Organisation

1

Child Marriage

"The greatest destroyer of peace is abortion because if a mother can kill her own child, what is left for me to kill you and you to kill me? There is nothing between."

- Mother Teresa

Introduction

A child is generally a human between the stages of birth and puberty. There are many social issues that affect children, such as childhood education, bullying, child poverty, dysfunctional families and in developing countries, hunger. The United Nations Convention on the Rights of the Child defines child as *"a human being below the age of 18 years unless under the law applicable to the child, majority is attained earlier."* Children generally have fewer rights than adults and are classed as those unable to make serious decisions, and legally must always be under the care of a responsible adult. Social attitudes toward children differ around the world in various cultures. These attitudes have changed over time. Protection of children from abuse is considered an important contemporary goal. The age at which children are considered responsible for their society-bound actions has changed over time and this is reflected in the way they are treated in courts of law.[1] Investing financial resources to help children survive and develop to their full potential is, first and foremost, a moral imperative. Programmes that invest in early childhood development could generate considerable cost savings for Government. Investments in children are increasingly seen as one of best and most valuable long-term investments we can make.[2] Although some may regard art education as a luxury, simple creative activities are some of the building blocks of child development. Learning to create and appreciate visual aesthetics may be more important than ever to the development of the next generation of children as they grow up.[3]

Marriage is a socially or ritually recognised union or legal contract between spouses that establishes rights and obligations between them, and their children, and between them and their in-laws. Individuals may marry for several reasons, including legal, social, libidinal, emotional, financial, spiritual, and religious purposes. Marriage can be recognised by a state, an organisation, a religious authority, a tribal group, a local community or peers. Since the late twentieth century, major social changes in western countries have led to changes in the demographics of marriage, with the age of first marriage increasing, fewer people marrying, and many couples choosing to cohabit rather than marry.[4]

What is Child Marriage?

Child marriage is defined as a formal marriage or informal union entered into by an individual before reaching the age of 18. While child marriage is observed for both boys and girls, the overwhelming majority of those affected by the practice are girls, most of whom are in poor socioeconomic situations. Child marriage, defined as a formal marriage or informal union before age 18, is a reality for both boys and girls, although girls are disproportionately the most affected. UNICEF works with communities to rise the age of marriage and address gender discrimination through awareness rising and community discussions at local and national levels and assists governments in strengthening national legislation, policies and services.[5] Early marriage refers to any marriage before the legal age which may differ from country to country. It is not only a violation of a girl's rights; it also seriously compromises with efforts to reduce gender-based violence, advance education, overcome poverty and improve health indicators for girls and women.

Reasons Behind

There are many factors which sustain the continuation of the practice of child marriage in India. Poverty and social norms intended to ensure family honour and protect girls are significant factors that increase the risks for a girl to be married while still a child.[6] There is a strong correlation between child marriage and education. Higher levels of education are associated with lower child marriage rates. Education can play an important role in empowering girls and offering them alternative opportunities for future. Drop-out trends show some associations with the trends in child marriage. While drop-out rates tend to increase the higher the class group, child marriage incidence tends to be higher in late adolescence, as suggested by the median age for marriage.[7] Bangladesh has one of the highest rates of child marriage in the world, with 20 per cent of girls becoming spoues before their 15th birthday, even though 18 is the minimum age allowed by law. It means they are totally dependent on their families to support, protect and pay their dowries. That's the money a father must pay to a future husband to secure a marriage.[8]

Global Perspectives

Child marriage is very common in poor countries of the Third World. Despite various government and non-governmental initiatives to stem child marriage, parents are continuing to marry off their underage daughters. Early marriage is a big problem for Bangladesh. According to UNICEF's 2011 State of the World's Children report, about a third of women in Bangladesh aged 20-24 are married by the age of 15, and 66 per cent of girls will double before their 18th birthday. The root causes of child marriage are continuing to prompt parents to marry girls off before they reach adulthood. According to the 1929 national Child Marriage Restraint Act, it is illegal for parents to marry off children under 18.[9] In Nepal, with a population of about 30 million, over half the adults married when they were still children. A UNICEF study reports that 60 per cent of Nepalese women were married by the time they reach 18. Now the Nepalese government and human rights groups are working together to help such children and teenagers. The key to the problem is getting children to stay in schools once they are there. According to Nepalese law, a person must be at least 20 years old to get married, but people are not punished, if they do not obey.[10]

The annual number of child marriages in Pakistan remains unknown. It is believed most such forced marriages, many occurring in relatively remote rural areas, go unreported. Amnesty International in a report in 2002 found such marriages widespread, despite increased awareness about violence against women in all forms. The United Nations Development Fund for Women has been campaigning against forced marriages in Pakistan, but for the present, despite these efforts, the trend continues. The Sindh and Southern Punjab region is one of the most impoverished in the country, and research carried out into the issue indicates this as a key factor in the increase in such unlawful unions, with parents often tempted to sell off young girls in exchange for the high price offered by grooms, often many times the age of their *'brides'*. Under Pakistani law, the Child Marriage Restraint Act of 1929 states no female under 16 or male less than 18 may marry. But like other pieces of legislation aimed at protecting the most vulnerable members of Pakistani society, the law is rarely enforced.[11]

Former British Prime Minister Gordon Brown has announced that *"child marriage-free zones"* are to be set up in Pakistan. Mr Brown, the UN's special envoy on global education, said the practice of forcing girls into marriage is *"not acceptable in the modern world"*. It deprives a girl of her education and her childhood. Child marriage-free zones have already been set up in other countries. There are groups in Pakistan who want to make it easier for people to sell off their children in marriage at an early age. It deprives a girl of her education and her childhood and indeed changes her life, and is something that is not acceptable in the modern world.[12]

The United Nations, government officials and rights bodies in the Afghan capital, Kabul, have expressed grave concern about the widespread practice of girls marrying early. Nearly 60 per cent of marriages in Afghanistan involve girls below the legal age of 16. Rights and health activists say that such marriages increase the maternal mortality rate and deny young women an education or any kind of independent life. Badakhshan [northeastern province] has the highest maternal mortality rate in the country and one of the main reasons is under-age marriage.[13]

Afghan civil law stipulates that a girl cannot legally marry until she is 16 unless her father choses her to marry at 15. Enforcing the rule of law in Afghanistan can be exceptionally challenging due to the ongoing security situation in the country, creating an environment for tribal traditions like child marriage to thrive. Girls are often married at a very young age to protect their sexual chastity; late marriage is considered shameful. Parents also marry off their daughters to repay debts, resolve tribal conflicts and boost family standing.[14]

The traditional practice, arranged marriages based on family and ethnic ties, has been replaced in the late twentieth century with marriages based on mutual affection. Marriages were usually arranged by the partners in contemporary Bhutan, and the minimum age was sixteen for women and twenty-one for men. The institution of child marriage once relatively widespread had largely declined as Bhutan modernised and there were only remnants of the practice in the late twentieth century. Polyandry was abolished and polygamy was restricted in the mid twentieth century, but the law in the 1990s still allowed a man to have as many as three wives, provided he had the first wife's permission. The first wife had the power to sue for divorce and alimony, if she did not agree. In the 1980s, divorce was common, and new laws provided better benefits to women seeking alimony.[15] The law pertaining to child marriage in Bhutan has evolved significantly over the last two decades. In order to comply with international standards, the government of Bhutan in 1996 raised the minimum legal age of marriage to 18 years for both boys and girls. According to the Child Care and Protection Act, marrying and having sex with a child is considered statutory rape. While the existence of laws is an important first step, enforcement remains weak in remote, rural areas. Marriage registration is also patchy, and systems and enforcement are unreliable, especially in regions where prevalence is deemed to be high.[16]

According to recent data released by Iran's Association of Children's Rights, the number of girls married in Iran under the age of 15 went from 33,383 in 2006 to 43,459 in 2009, a 30 per cent increase in three years. The alarming figures were accompanied by an official statement from the Iranian parliament's legal affairs committee that the Islamic Republic will lower the legal marriage for girls to nine (before they reach puberty) from the current thirteen. More importantly, as there is no protection for the age of consent within marriage, these young girls have no means and rights to protect themselves against unwanted sex or pregnancy leaving some of them to die of painful childbirth when they are as young as 14.[17] Traditions that further fuel child marriage in Iran include the practice of *"temporary marriages"* for which men pay a family to take a girl on as his short-term bride. Registration is legally required for transactions, which often occur covertly, making it difficult to track or determine the number of young girls it affects. Child marriage law in Iran has changed many times over the last century. Before the 1979 Iranian revolution, the legal age of marriage for boys and girls was 18 and 16, respectively. Shortly after the revolution, the age of marriage for girls was lowered to nine, subject to competent approval and *'physical maturity'*. In 2003, female parliamentarians successfully pushed through legislation that raised the legal age of marriage for girls to 13.[18]

In response to calls for stricter Islamic or sharia law in the Republic of Maldives, an island nation in the Indian Ocean that already prohibits the worship of any religion other than Islam. In his candor, this Muslim President of an entirely Muslim nation has admitted to the world's press that Islamic/Sharia law bans music, mutilates girls' genitals, allows nine-year-old to be married, forbids art and allows *"concubines."*[19] The legal system in the Maldives is based on a mixture of Islamic law and English common law, with the latter being more influential in regulating commerce and other activities that fall outside the social realm. In relation to personal status, Sharia law is more dominant, as adapted to the modern Maldivian judicial system. Many studies in Southern Asia report that child marriage may be higher in those Islamic communities that follow Sharia law, which allows girls to marry at age 15. In the Maldives, premarital sex is not legal, but flogging is an accepted punishment. The girl had been under house arrest on an island near the capital, Malé, since her sentencing. According to the Constitution, the Maldives is a democratic republic based on the principles of Islam. Article 7 states that Islam is the state religion and Article 16 states that it allows for criminal defense in accordance with Sharia.

According to Maldives's customs, the minimum age for marriage is 15, but the local Protection of the Rights of the Child law discourages marriage before the age of 16.[20]

UNICEF released a report on *"Emerging concerns and case studies on child marriage in Sri Lanka"* revealing statutory rape and early marriage in certain districts. The study highlighted the increasing cases of child abuse and the *"grossly inadequate"* measures available for dealing with the problem. The number of crimes against children increased by 64 per cent in 2012, from a year earlier with three to five children being raped every day.[21] In 1995, the minimum age of marriage for both boys and girls was set at 18 years for the majority of the population. The National Child Protection Authority has noted that some underage marriages continue because of accepted cultural norms in some regions, especially in the Badulla and Polonnaruwa regions.[22]

Child Marriage in India

Worldwide one of the key indicators to measure the incidence of child marriage is the percentage of currently married women in the age group 20-24 years who were married before the legal age of 18 years. As far as India is concerned, the data from three rounds of NFHS portrays declining trend, yet the rate of decline has been very slow, at less than one percentage point per year. There are more child marriages in rural areas than in urban areas.[23] The states with the highest incidence of child marriage in the country are Bihar, Rajasthan, Jharkhand, Uttar Pradesh, West Bengal, Madhya Pradesh, Andhra Pradesh and Karnataka.[24]

Child marriage, also known as Bal Vivaha, is believed to have begun during the medieval ages of India. At this time, the political atmosphere was turbulent and ruled by Delhi Sultans in an absolute monarchy government. Indian feudalistic society became present, where characteristics such as honour, rivalry, and animosity were important qualities to possess, and because of this, families and kingdoms created strong military alliances to preserve or destroy power in between them. To ensure the alliance upheld by both sides, each family was exchanged an young member of their household reared and educated at the other family's estate. Child marriage tradition in India has social reasons too. Indians performed child marriages to get their girls protected against rape and abduction by foreign rulers. The caste system is also believed to have contributed to the growth of child marriage.[25] The problem of child marriage in India remains rooted in a matrix of religious traditions, social practices, economic factors and deeply-rooted prejudices. Regardless of such roots, child marriage constitutes a gross violation of human rights, leaving physical, psychological and emotional scars for life. Sexual activity starts soon after marriage, and pregnancy and childbirth at an early age can lead to maternal as well as infant mortality.[26]

The Effects

The consequences for girls are especially dire, as they are usually compelled into early childbearing and social isolation. Child brides will frequently drop out of school and were exposed to high risk of domestic violence and abuse, increased economic dependence, denial of decision-making power, inequality at home, which further perpetuates discrimination and low status of girls/ women. Child marriage is associated with several health risks for the young mother, as early marriage may translate into repeated pregnancies at tender age when the body is not fully equipped for child bearing. Girls who are married at younger age are more likely to be victims of violence and abuse and are often forced to obey by the household rules as they have less power and negotiating skills.[27]

Child marriage affects both boys and girls but impacts girls with higher incidence and more intensity. It has important consequences on the development and full growth of the girl as it is associated with increased risks of maternal and child mortality, low levels of education, and exposure to violence, isolation and confinement. Spousal violence, especially sexual violence (forcing to have sexual intercourse or perform sexual acts without consent) perpetrated by the husband has severe and damaging consequences. Evidence suggests that child brides are more likely to be exposed to violence or abuse.[28] Early marriage leads to early pregnancy. One third of teenage girls aged 15 to 19 are mothers or are already pregnant. Adolescent mothers are more likely to suffer from birth-related complications of adult woman.[29]

Legal Mechanism

Child marriage is a major social concern. It is a violation of children's rights, whether it happens to a girl or a boy. It denies the basic rights to health, nutrition, education, freedom from violence, abuse and exploitation and deprives the child of his/ her childhood. The government of India has adopted the Prohibition of Child Marriage Act in 2006, replacing the Child Marriage Restraint Act, 1929. Complementarily, the Compulsory Registration of Marriages Act, 2006. The Dowry Prohibition Act, 1961 and Right to Free and Compulsory Education Act, 2009 reinforce India's legal framework against child marriage. Following the adoption of the Prohibition of Child Marriage Act, 2006 State Governments/union Territories are required to appoint Child Marriage Prohibition Officers and to frame Rules. So far, 21 states have framed their Rules and 15 have appointed prohibition officers. UNICEF has been working with Government and civil society to foster a change in social norms and behaviours with regard to child marriage in addition to promoting institutional capacity and law enforcement.[30] Child marriage is an appalling violation of human rights and robs girls of their education, health and long-term prospects.

Child Marriage Restraint Act, 1929

Child Marriage Restraint Act, 1929 popularly known as the Sarda Act after its sponsor Rai Sahib Harbilas Sarda to the British India Legislature in India was passed on September 28, 1929, fixed the age of marriage for girls at 18 years and boys at 21 years. It came into effect six months later on April 1, 1930. It applies to all of British India, not just to Hindus. It was the first social reform issue, taken up by the organised women in India. To eradicate the evil of child marriage, the Child Marriage Restraint Act was passed in 1929. The object was to eliminate the special evil was which had the potentialities of dangers to life and health of female child, who seldom withstand the stress and strains of married life and to avoid early death of such minor mothers. A male above eighteen years of age and below twenty one, contracts child marriage shall be punishable with simple imprisonment, which may extend to fifteen days, or with fine which may extend to one thousand rupees, or with both. A male above twenty-one years of age, contracts child marriage shall be punishable with simple imprisonment which may extend to three months and shall be liable also to fine. Where a minor contracts child marriage, any person guarding the minor, whether as parent or guardian or in any other capacity, lawful or unlawful, who does any act to promote the marriage or permits solemnisation, or negligently fails to prevent from being solemnised shall be punishable with simple imprisonment, which may extend to three months and shall be liable also to fine. No court shall take cognizance of any offence under this Act after the expiry of one year from the date on which the offence is alleged to have been committed.[31]

Prohibition of Child Marriage Act' 2006

It extends to the whole of India except the state of Jammu and Kashmir. It applies also to all citizens of India from within and beyond India. "Child means a person who, if a male, has not completed twenty-one years of age, and if a female, has not completed eighteen years of age. Child marriage" means a marriage to which either of the contracting parties is a child. Every child marriage, whether solemnised before or after the commencement of this Act, shall be voidable at the option of the contracting party, who was a child at the time of such marriage. The District Magistrate shall have additional powers to stop or prevent solemnisation of child marriages and for this purpose, he may take such appropriate measures and use the minimum force required. The state government shall, by notification in the official gazette, appoint for the whole state, or such part thereof may be specified in that notification, an officer or officers to be known as the child marriage prohibition officer having jurisdiction over the area or areas specified in the notification.[32]

Conclusion

Child marriage is a major social concern and a violation of children's rights. The states with the highest incidence of child marriage in the country are Bihar, Rajasthan, Jharkhand, Uttar Pradesh, West Bengal, Madhya Pradesh, Andhra Pradesh and Karnataka. Poverty and social norms intended to ensure family honour and protect girls are significant factors that increase the risks for a girl to be married while still a child. Child marriage affects both boys and girls but impacts girls with higher incidence and more intensity. It has important consequences on the development and full growth of the girl, as it is associated with increased risks of maternal and child mortality, low levels of education, and exposure to violence, isolation and confinement. To eradicate the evil of child marriage, the Child Marriage Restraint Act was passed in 1929. The object is to eliminate the special evil which had the potentialities of dangers to the life and health of female child, who could not withstand the stress and strains of married life and avoid early deaths of such minor mothers.

REFERENCES

1. *Child (2014)*. Retrieved from http://en.wikipedia.org/wiki/Child
2. *Importance of investing in children (2014)*, Retrieved from http://www.unicef.org/socialpolicy/index_53294.html
3. Grace Hwang Lynch (2014). *The Importance of Art in Child Development*, Retrieved from http://www.pbs.org/parents/education/music-arts/the-importance-of-art-in-child-development/
4. *Marriage (2014)*. Retrieved from http://en.wikipedia.org/wiki/Marriage
5. *Child Marriage-UNICEF*, Retrieved from http://www.unicef.org/protection/57929_58008.html
6. *Child Marriage (2014)*. Retrieved from http://www.unicef.org/india/Child_Marriage_Fact_Sheet_Nov2011_final.pdf
7. *Child Marriage in India: An analysis of available data (2012)*, Retrieved from http://www.unicef.in/documents/childmarriage.pdf
8. *Angus Crawford / (2012)*. Child marriages blight Bangladesh, Retrieved fromhttp://www.bbc.com/news/magazine-17779413
9. *Bangladesh: Parents still not heeding child marriage warnings*, Retrieved from http://www.irinnews.org/report/92375/bangladesh-parents-still-not-heeding-child-marriage-warnings
10. *Child marriage in Nepal (2014)*. Retrieved from http://www.english-online.at/news-articles/people/child-marriage-in-nepal.htm
11. *Pakistan: Child marriages on the rise across rural Sindh*, Retrieved from http://www.irinnews.org/report/33985/pakistan-child-marriages-on-the-rise-across-rural-sindh

12. *Gordon Brown: Create Pakistan child marriage-free zones (2014).* Retrieved from http://www.bbc.com/news/world-26801597
13. *Afghanistan: Child marriage still widespread,* Retrieved from http://www.irinnews.org/fr/report/28727/afghanistan-child-marriage-still-widespread
14. *Child Marriage in Southern Asia: Context, Evidence and Policy Options for Action,* Retrieved from http://reliefweb.int/sites/reliefweb.int/files/resources/Child_Marriage.pdf
15. *Bhutan-Marriage and Family Life,* Retrieved from http://www.mongabay.com/history/bhutan/bhutan-marriage_and_family_life.html
16. *Child Marriage in Southern Asia: Context, Evidence and Policy Options for Action,* Retrieved from http://reliefweb.int/sites/reliefweb.int/files/resources/Child_Marriage.pdf
17. Vivian Tsai (2012). *Child Bride Practice Rising In Iran, Parliament Seeks To Lower Girl's Legal Marriage Age To Nine,* Retrieved from http://www.ibtimes.com/child-bride-practice-rising-iran-parliament-seeks-lower-girls-legal-marriage-age-9-760263
18. *Child Marriage in Southern Asia: Context, Evidence and Policy Options for Action,* Retrieved from http://reliefweb.int/sites/reliefweb.int/files/resources/Child_Marriage.pdf
19. Maldivian president: Islamic law bans music and art, mutilates girls' genitals, allows child marriage and concubines, See http://freethoughtnation.com/maldivian-president-islamic-law-bans-music-and-art-mutilates-girls-genitals/
20. Mohshin Habib (2013). *Solving the Problem of Child Marriage,* Retrieved from http://www.gatestoneinstitute.org/3981/child-marriage
21. See http://www.therepublicsquare.com/politics/2013/08/14/sri-lanka-child-abuse/
22. *Child Marriage in Southern Asia: Context, Evidence and Policy Options for Action,* Retrieved from http://reliefweb.int/sites/reliefweb.int/files/resources/Child_Marriage.pdf
23. *Child Marriage in India: An analysis of available data (2012),* Retrieved from http://www.unicef.in/documents/childmarriage.pdf

24. *Child Marriage (2014)*. Retrieved from http://www.unicef.org/india/Child_Marriage_Fact_Sheet_Nov2011_final.pdf
25. *Child marriage in India (2014)*. Retrieved from http://en.wikipedia.org/wiki/Child_marriage_in_India
26. *Child marriage in India (2014)*. Retrieved from http://www.csrindia.org/index.php/child-marriage-in-india
27. *Child Marriage (2014)*. Retrieved from http://www.unicef.org/india/Child_Marriage_Fact_Sheet_Nov2011_final.pdf
28. *Child Marriage in India: An analysis of available data (2012)*, Retrieved from http://www.unicef.in/documents/childmarriage.pdf
29. *Early Marriage (2014)*. Retrieved from http://www.unicef.org/bangladesh/children_4866.htm
30. *Child Marriage (2014)*. Retrieved from http://www.unicef.org/india/Child_Marriage_Fact_Sheet_Nov2011_final.pdf
31. *Child Marriage Restraint Act 1929*, Retrieved from http://wcd.nic.in/cmr1929.htm
32. *Prohibition of Child Marriage Act in 2006*, Retrieved from http://wcd.nic.in/cma2006.pdf

2

Bonded Labour

"Parents and schools should place great emphasis on the idea that it is all right to be different. Racism and all the other 'isms' grow from primitive tribalism, the instinctive hostility against those of another tribe, race, religion, nationality, class or whatever. You are a lucky child if your parents taught you to accept diversity."

- Roger Ebert

Introduction

Slavery is considered to be one of the worst human rights violations alongside torture and the death penalty. Freedom from slavery is often referred to as a *fundamental right* or *basic human right*. Slavery is the denial of a person's humanity by depriving the individual of individuality and it 'continues[s] to be among the greatest human rights challenges facing the international community. Freedom from slavery and objection to any kind of servitude is a human right.[1] Though the bonded labour system is deeply embedded in feudal and semi-feudal social structure; it is prevalent in advanced agriculture with landlord serf relation and in the non-agricultural sectors. Bonded Labour System is not a one time or one occupation phenomenon. It may recur at any point of time in any industry, occupation or process.

In some cases, this occurs because the labour of the child alone, or of the entire family, is directly purchase. In other cases, bondage is intergenerational: once a parent is no longer able to work, debts are passed down from parent to child. Bonded labour has been widespread since ancient times and has flourished at various periods in most countries. At the origin of bonded labour lies a loan that a family takes from an employer. Bonded labour can sometimes permit Pareto improving transactions that would not otherwise occur. For assetless individuals, pledging one's labour could be the only way to obtain much needed loans. Sometimes, a child's labour is directly pledged as security for loan. In other situations, the condition of bonded labourer is intergenerationally transmit to the child after the death of his parent. In all cases of child bonded labour, that a parent can use one's child as collateral raises serious questions.

Who are Bonded Labourers?

Bonded labour refers to a situation in which a person owing money pledges personal services or those of someone under his/her control as collateral against a debt. Either the remuneration for the labour is not reasonably assessed for paying the debt off or the duration and type of services are not clearly limited and defined. By using a system of advances that bond labourers and their families, kiln owners are able to ensure regular labour at a low cost. Throughout the global brick industry, advances are commonly used to tie workers and their families to a kiln and keep wages low. Alternative means of securing regular labour such as improving on their wages and conditions are currently not feasible given the current conditions of the brick industry. High levels of competition and notoriously low profit margins maintain significant pressure on operating costs, notably of their wages. Therefore, kiln owners cannot increase wages or improve conditions without raising brick prices, effectively pricing themselves out of the market.[2]

Bondage is the state of subjection to an influence or force. In its basic sense, it denotes the state of being bound to an unfree labour system. It is a form of indenture. The indentured servants are under contract of an employer for a certain period of time. During this period, they have to work in exchange for their food, clothing, lodging, transportation and other requirements. If the labourer has taken loan from the employer, the employer may forgive the debt in exchange for the labour which sometimes continues indefinitely.[3]

Reasons Behind

One mechanism often claimed to be the source of bondage is that the labourer owes the employer using his future labour services as collateral. If the labourer is not able to repay the loan, he looses his collateral, and is deemed to work for the employer and only having his basic needs covered. However, debt bondage created by the inability of a borrower to service his debt is not a new phenomenon.[4] Bonded labour in South Asia happens as a result of poverty, social exclusion and the failure of governments to act against the practice and its causes. People in bonded labour are the poorest in society with nothing to sell except them. Around 90 per cent of those in bonded labour are from the lowest caste groups known as *dalits*. Bonded labourers work in different jobs including brick kilns, domestic work and construction.

In bonded labour, the control of labourers is established from the outset at recruitment. The absence or lack of labour standards paves the way for unequal power relationships between labourers and employers, and increases the latter's control over the former. In some unregulated sectors, mostly in isolated work environments and where workers are required to live in work premises; they also face intimidation by security personnel and other armed individuals as a way of controlling them, especially in the brick-kiln industry. Social practices may also be used to ensure that certain groups carry out tasks for the entire community. The use of children and women in work assigned to a family, without accounting for their contributions, for example, reinforces exploitative conditions.[5]

Global Perspectives

Bonded labour remains a widespread problem. The UN has estimated that some 20 million people are held in such working conditions around the world. Many reports on the livelihood of people indicate that they are deprived of basic liberties, and many live in destitution. This has spurred several governments of countries, where bonded labour is a large problem to ban the institutions, and also some regional agreements to prohibit forced labour.[6] Nowadays, forced labour is present in some form on all continents, in almost all countries, and in every kind of economy. There are persistent cases of what may be termed *traditional* forms of forced labour. These include entrenched bonded labour systems in parts of South Asia, debt bondage affecting mainly indigenous peoples in parts of Latin America, and the residual slavery-related practices most evident today in certain parts of Africa. In numerous countries, domestic workers are trapped in situations of forced labour, and they are restrained in many cases from leaving the employers' homes through threats or violence. Forced labour today also affects sizeable numbers of migrant workers who are transported away from their countries or communities of origin.[7]

Slavery existed within sub-Saharan African societies before the arrival of Europeans is a hotly contested point between Afro-centric and Euro-centric academics. Africans were subjected to several forms of slavery over the centuries, including chattel slavery under both the Muslims with the trans-Saharan slave trade, and Europeans through the trans-Atlantic slave trade. Slavery still exists in Islamic North Africa, in such countries as Mauritania and Sudan (despite both countries being participants in the 1956 UN slavery convention).

Bonded labour is a contemporary form of slavery, which continues to thrive in South Asian countries despite its illegality. Historically associated with agriculture, bonded labour is in the 21st century both a rural and urban phenomenon practiced in almost all sectors of the South Asian economy. The debt bondage of labourers exists in many forms. It can be intergenerational, when the burden of labour and debt are transferred to the next generation. Increasingly generational and family bondage has given way to more individualised and temporary forms of bondage such as seasonal bondage; where a worker is bound by an advance to an employer for a restricted period but where the employee uses that advance or debt to exploit the worker. There is no consensus on the total number of people in bonded labour in South Asia. However, the ILO estimates a minimum of 9.5 million people are in forced labour, in the Asia Pacific region, the majority of whom are in debt bondage. The lack of consensus on the numbers in bonded labour reflects consistent failure by the Governments of India, Nepal and Pakistan to take a systematic and sustained approach against bonded labour, including serious investigation into the scale of bonded labour. Moreover, it reflects a tendency by government authorities to conceal the incidence of bonded labour and a failure to recognise bonded labour, demonstrated by disputes in South Asian courts over the definition of bonded labour.[8]

South Asia is believed to have 9.5 million people in forced labour, the majority of whom are in debt bondage. These statistics are either ignored or downplayed by Government authorities in Nepal, Pakistan and India, making these governments complicit with the business, intentionally or not. Recently, as agriculture in South Asia undertook structural change, moving to cash-cropping for example, some impacts were felt on bonded labour itself. With the decline in the agricultural labour force as a result of mechanisation, agricultural work has become more and more seasonal. This puts strains on the population working in the primary sector as they have to take advances on their remuneration, which then requires them work the full season to receive the rest.

Most households working in brick kilns in Afghanistan fell vulnerable to debt bondage when living in Pakistan as refugees or migrants. With large families to feed, limited skills and almost no access to credit, households turned to brick kilns, because they are one of the few places where they can receive advances as well as payments in-kind such as shelter and water. Households take on debt from brick kilns to pay for basic needs such as food, medical bills, as opposed to investments in shelter or entrepreneurial activities. Fifty-six per cent of brick makers in Afghan kilns are children, and a majority of workers are 14 and under.[9] The main obstacle in Afghanistan is not policy making or establishing laws on bonded and child labour; rather it is one of implementation, monitoring and enforcement of said laws. Despite existing conventions and laws, the Afghan government has suffered from a lack of capacity to clearly understand, uphold and prioritize these standards. The government of the Islamic Republic of Afghanistan does not have laws that specifically address bonded labour. The Afghan Labour Law does address compulsory work, which would be applicable in those cases of bonded labour that can also be deemed forced labour. Article 4 of the Labour Law prohibits compulsory work, which it defines as activities performed under threat or against the will of the worker. ILO standards unequivocally condemn forced labour and the use of children in slavery and/or debt bondage. ILO Convention No. 105 requires the immediate and complete abolition of forced and compulsory labour.[10]

This rapid assessment examines the incidence of bonded labour in the mining industry of Pakistan. Of the sectors where bonded labour is suspected, mining appears to be the one that has received least exposure, despite conditions in the mining sector must be regarded as amongst the most hazardous. Pakistan, with more than 600,000 sq. kms of outcrop area is endowed with significant mineral resources. In addition to the world's second largest reservoir of salt in Khewra (Punjab), there are significant deposits of coal and other industrial and construction minerals.[11] The first Indian Mines Act, passed in 1901, contained provisions on safety and health, but it was not until the Mines Act of 1923 that any restrictions were imposed on the employment of labour. The 1923 Act, contains *inter alia* provision for the exclusion of children under 13-years, the grant of a weekly holiday and the limitation of weekly hours to 60 above ground and 54 below ground. The Act was supplemented by two elaborate series of regulations; one relating to coal mines and one to other mines. In addition, rules were framed by provincial governments. After 1923, two important changes were made in the law. The amending Act of 1928 provided that no mine shall be open more than 12 hours in 24, unless on a system of shifts and that shifts must not exceed 12 hours and must not overlap. The regulations of March 1929 prohibited the employment of women underground.[12] Bonded labour is generally alleged to exist in agriculture. Some recent studies have identified agriculture as major location for debt bondage of sharecroppers, particularly in Sindh, and this may be the case for other areas of the country as well. The Constitution of Pakistan prohibits all forms of forced labour. The Bonded Labour System (Abolition) Act 1992 declares all arrangements that impose restrictions on labour or services illegal as a condition for loans and advances.[13]

Bonded labour in Nepal has arisen out of unequal agrarian relations. Landless lower castes are often forced by circumstances to borrow sums of money from rich land owners, to meet subsistence needs. Eventually, they end up pledging physical labour as interest towards repayment of loan. Often, generations of family get trapped in this cycle of loan repayment and working as labourers without pay for landlords. This vicious cycle does not allow them life of dignity. In Nepal, bonded labourers are referred to as Haruwa/Charuwa, Kamaiya or Haliya in different parts of the country. The Tarai is the flat agricultural area that spans the length of Nepal, bordering the Indian states of Bihar, Uttar Pradesh and Uttarakhand. But this tranquil rural setting harbours an age-old problem: the Haruwa-Charuwa system of bonded labour. A recently launched ILO report that examines conditions in the twelve districts where these systems of bonded labour are most prevalent found that 12 per cent of the estimated 942,000 households were affected by forced labour. That means that at least one member of the family whether it was an adult or child was working under forced labour conditions. However, when looking only at the Haruwa-Charuwa and Haliya households, the proportion was higher, at 94 per cent. Children are part of this system of bonded labour and have to work from early morning till evening, thus excluding them from school.

The Government of Nepal has taken important steps to tackle bonded labour. Following the liberation of the Kamaiyas, the Haliyas organised themselves and put up similar demands to be freed. As a result, the government announced their liberation in September 2008 and is in the process of approving a National Plan of Action for rehabilitation. But much more needs to be done, especially regarding the Haruwa-Charuwa system. Despite the legal prohibition on bonded labour, these practices persist in different locations in the country. The implementation of the Kamaiya Labour (Prohibition) Act 2001 was taken up by way of identification, resettlement and rehabilitation of Kamaiyas, which was aided by giving land and skill training to some Kamaiyas.

Tens of thousands of people are working as bonded labourers in rural Bangladesh. Even though it is illegal, entire families, including children, are bonded to employers while they struggle to pay back loans. Thousands of children are being forced into bonded labour every day, because of poverty and their parents' unemployment," Sumaiya Khair, a human rights activist and researcher into child labour in Dhaka, the capital. Unlike in cities where workers are paid daily or fixed wage, the rural workforce mostly has to make verbal arrangements for wages, which are manipulated often by unscrupulous landlords and loan sharks, known as Mahajan. Many, mostly women and children, end up as domestic servants, working in conditions that resemble servitude. Many suffer from physical abuse, sometimes resulting in death. Domestic servants, especially the women and children are often exposed to inhuman treatment. Few, if any, are concerned with this matter unless tragedy like death by torture becomes public. Forced labour has been present in Bangladesh for centuries. After the liberation of Bangladesh, it has changed form and has taken the new face of various 'contracts' associated with loans taken by poor farmers from the usurers.

Bangladesh is primarily affected by modern slavery for sexual exploitation, forced labour and bonded labour, both within its borders and overseas. Some of these migrant workers, men, women and children are in bonded labour, debt bondage, and forced labour in a variety of industries throughout Bangladesh. Debt bondage has been reported in the shrimp and tea industries, as well as in brick making and forced begging. Some victims are forcibly trafficked internationally. Large numbers of women and girls are reportedly trafficked to India and Pakistan annually. Some Bangladeshi women are vulnerable to enslavement for sexual exploitation within Bangladesh's borders. Although, a strong set of laws and judicial guidelines exist to tackle violence against women, implementation of systems remains poor, while violence against women, illegal punishments, such as fatwas, and sexual harassment continue. In 1972, Bangladesh ratified both ILO Convention No. 29 (1930), the Forced Labour Convention and ILO Convention No. 105 (1957), the Abolition of Forced Labour Convention. The law prohibits forced or bonded labour and the Factories Act and Shops and Establishments Act provide for inspection mechanisms to strengthen laws against forced labour.

The System in India

The National Commission on Rural Labour (NCRL) saw bondage of agricultural labourers as still being the main form of bondage in India. The Commission concluded that agricultural labour bondage was higher in states and districts characterised by high percentage of rural labourers, low irrigation and agricultural productivity and poor infrastructure. However, there were bonded labourers in the plantation sector: for example, bonded labourers from Orissa and Bihar were employed in the sector in Assam and Tripura. The NCRL found a high incidence of migrant bonded labour: Bihari labour in the fields of Punjab, Haryana and Uttar Pradesh; in brick kilns of these states; in sugarcane fields in Gujarat; in stone and slate quarries and mines; in plantations of Assam; and even in the seaports of Gujarat. The Commission highlighted bondage among women on account of social as well as economic factors and mentioned the *Joginis* of Andhra Pradesh and the *Devdasis* of Karnataka. The regional picture that emerges is indeed the high concentration of bonded labourers in the three southern states of Andhra Pradesh, Tamil Nadu and Karnataka and in Uttar Pradesh. In Punjab, where the state government has quite recently denied the existence of bonded labour, the NHRC has been assiduously pursuing complaints regarding bonded labour in agriculture, brick kilns and other sectors, and has upheld complaints in a few cases.

Labour bondage draws heavily upon traditional social relations and the caste system, even in the non-agricultural sector, but can be seen most directly in agriculture and in bonded labour relation involving tribal. The uneven pace of modernisation of agriculture has created new demands for stable and servile labour force, which in some cases is obtained through credit bondage and elements of force, deceit and compulsion. The incidence of bonded labour perhaps is the highest in the unorganised and informal sector in India. And among the unorganised sectors, the incidence of bondage is probably the highest in quarries and open mines. The nature of bondage among local agricultural labour, mostly are drawn from the low castes. In the case of western Uttar Pradesh, where the decline of traditional attached labour relations had earlier been reported by Srivastava (1989), later studies have reported a system of recruitment of attached labour from Bihar and Nepal, with workers under bondage, made to work for long hours and denied wages. Tribals have long been subject to exploitative debt relations in several parts of the country, resulting in bondage. In the state of Madhya Pradesh, cases of bonded agricultural labour came to light in Harda (an area where agriculture is rapidly developing due to profitable oilseed cultivation) and adjoining districts, when a local NGO took initiative (on the plea of relatives) to get the labourers released.[14]

Effects of System

Bonded labour is a serious cause for concern. The reasons for the prevalence of bonded labour even today, its cascading effects and the consequences should be analysed and remedies found. Large number of people work as bonded labourers in various sectors without realising they were subjected to modern form of slavery. As a result of indebtedness, the farmers are not able to improve the agricultural produce. As a result of indebtedness, the farmers have to work as slaves of the money lender. The burden of indebtedness cast the farmers neither look after health nor get proper diet. The consequences of indebtedness are the poverty. Since the village people in spite of hard labour neither repay the loan nor improve their economic condition.[15]

Legal Mechanism

Freedom from forced or compulsory labour is one of the most important human rights within the sphere of competence of the International Labour Organisation (ILO). Historically, it was the first basic human rights within the organisation's mandate to be dealt within international labour standards. Today, forced or compulsory labour is universally banned, and the two ILO Conventions on the subject are the widely ratified of all International Labour Conventions. Moreover, in the ILO Declaration on Fundamental Principles and Rights at Work, adopted by the International Labour Conference at its 86th Session in 1998, the International Labour Conference "*Declares that all members, even if they have not ratified the Conventions in question, have an obligation, arising from the very fact of membership in the Organisation, to respect, to promote and to realise, in good faith and in accordance with the Constitution, the principles concerning the fundamental rights which are the subject of those Conventions, namely: ... the elimination of all forms of forced or compulsory labour ...*".[16]

The ILO Conventions on Forced Labour and relevant UN Conventions define and prohibit various types of forced labour, slavery and servitude, and debt bondage. Debt bondage is a specific form of forced labour, in which the element of compulsion is derived from debt. The UN Supplementary Convention on the Abolition of Slavery, the Slave Trade and Institutions and Practices Similar to Slavery (1956) defines debt bondage as "*the status or condition arising from a pledge by a debtor of his personal services or those of a person under his control as security for a debt, if the value of those services as reasonably assessed is not applied towards the liquidation of the debt or the length and nature of those services are not respectively limited or defined" (Article 1(a)). Forced labour violates the fundamental rights guaranteed to all citizens by the Indian Constitution. Article 23(1) in Part III of the Indian Constitution, relating to Fundamental Rights, states that "Traffic in human beings and begars and other forms of forced labour are prohibited and any contravention of the provision shall be an offence, punishable by law."*[17]

The Universal Declaration and the International Covenant on Civil and Political Rights contain provisions prohibiting slavery, servitude and forced labour in all their forms and acknowledge the special place of children in society. Article 24 of the International Covenant declares that every child has the "*right to such measures of protection as are required by his status as a minor". In addition to the general prohibitions on slavery and forced labour, which are applicable to children as well as adults, the Supplementary Convention of 1956 specifically defines a servile status that is restricted to children alone. The International Covenant on Economic, Social and Cultural Rights echoes the requirement of numerous ILO conventions that States should specify a minimum age below which "the paid employment of children should be prohibited and punishable by law"*.[18]

India's Labour Policy is mainly based on Labour Laws. The labour laws of independent India derive their origin, inspiration and strength partly from the views expressed by important nationalist leaders during the days of national freedom struggle, partly from the debates of the Constituent Assembly and partly from the provisions of the Constitution and the International Conventions and Recommendations. The relevance of the dignity of human labour and the need for protecting and safeguarding the interest of labour as human beings has been enshrined in Chapter-III (Articles 16, 19, 23 & 24) and Chapter IV (Articles 39, 41, 42, 43, 43A and 54) of the Constitution of India keeping in line with Fundamental Rights and Directive Principles of State Policy. The Labour Laws were also influenced by important human rights and the conventions and standards that have emerged from the United Nations. Under the Constitution of India, Labour is a subject in the concurrent list, where both the central and state governments are competent to enact legislations.[19]

The Constitution of India guarantees all its citizens - justice - social, economic and political; freedom of thought, expression, belief, faith and worship; equality of status and of opportunity and fraternity, dignity of individual and unity of the nation.

1. *Article 23:* Prohibition of traffic in human beings and forced labour- (a) Traffic in human beings and *beggar* and other similar forms of forced labour are prohibited and any contravention of this provision shall be an offence punishable in accordance with law. (b) Nothing in this article shall prevent the state from imposing compulsory service for public purposes, and imposing such service in the state shall not make any discrimination on grounds of religion, race, caste or class or any of them.
2. *Article 39:* Certain principles of policy to be followed by the states- Article 39(a) provides that the citizens, men and women equally, have the right to an adequate means of livelihood; Article 39 (d) provides that there is equal pay for equal work for both men and women and Article 39 (e) provides that the health and strength of workers, men and women, and the tender age of children are not abused and that the citizens are not forced by economic necessity to enter avocations unsuited to age or strength.
3. *Article 42:* Provision for just and humane conditions of work and maternity relief- The state shall make provision for securing just and humane conditions of work and maternity relief.
4. *Article 43:* Living wage etc. for workers: The state shall endeavour to secure, by suitable legislation or economic

> organisation or in any other way, to all workers, agricultural, industrial or otherwise, work and living wage, conditions of work ensuring a decent standard of life and full enjoyment of leisure and social and cultural opportunities and, in particular the state shall endeavour to promote cottage industries on an individual or co-operative basis in rural areas.[20]

The first survey to assess the nature and magnitude of bonded labour was undertaken in 1978. Subsequently, the Supreme Court of India has pronounced number of judgements to clarify the meaning of the term bonded labour. It has appointed commissioners to the Court and extended number of directives to central and State governments to indicate the incidence of bonded and forced labour and to vigorously implement the Bonded Labour System (Abolition) Act, 1976. Since 1997, the National Human Rights Commission (NHRC) has been given a pivotal role in monitoring the implementation of the Bonded Labour System (Abolition) Act and in ensuring the directives of the Supreme Court are followed by the central and state governments. The law dealing with bonded and forced labour was legislated by the Indian Parliament in 1976. The Bonded Labour System Abolition Act (1976) of India is quite extraordinary in that it recognises (a) the overlap between forced labour and bonded labour in customary relations, and also (b) the manifestation of these relations in contract labour and inter-state migration, and (c) considers the nature of restraints suffered by the labourer as a result of the bonded/forced labour relations, and makes all of these illegal.[21]

In order to assist the state governments in their task of rehabilitation of released bonded labourers, the Ministry of Labour launched a centrally sponsored scheme in May 1978 for rehabilitation of freed bonded labourers. The Supreme Court has requested the National Human Rights Commission to be involved in dealing with the issue of bonded labour. A Central Action Group (CAG) has been constituted in the National Human Rights Commission. This group holds regular meetings/sensitisation workshops at various places in collaboration with the Ministry of Labour and Employment and the matter is being pursued with the state governments.[22]

The Government of Nepal abolished the Kamaiya system (a form of bonded labour in agriculture) in July 2000 through an enactment: *"The Kamaiya Labour Prohibition Act-2001"*. Although the Act is named after one system of bonded labour (the Kamaiya system), it covers other forms of bonded labour such as Bhaisabar (buffalo herder), Gaibar (cow herder), Chhekarabar (goat herder), Haruwa (tiller), Charuwa (herder), Hali (tiller), Gothalo (herder). The Government of Nepal has started initiatives to address the issue of bonded labour (Kamaiya system) in coordination with development agencies (including ILO-IPEC) in the western part of Nepal.[23]

Bonded Labour System (Abolition) 1976

Bonded Labour System (Abolition) Act was passed in 1976. This abolished the practices of bonded labour, bonded labour system and bonded debt throughout India from October 25th. The Act has provided for Vigilance Committees at the district and sub-divisional levels under the chairmanship of district and sub-divisional magistrates. A complaint under the law can be filed before the Vigilance Committee under the Act. Executive Magistrates are empowered under the Act to conduct a trial of offences and to release the bonded labourers(s). The Act also lays down stringent penal provisions against offending employers. These penalties include imprisonment for a term which may extend to three years and also with a fine.[24] The law provides for the duties and responsibilities of the district magistrate and every officer specified by him. The law also provides for the constitution of vigilance committees at the district and sub-divisional level, duties and responsibilities of such committees in the area of identification and rehabilitation of freed bonded labourers. The Act provides for punishment for compelling any person to render any bonded labour. It also provides for (a) punishment for advancement of bonded debt, (b) punishment for extracting bonded labour system, (c) punishment for omission or failure to restore possession of property of bonded labourers and (d) abatement.

International Labour Organisation

The International Labour Organisation (ILO) is the oldest UN agency. It was established in 1919. The primary reason for its creation was to promote global peace and harmony by promoting social justice. The preamble to the Constitution of ILO states that *"Universal and lasting peace can be established only if it is based upon social justice"*. Since inception, the ILO has maintained and developed a system of international labour standards aimed at promoting opportunities for women and men to obtain decent and productive work, in conditions of freedom, equity, security and dignity. The Decent Work Agenda of ILO aims to achieve decent work for all by promoting social dialogue, social protection and employment creation, as well as respect for international labour standards. In the ILO's Declaration of Philadelphia of 1944, the international community recognised that *"labour is not a commodity"*. Conventions and recommendations are drawn up by representatives of governments, employers and workers and are adopted at the ILO's annual International Labour Conference. The ILO's governing body has identified eight conventions as fundamental, covering subjects that are considered as fundamental principles and rights at work: freedom of association and the effective recognition of the right to collective bargaining; the elimination of all forms of forced or compulsory labour; the effective abolition of child labour; and the elimination of discrimination in respect of employment and occupation. There are two main ILO Conventions on forced labour. Convention 29 of 1930, ratified by 161 countries including Pakistan (December 23, 1957) and Convention 105 of 1957, ratified by 158 countries including Pakistan (February 15, 1960). Forced labour is defined in Convention 29 as *"all work or service ...exacted ... under the menace of any penalty and for which the said person has not offered himself voluntarily"*.[25]

Conclusion

Bonded Labour is one of the forms of slavery, which still persists. It is illegal but present in many of the South Asian countries, for example in India, Pakistan, Cambodia, Nepal and Bangladesh. Bonded labour is increasingly found in urban industries. While generational and family bonded labour has decreased, new forms of bonded labour have emerged. Bonded labour is a feature of many sectors of the economy in South Asia. It is still predominantly an agricultural phenomenon, affecting the chronically poor and landless. Bonded labour occurs for a variety of reasons, but reviewing the realities of bonded labourers' lives suggests three major factors contributing to the phenomenon of bondage in South Asia: poverty, discrimination, and government failure to protect the rights of its vulnerable citizens. Bonded labour system has been abolished in India and bonded labourers were freed from any obligation to render bonded labour and payment of debt with the commencement of the Bonded Labour System (Abolition) Act, 1976. Any custom, agreement or other instrument by virtue of which, a person is required to render any service as bonded labour became void.

REFERENCES

1. Christine Molfenter (2011). *Bonded Child Labour in Pakistan: The State's Responsibility to Protect from an Institutional Perspective,* Retrieved from http://www.academia.edu/1973698/Bonded_Child_Labour_in_Pakistan-The_States_Responsibility_to_Protect_ from_an_Institutional_Perspective
2. *Buried in Bricks: A rapid assessment of bonded labour in Afghan brick kilns,* Retrieved from http://www.indianet.nl/pdf/BuriedInBricks.pdf
3. Shujaat Ali Shah, *The State of Bonded Labour in Pakistan,* Retrieved from http://www.ilo.org/wcmsp5/groups/public/@ed_norm/@declaration/documents/publication/wcms_096991.pdf
4. Espen Villanger (2006). *Is Bonded Labor Voluntary? A Framework against Forced Work,* Retrieved from http://www.cmi.no/publications/publication/?2142=is-bonded-labor-voluntary
5. Krishna Prasad Upadhyaya (2008). *Poverty, Discrimination and Slavery: The reality of bonded labour in India, Nepal and Pakistan,* Retrieved from http://www.antislavery.org/includes/documents/cm_docs/2009/p/povertydiscriminationslaveryfinal.pdf
6. Espen Villanger (2006). *Is Bonded Labor Voluntary? A Framework against Forced Work,* Retrieved from http://www.researchgate.net/publication/4932467_Is_bonded_labor_voluntary_A_framework_against_forced_work

7. Report III (Part 1B): *General Survey concerning the Forced Labour Convention, 1930 (No. 29), and the Abolition of Forced Labour Convention, 1957 (No. 105),* Retrieved from http://www.ilo.org/public/english/standards/relm/ilc/ilc96/pdf/rep-iii-1b.pdf
8. Krishna Prasad Upadhyaya (2008). *Poverty, Discrimination and Slavery: The reality of bonded labour in India, Nepal and Pakistan,* Retrieved from http://www.antislavery.org/includes/documents/cm_docs/2009/p/povertydiscriminationslaveryfinal.pdf
9. *Buried in Bricks: A rapid assessment of bonded labour in Afghan brick kilns*, Retrieved from http://www.indianet.nl/pdf/BuriedInBricks.pdf
10. *Buried in bricks: A rapid assessment of bonded labour in brick kilns in Afghanistan*, Retrieved from http://www.ilo.org/wcmsp5/groups/public/—asia/—ro-bangkok/documents/publication/wcms_172672.pdf
11. Ahmad Saleem (2004). *A Rapid Assessment of Bonded Labour in Pakistan's Mining Sector*, Retrieved from http://www.ilo.org/wcmsp5/groups/public/—ed_norm/—declaration/documents/publication/wcms_082032.pdf
12. Ahmad Saleem (2004). *A Rapid Assessment of Bonded Labour in Pakistan's Mining Sector*, Retrieved from http://www.ilo.org/wcmsp5/groups/public/—ed_norm/—declaration/documents/publication/wcms_082032.pdf
13. G. M. Arif (2004). *Bonded Labour in Agriculture: A Rapid Assessment in Punjab and North West Frontier Province, Pakistan,* Retrieved from http://www.ilo.org/wcmsp5/groups/public/—ed_norm/—declaration/documents/publication/wcms_082027.pdf
14. Ravi S. Srivastava (2005). *Bonded Labour in India: its Incidence and Pattern*, Retrieved from http://digitalcommons.ilr.cornell.edu/cgi/viewcontent. cgi?article=1017&context=forcedlabor
15. *What are the Effects and Consequences of Indebtedness?* Retrieved from http://www.preservearticles.com/201105076364/what-are-the-effects-and-consequences-of-indebtedness.html
16. Report III (Part 1B): *General Survey concerning the Forced Labour Convention, 1930 (No. 29), and the Abolition of Forced Labour Convention, 1957 (No. 105),* Retrieved from http://www.ilo.org/public/english/standards/relm/ilc/ilc96/pdf/rep-iii-1b.pdf

17. Ravi S. Srivastava (2005). *Bonded Labour in India: Its Incidence and Pattern,* Retrieved from http://digitalcommons.ilr.cornell.edu/cgi/viewcontent.cgi? article=1017&context=forcedlabor
18. David Weissbrodt and Anti-Slavery International (2002). *Abolishing Slavery and its Contemporary Forms,* Retrieved from http://www.ohchr.org/Documents/Publications/slaveryen.pdf
19. *Report of the working group on labour laws & other regulations for the Twelfth five year plan (2012-17),* Retrieved from http://planningcommission.gov.in/aboutus/committee/wrkgrp12/wg_labour_laws.pdf
20. Bonded Labour (2010). *National Human Rights Commission, India,* Retrieved from http://www.nhrc.nic.in/Documents/Publications/KYR%20 Bonded%20Labour%20English.pdf
21. Ravi S. Srivastava (2005). *Bonded Labour in India: Its Incidence and Pattern,* Retrieved from http://digitalcommons.ilr.cornell.edu/cgi/viewcontent.cgi? article=1017&context=forcedlabor
22. *Bonded Labour in India,* Retrieved from http://nhrc.nic.in/Documents/SPEECH_2012_10_25.pdf
23. *Sustainable Elimination of Child Bonded Labour in Nepal: Phase II*, Retrieved from http://www.ilo.org/wcmsp5/groups/public/—ed_mas/—eval/documents/publication/wcms_171921.pdf
24. *Bonded Labour in India*, Retrieved from http://nhrc.nic.in/Documents/SPEECH_2012_10_25.pdf
25. Saeed Ahmed Awan, *Addressing bonded labour and gender concerns at work*, Retrieved from http://www.ciwce.org.pk/Publications/bonded_labour/Training_module_on_role_of_labour_inspectors_in _addressing _bonded_labour.pdf
26. *Types of Slavery in Africa,* Retrieved from http://africanhistory.about.com/od/slavery/p/SlaveryTypes.htm
27. Garance Genicot, *Child Bonded Labor,* Retrieved from http://faculty.georgetown.edu/gg58/CBL.pdf
28. *Bonded labour*, Retrieved from http://www.un.org.np/oneun/bondedlabour
29. *Bonded Labour in South Asia,* Retrieved from http://weeklybolshevik.com/2013/06/10/bonded-labor-in-south-asia/
30. *Fighting Bonded labour in Nepal*, Retrieved from http://www.ilo.org/global country/bangladesh/

3

Child Labour

"The first question which the priest and the Levite asked was: 'If I stop to help this man, what will happen to me?' But ... the Good Samaritan reversed the question: 'If I do not stop to help this man, what will happen to him?'"

- Martin Luther King

Introduction

The child is the most precious human resource. Childhood represents the most tender, most formative and most impressionable stage of human development. It is a time of innocence, vulnerability, dependency, curiosity, activity, and hope for the future. It should be a moment of joy and peace, playing, learning and growing. Child labour is an integral part of labour force, especially in poor countries. These children are the most deprived section of population forced to enter labour market at tender age to earn a pittance or to contribute to family work, sacrificing personal development. Such labour has been the subject of public health discourse especially in countries with poor economies.[1] Child labour is a multi-faceted issue that has been addressed at both the international and national levels. Globalisation and the collateral indebtedness and the widening income gap between rich countries and the countries in the Third World may have exacerbated the problem, despite all good intentions. The highest incidence of child labour is to be found in the poorest countries of the world, particularly in poorest regions of the countries. The growth of child labour world-wide is the result of globalisation. The phenomenon of child labour, like all other social phenomena is historically and socially conditioned. Magnitude of child labour may be ascertained by (a) considering the number of child labourers, (b) the percentage of children who work as labourers (i.e., the participation rate), and (c) the child participation rate as percentage of overall participation rate.

The domestic workload can be extremely heavy. Children engaged in these activities especially girls are easy to hire; they come in cheap; and they can be easily moulded and conditioned to customize needs.[2] Child labour is a widespread and growing phenomenon in the developing world. It is problematic on a number of counts, ranging from the welfare, health and physical integrity of the affected children to downward pressure on adult wages. In recent years, the impact of globalisation on the incidence of child labor has started to spark both public and academic debate, and has become an issue that invokes passion because it brings together people concerned about the exploitation of children on moral and ethical grounds and organised labour interested primarily in protecting jobs.[3]

Who is Child Labourer?

Child labour is multi-dimensional and multi-layered in nature. International Labour Office (ILO) defines child labourer as any activity other than study or play, paid or unpaid, that is carried out by a person under the age of 15 (14 in certain countries). Children are often prompted to work by their parents. Child labour means employment of children in gainful occupations, which are injurious to their physical, mental moral and social development. According to Homer Folks, the chairman of the US National Child Labour Committee, the term 'child labour' is generally used to refer, *"any work by children that interfere with their full physical and mental development, the opportunities for a desirable minimum of education and of their needed recreation."* According to Francis Blanchard (former director of ILO) *"Child labour includes children prematurely leading adult lives, working long hours for low wages under conditions damaging to their health and to their physical and mental development, sometimes separated from their families, frequently deprived of education and training apprentices that could provide them a better future."*[4] UNICEF has given a comprehensive formulation in its attempt at defining child labour Accordingly; child labour is exploitative if it involves: full time works at too early an age; too many hours spent for working; work that exerts undue physical, psychological and social stress; work and life on the streets in bad conditions; inadequate pay: too much responsibility; work that hampers access to education; work that undennines children's dignity and self-esteem, such as slavery or bonded labour and sexual exploitation; and work that is detrimental to full social and psychological development.[5]

Reasons Behind

Different socio-economic factors can be held responsible for the prevailing poverty, illiteracy, unemployment, lack of family planning, dissatisfaction about education system, absence of social security mechanism and many others. Now it is the responsibility of the government to provide children with their rights and to protect them from all sorts of exploitation, because the future of mankind and civilization lies in children. The main reason why children start work instead of attending school, or leave school before completing primary education is that their families are poor and cannot pay basic costs of food and housing without their child earning something. Families break down for many reasons, leaving the household short of income. Sometimes, divorce leaves one parent looking after more children than s(he) can afford to feed. Divorce is sometimes brought about by domestic violence, which also directly drives children to leave home when they are still young. The relatively low wages paid to children are often a reason why employers prefer. Another factor is the practical difficulty of establishing a child's actual age in countries, where the infrastructure may not be in place for e.g. systematic birth registration.[6]

Poverty is generally considered as the most important reason for which children work at inappropriate jobs. But, there are other reasons as well, like as family expectations and traditions; abuse of the child; lack of good schools and day care; lack of other services, such as health care; public opinion that downplays the risk of early work for children; uncaring attitudes of employers; and limited choices for women.[7]

Global Perspectives

According to ILO estimates, there are some 250 million children between the ages of five and fourteen years who are in economic activities in developing countries alone. For 120 million, work is a full-time activity. The remainder combines work with schooling or other non-economic activities. In absolute terms, Asia, being the most densely populated region of the world has the largest number of child workers. The relative level of the child workforce in any economic activity can vary widely from one country to another. The largest proportion of child workers is in economic activities and occupations related to agriculture. Many children work for long hours every day of the week.[8] According to a recent ILO report, boys continue to be more exposed than girls to child labour, particularly work of some hazardous nature. The child labour participation rates decrease in the world in general and this tendency is explained with economic growth by some economists. Although, child labour shows a decreasing trend according to world statistics, the detailed regional studies get some evidence about increases in child labour participation rates with economic growth in that regions.[9]

The fall of the Soviet Union and the ensuing transition of countries in Central and Eastern Europe from planned to market economies increased interest in the regions on their experiences. For these middle-income countries, the process of transition entailed massive reallocation of resources across sectors of the economy, and this has led to dramatic increase in labour market risk for workers. To ameliorate the effects of such increased risk, policymakers were faced with the challenge of designing new labour market institutions.[10] Compared with other continents; African countries are more rural, and dominated still by household production, not large land holdings combined with labour markets. All factors cause high child participation rates. There are also cultural factors and norms that pull children toward the labour force. Several recent anthropological studies have confirmed that women in African agricultural households do larger share of tasks. The *high birth rate* is another influencing factor at the macro level. Child labour has a long history in most countries, and changes in participation rates are naturally regarded as a long-term growth issue. Most child labor in Africa takes place at home. Some labor might be harmful, while other kinds of labour are either harmless or develop skills. Furthermore, the health and the nutritional status of the individual child greatly affect to what degree the same labour is harmful or helpful. As in other countries studied, child work is more extensive in rural than urban areas of Africa. More serious than the lack of information is the possibility of exploitation. Children are within the guardians' control for a limited period of their economic life, while the eventual negative effects on the children's future productivity of non-schooling will become the burden of the children themselves. No reasonable estimates exist of the size of the child labour problem in Africa. For various reasons, many children are sent away from parents or guardians and have to survive on their own. The child-controlled labour supply is a form of child labour that we believe to be more prevalent in at least some African countries than elsewhere.[11]

With the heralding of new millennium, the problem of child labour stands as one of the important global challenges. Children in Cambodia are exploited in the worst forms of child labour, many of them in agriculture, including on rubber plantations. Children's work in agriculture commonly involves harmful activities, such as the use of potentially dangerous machinery and tools, carrying of heavy loads, and the application of harmful pesticides.[12]

Social norms and economic realities mean that child labour is widely accepted and very common in Bangladesh. Many families rely on the income generated by their children for survival, so child labour is often highly valued. Child labour is a visible part of everyday life in Bangladesh: young children serve at roadside tea stalls, and weave between cars selling goods to motorists. Other children work in jobs that are hidden from view, such as domestic work, which makes monitoring and regulation difficult. Many of the jobs that children perform are considered hazardous, and put their physical and mental development at risk.

Bangladesh enacted the Labour Act in 2006, which includes a chapter on child labour. This new law prohibits employment of children under 14 years of age, as well as prohibiting hazardous forms of child labour for persons under age 18. However, children who are aged 12 and above may be engaged in "light work" that does not pose a risk to their mental and physical development and does not interfere with their education. The Ministry of Labour and Employment has recently adopted a National Child Labour Elimination Policy 2010, which provides a framework to eradicate all forms of child labour by 2015. According to the new National Education Policy, education is free and compulsory upto grade eight, however it is estimated that more than one million children have never been to school. Bangladesh's 421,000 child domestic workers (three-quarters are girls) face particular vulnerabilities, because they work behind closed doors.

Though child labour is illegal in Nepal, an estimated 1.6 million children between the ages of five and 17 years are in the work force, according to the National Child Labour Report. Children working in rag-picking, tea-shops and restaurants, porter, scavenging, shoe shinning, street vendoring, rickshaw pulling etc. Children are working at road, house, sewage, hydropower construction, production of tea, sugarcane, tobacco etc. Children, especially girls, provide domestic services for child care, kitchen work, house cleaning, grazing cattle, etc. 1.7 million working children do not have any access to education. And these, out of school children are involved in different forms of child labour for survival and family subsistence. Number of girls, who drop out of school, are more than the boys since girls are more involved in child labour than boys. The issue of trafficking in children and child sex abuse is traditionally viewed as welfare issue than a rights issue. Child workers are a frequent sight on Kathmandu's streets, whether cleaning dishes in local restaurants or making a living as conductors on the city's public transport. Many are employed in the carpet, brick and garment industries, or in private homes as domestic workers. Thousands of children continue to work as breadwinners for their families. While Nepal's Interim Constitution of 2007 guarantees the rights of children, and the country has signed major international conventions against child labour, enforcement is weak. Under its National Master Plan on Child Labour, the country has identified the worst forms of child labour—bonded labour, domestic child labour and carpet weaving among them—and aims to eliminate them by 2016.

Human rights groups in Pakistan say the country's labour laws ignore the abuse of children who, from an young age, are working on the streets or in the homes of middle-class families. There are an estimated 12 million child workers in Pakistan, many enduring unsafe or harsh conditions. Up to 1.7million children from the age of five are working in illegal brick factories in Pakistan and are denied their basic right to childhood, to an education and to play. Forced into labour by severe poverty, children work up to 14 hours a day with scarce food, no sanitation and little pittance. And with nearly a quarter of Pakistan's population living below poverty line, many adult workers are forced to work in unsafe conditions, with their most basic rights denied.

In the rural Bhutanese context, where small families depend on members to the contribution of labour, 'child work' is perhaps seen as natural part of life. Children are engaged in carrying out household chores, agricultural works, maintenance of livestock and other activities. Children as young as six to seven years of age form part of this labour force. Child labour is significant in Bhutan. Children in Bhutan are engaged in the worst forms of child labour, especially in agriculture and domestic service. Girls are more likely to be employed as child domestic workers in homes where, they may be subjected to abuse and exploitation. Some children in Bhutan work in unregulated activities such as rag picking. Urban children sometimes work as street vendors. Children working on the streets may be involved in vehicle accidents or exposed to dangers including severe weather and criminal elements. The 2007 Labour and Employment Act of Bhutan sets the minimum age for work at age 18. However, children ages from 13 to 17 can work provided they are not exposed to physical harm, dangerous machinery or some unhealthy working environment.

Children in Sri Lanka are engaged in dangerous activities in manufacturing and agriculture. Children working in agriculture may use dangerous tools, carry heavy loads, and apply harmful pesticides. Children, predominantly boys, are exploited in prostitution in coastal areas as part of sex tourism. Children are also employed in domestic service, a largely unregulated and undocumented sector. There are reports that children are subjected to bonded and forced labour on dry zone farming areas (tea estates). The Employment of Women, Young Persons, and Children Act has set the minimum age for employment at 14 and that for employment in hazardous work at 18. The minimum age for voluntary recruitment in the armed forces is 18; there is no conscription into the military. Education in Sri Lanka is compulsory and free until the age of 15. The National Steering Committee on Child Labour (NSC) coordinates with the implementation of the Roadmap to End the Worst Forms of Child Labour (2011-2016), the government's key mechanism for the elimination of the worst forms of child labour.

There are reports of limited numbers of children engaged in the worst forms of child labour in the Maldives, particularly girls found in commercial sexual exploitation and working as domestic maids in private households. There is information that children work in potentially dangerous activities in fishing. These children may work to long hours, perform physically demanding tasks, and face dangers such as drowning. In January 2013, the government ratified ILO Convention 138 and ILO Convention 182. The Employment Act establishes 16 as the minimum age for work and 18 as the minimum age for work that may have a detrimental effect on a child's health, education, safety, or conduct. The Constitution establishes the right to free education. The Employment Act and the Constitution both prohibit forced labour, and the Constitution prohibits slavery and servitude.

Indian Scenario

In India, child labour is not a new phenomenon. It has been in existence since time immemorial in one form or the other and has been changing from time to time. With the advent of industrialisation and urbanisation in the early nineteenth century, the factory and industry began replacing handicrafts. Agriculture became more mechanized.[13] In South Asia, the highest incidence of child labour is to be found in India. It is ironical that there are 55 million child labourers in India while

55 million unemployed youth are also looking for jobs. Child labour has dramatically increased in South Asia mainly due to the expansion of government exports to the West. Child labour increased with international demand in sectors, where child labour was not prevalent previously. According to the Census 2001 figures, there are 1.26 crore working children in the age group of 5-14 as compared to the total child population of 25.2 crore. There are approximately 12 lakh children working in the hazardous occupations/processes, which are covered under the Child Labour (Prohibition & Regulation) Act i.e. 18 occupations and 65 processes. However, as per survey conducted by National Sample Survey Organisation in 2004-05, the number of working children is estimated at 90.75 lakh. It shows that the efforts of the government have borne the desired fruits.[14]

Asia contributes 61 per cent of global child labour while Africa 30 per cent. It has been over 25 years since the government of India banned child labour but the scourge continues. Even in cities like Nagpur, child labourers are working right under the nose of government authorities and in their own projects.[15] Poverty can be termed as the main reason for child labour in India. Though, the country has achieved commendable progress in industrialisation, the benefits of the same have not been effectively passed on to the lower strata of society. The average earning of a poor industrial worker are still about 2 dollars per day even in suburban areas around Mumbai and other metropolitan cities of India. This helps the industries to keep their labour costs down at the cost of the poor labourers. In effect what happens is that the children of these poor unorganised labourers have to find some work to help run the family. The industrialists in India have been successful in taking advantage of this disadvantage faced by job seekers. Due to high population, the job seekers not in a position to bargain a higher wage. As a result, the poor remain poor working for low wages.[16]

Effects of Child Labour

Childhood is the most innocent stage in a human life. It is that phase of life where a child is free from all the tensions, fun-loving, play and learn new things, and is the sweetheart of all the family members. Child labour is not only affecting under-developed and developing countries, but developed countries are also facing this though the rate is comparatively very less.[17] Working conditions that are safe and healthy for adults may not be safe and healthy for children because of their physical differences. Risks may be greater for children at various stages of development and may have long-term effects.[18] It might under-estimate the harm of child work, because children that work as well as going to school may find themselves less able to learn, as a result of exhaustion or insufficient time to complete homework.[19]

Child labour hampers the normal physical, intellectual, emotional and moral development of a child. Children who are in the growing process can permanently distort or disable their bodies when they carry heavy loads or are being forced to adopt unnatural positions at work for long hours. Children are more vulnerable, because they are less resistant to diseases and suffer more readily from chemical hazards and radiation than adults.[20] Child labour harms not only the present generation but also the posterity. Child Labour has become a growing phenomenon across the world. Millions of children are working in hazardous and exploitative conditions harmful to their physical, mental and moral development.[20] Child labourers suffer from extreme indisposition and injury rates in underground mines, opencast mines, and quarries. Children as young as six or seven years old break up rocks, and wash, sieve, and carry ore. Many children, especially girls work in domestic service, sometimes starting as young as five or six. This type of child labour is linked to child trafficking. Domestic child labourers can be victims of physical, emotional, and sometimes sexual abuse. Millions of children are involved in work that, is considered unacceptable for children under any circumstance, including the sale and trafficking of children into debt bondage, serfdom, and forced labour.[21]

International Labour Organisation

The International Labour Organisation (ILO) is central in global efforts to eliminate child labour. Standard setting and research as well as activities through the International Programme on the

Elimination of Child Labour are significant. ILO has mainstreamed child labour into its activities to raise the profile of the issue and ensure greater impact.[22] UNICEF is another key organisation, addressing the issue from the perspective of protecting the child through awareness raising and assistance activities. UNICEF's comparative advantage lies in particular supporting basic education as both a preventive and protective strategy, but also in its strong country presence. Its focus lies on the rights and protection of the child. Other important actors within the United Nations system are UNESCO, WHO, UNDP as well as the World Bank.[23]

Effective Measures

There are a number of measures that can be taken immediately to reduce the impact of poverty and help protect children and families from exploitation. Income-generating and credit schemes can alleviate some of the greatest pressures on poor people. The provision of basic services such as safe water, health care and education are such schemes. In fact, education is key to keeping children out of labour. Investments in primary and lower secondary education including efforts to reduce indirect costs are strongly correlated with a decrease in children's work. Trade Unions have played an important role in the fight against child labour. A number of civil society organisations are actively engaged in rising awareness and providing information to policy makers together with projects in developing countries. NGOs have been engaging locally in developing countries and have been at the forefront of developing new approaches to eliminating child labour.[24] At the administrative level, child labour is considered a *'harsh reality'*. The focus will be on preventing the more *'exploitative'* aspects of child labour like the employment of children in so-called hazardous industries.[25] Economists seeking government intervention in the child-labour market have typically justified their recommendation by claiming that there are externalities to child labour or that private returns to education are smaller than social returns.[26]

The Convention and Its Implications

The United Nation has implemented the convention on the rights of the similar child in 1989 to endow children with rights;

as adult and comfort; having a fragile status which protect them. The convention comprises 54 articles and two protocols. The convention is based on five fundamental principles. It stipulates that children throughout the world regardless of race, colour, religion, ethnic, caste, opinion, gender, wealth must beneficiate of the right to survival, to develop to the fullest, to be protected from harmful influences, abuse and exploitation, to participate fully in family, cultural and social life. The survival of children is the main problematical issue. The second problem faced by the convention is its objective of *"to develop to the fullest"*. The third problem addressed by the UN convention is those of exploitation and child abuse. The convention on the child rights gives a universal concept of childhood. Every child in every part of the world must have the same childhood which consists in going to school for basic education, playing game for the physical and mental development. The UN defines child as a person being under the age of 18.[27]

Legal Mechanism

Gangabhushan M. Molankal in his paper Child Labour in India: An Overview discusses details about various acts implemented in India for preventing child labour. Several preventive measures have been initiated in India for regulating child labour during the pre-independence period by enacting important legislations like The *Indian Factory Act 1881*. The Act defined *"child"* to be any young person below 12 years of age, and fixed the minimum and maximum ages for employment at seven and twelve respectively, and the hours of work at nine a day with an interval for rest of one hour, and a weekly holiday. *The Children (Pledging of Labour) Act, 1933* came into being to prohibit the pledging of labour of children. The Act lays down that an agreement, oral or written, expressed or implied, made by parent or guardian of child in consideration of some payment or benefit for causing or allowing the services of a child to be utilised in any employment, shall be void (Section-3). In consonance with the recommendations made by The Twenty Third Session of the International Labour Conference held in 1937, India passed the *Employment of Children Act, 1938.* The Act prohibits the employment of children who have not completed 15 years of age in any occupation connected with the transport of passengers, goods or mails by railways; or connected with cinder picking, clearing of an ash pit or building operation in the railway premises; or connected with the work in a catering establishment at a railway station, involving the movement of the vendor or any other employee of the establishment for one platform to another or into or out of the moving train; or connected with the work relating to the construction of railway station or with any other work where such work is done in close proximity or between the railway lines; or connected with a port authority within the limits of any port [Section- 3(1)].

The Factories Act, 1948 prohibits the employment of child under 14 years of age in factories (Section- 67). A child who has completed the age of 14 years is not permitted to work in a factory for more than four hours any day (Section- 71(1) (a)). They should not work at night i.e., twelve consecutive hours including the period from 10 p.m. to 6 a.m. (Section- 71(1) (b)). The period of work is to be limited to two shifts, which should not overlap and spread over more than five hours (Section- 71(2)). *Minimum Wages Act, 1948* provides for the fixation of minimum rates of wages in certain employments which have been specified by appropriate government in the schedule of the Act. The Act made provisions for fixing minimum rates of wages for adults, adolescents and children (Section- 3). According to *the Plantation Labour Act, 1951*, a child (below 14 years) or an adolescent between 15-18 years cannot be employed for work unless he is certified fit for work by a surgeon (Section- 26). *The Mines Act, 1952* provides for some more stringent provisions. The Act prohibits employment of persons (below 18 years) in any mine or part thereof (Section 40) and also their presence in any part of the mine above ground; where any operation connected with or incidental to any mining operation is being, carried out (Section- 45).

The Motor Transport Workers Act, 1961 covers every motor transport undertaking employing five or more persons. The Act prohibits employment of persons under 14 years of age in any capacity in the motor transport undertaking (Section 21). *The Beedi and Cigar Workers (Conditions of Employment) Act, 1966* covers all industrial premises wherein any manufacturing process connected with making of beedi or cigar or both is being, or is ordinarily carried on with or without the aid of power. The Act prohibits the employment of children below 14 years in any such premises (Section 24). The employment of young persons between 14 to 18 years is prohibited between 7 p.m. to 6 a.m. *The National Policy for Children,* as adopted on August 22nd August, 1974, stands as the basis of several national policies and programmes initiated in the last few decades to address the varied needs of children, and is the policy framework for this plan. Based on the recommendations of Gurupadaswamy Committee, *the Child Labour (Prohibition and Regulation) Act, 1986* was enacted. The Act prohibits employment of children in certain specified hazardous occupations and regulates the working conditions in the jobs that it permitted, and put greater emphasis on health and safety standards. The *National Plan of Action for Children, 2005* emphasizes the role of Government to ensure all measures and an enabling environment for survival, growth, development and protection of all children, so that each child can realize his or her inherent potential and grow up to be a healthy and productive citizen.[28]

Employing children below 14 years will now attract a maximum jail term of three years or a fine of up to Rs 50,000 with the Union Cabinet clearing a proposal by the Labour Ministry to completely ban employment of children below that age in all occupations and processes. The Child Labour (Prohibition and Regulation) Act, 1986, will be amended to incorporate the changes and will be renamed as Child and Adolescent Labour (Prohibition) Act. Giving more teeth to the Act, offences under it have been made cognizable and the punishment increased. Presently, children under the age of 14 are prohibited from employment in *"hazardous occupations and processes"* while their conditions of work in non-hazardous occupations and processes are merely regulated. Sources said the amendments include increasing the age of prohibition for employment of children and adolescents in hazardous occupations such as mining from 14 to 18. Employment of children below 14 years is presently prohibited in 18 occupations and 65 processes. Employment of children as domestic help and at road-side eateries, restaurants and tea stalls was banned in 2006. Labour Ministry officials said the maximum punishment for offences under the Act has been increased from one year to two years of imprisonment and from Rs 20,000 to Rs 50,000 fine or both. For repeated offences, it has been raised to three years of imprisonment.[29] Children between 14-18 years have been defined as *"adolescents"* in the Child and Adolescent Labour (Prohibition) Bill, 2012. Employing a child below 14 years in any kind of occupation is set to become a cognisable offence, punishable with a maximum three years imprisonment or fine up to a maximum of Rs. 50,000. Ministry officials said that banning any employment of children below 14 years will go a long way in enforcing the Right to Education Act, 2009 which mandates free and compulsory education of all children in the age group of 6-14 years.[30]

National Child Labour Project

National Child Labour Project is a government-sponsored scheme meant for such children, who were living like an adult life in childhood. Special schools were opened under the scheme where working children were enrolled, provided with education, nutritive food, monthly stipend, health care facilities and marketable vocational skill and finally after three years mainstreamed into the regular schools. These special schools act like a bridge for such children which make them students from labourers, give them education from exploitation and admit them in a school instead of engaging at workplace.[31]

Conclusion

The attempts to assert human rights or child's rights are often confronted with the accusation of violation and non respect of countries cultural specificities. Child labour is a global crisis. Global response is needed. No nation, community or household can expect to achieve sustainable human development if it tolerates child labour, if it neglects the development of human resources and if it squanders most valuable resource, namely the potential capabilities embodied in children.[32] The international consensus on the elimination of child labour is built around three main concerns: the protection of children, their mental and cognitive development, and the economic impact of child labour. Child labour laws should aim to protect children who work, instead of trying to remove children from work.

REFERENCES

1. F. O. Omokhodion, S. I. Omokhodion, and T. O. Odusote (2005). *Perceptions of child labour among working children in Ibadan, Nigeria*, Retrieved from http://www.ncbi.nlm.nih.gov/pubmed/16634973
2. *Whole Time Domestic Child Labor in Metropolitan City of Kolkata (2008).* Retrieved from http://library.isical.ac.in/jspui/bitstream/10263/5432/1/IP-45-2008-579-582%20(2).pdf
3. *Trade Openness, Foreign Direct Investment and Child Labor,* Retrieved from http://eprints.lse.ac.uk/625/
4. B. A. Bhat and T. A. Rather (2009). *Child labour in the handicrafts home industry in Kashmir: A sociological study,* Retrieved from http://www.academia.edu/4133316/Child_labour_in_the_handicrafts_home_industry_in_Kashmir_A_sociological_study
5. *Chapter III, Child Labour in India - Issues, Dimensions and Determinants,* Retrieved from http://shodhganga.inflibnet.ac.in/bitstream/10603/648/8/08_chapter3.pdf
6. Professor Himayatullah Khan, *Child labour in Pakistan and other developing countries,* Retrieved from
7. Protect children: World day against child labour, Retrieved from http://www.ilo.org/ipec/Campaignandadvocacy/WDACL/lang—en/index.htm
8. *Facts and figures on child labour,* Retrieved from http://www.ilo.org/global/about-the-ilo/media-centre/issue-briefs/WCMS_206127/lang—en/index.htm
9. Ozcan Dagdemir, Hakan Acaroglu (2010). *The effects of globalization on child labor in developing countries,* Retrieved from http://econpapers.repec.org/article/pdcjrnbeh/v_3a2_3ay_3a2010_3ai_3a2_3ap_3a37-47.htm
10. Tito Boeri, Brooke Helppie & Mario Macis (2008). *Labor Regulations in Developing Countries: A Review of the Evidence and Directions for Future Research,* Retrieved from http://siteresources.worldbank.org/SOCIALPROTECTION/Resources/SP-Discussion-papers/Labor-Market-DP/0833.pdf
11. Jens Chr. Andvig, Sudharshan Canagarajah & Anne Kielland (2001), *Issues in Child Labor in Africa, Africa Region Human Development Working Paper Series.*

12. *Cambodia-Child Labour*, Retrieved from http://en.wikipedia.org/wiki/Child_labour_in_Cambodia
13. European Commission (2010). *Commission Staff working documents-Child Labour,* Retrieved from
14. About child labour, *Ministry of labour and employment, Government of India*, Retrieved from http://labour.nic.in/content/division/child-labour.php
15. *The Times of India (Feb 1, 2014).* Child labour: A menace that continues unabated, Retrieved from http://timesofindia.indiatimes.com/city/nagpur/Child-labour-A-menace-that-continues-unabated/articleshow/29685779.cms
16. *Child labour in India and its causes*, Retrieved from http://vegaselias.hubpages.com/hub/CHILD-LABOR-IN-INDIA-AND-ITS-CAUSES
17. *Child Labor – A Challenge the World is Facing,* Retrieved from http://anujagarwal.hubpages.com/hub/Cause-and-effects-of-Child-Labour
18. *Physical Differences between Children and Adults May Increase Children's Work-related Risks,* Retrieved from https://www.continuetolearn.uiowa.edu/laborctr/child_labor/about/health_issues.html
19. See http://www.unicef-irc.org/publications/pdf/iwp79.pdf
20. European Commission (2010). *Commission Staff working documents-Child Labour,* Retrieved from http://trade.ec.europa.eu/doclib/docs/2010/february/tradoc_145803.pdf
21. Dr Sharmistha Bhattacharjee, *Child labour in India: a health and human rights perspective.*
22. What is Child Labour? Retrieved from https://www.continuetolearn.uiowa.edu/laborctr/child_labor/about/what_is_child_labor.html
23. European Commission (2010). *Commission Staff working documents-Child Labour,* Retrieved from http://trade.ec.europa.eu/doclib/docs/2010/february/tradoc_145803.pdf
24. *Ibid*
25. *Ibid*
26. Devendra Mishra and Prem Arora (2007). *Domestic Child Labor*, Retrieved from http://endchildlabor.org/?page_id=407

27. *The Economics of Child Labor,* Retrieved from http://qed.econ.queensu.ca/pub/faculty/sumon/basu_childlabor.pdf
28. Child Labour, *Human Rights and the Capability Approach,* Retrieved from http://cornell.lawreviewnetwork.com/files/2013/02/Dixon-Nussbaum final.pdf
29. Gangabhushan M. Molanka, *Child Labour in India: An Overview,* Retrieved from http://www.childjustice.org/wsecl/papers/Molankal2008.pdf
30. *The Indian Express (Aug 29, 2011).* Govt nod to total ban on child labour, Retrieved from http://archive.indianexpress.com/news/govt-nod-to-total-ban-on-child-labour/994513/
31. See http://bba.org.in/?q=content/india-moves-ban-all-forms-child-labour
32. Dharmendra Kumar Mishra (2012). *Strengthening Government's Action Against Child Labour : The Milestones, Odisha Review,* Retrieved from http://orissa.gov.in/e-magazine/Orissareview/2012/May/engpdf/19-24.pdf
33. Chapter I, *S7ntroduction and Review of Literature,* Retrieved from http://ietd.inflibnet.ac.in/bitstream/10603/648/6/06_chapter1.pdf
34. *Child labour in Bangladesh,* UNICEF, Retrieved from http://www.unicef.org/bangladesh/Child_labour.pdf
35. *Child labour in Nepal,* Retrieve from http://www.darvag.com/jamiat/bultan/wc-nepal.pdf
36. Bibek Bhandari (Aug 15, 2013), *No life for a child: The grim reality of Nepal's child laborers,* Retrieved from http://edition.cnn.com/2013/08/14/world/asia/nepal-child-labor/
37. *Pakistan's labour laws 'ignore abuse of children' (January 10, 2014),* BBC News, Retrieved from http://www.bbc.com/news/world-asia-25678508
38. Richard C.W. Miller (2014), *Work or Starve: Child Labour in Pakistan's Brick Kilns,* Retrieved from http://www.huffingtonpost.co.uk/richard-cw-miller/child-labour-pakistan_b_4694541.html
39. Kishore Kumar Chhetri (2011), *Child Labour in Bhutan: The Challenges of Implementing Child Rights in Bhutan,* Retrieved from http://munin.uit.no/bitstream/handle/10037/3501/thesis.pdf?sequence=1

40. *Bhutan Child labour,* Retrieved from http://www.refworld.org/docid/4e8c397319.html
41. *Sri Lanka: 2012 Findings on the Worst Forms of Child Labour,* Retrieved from http://www.dol.gov/ilab/reports/child-labor/sri_lanka.htm
42. *Maldives: 2012 Findings on the Worst Forms of Child Labour,* Retrieved from http://www.dol.gov/ilab/reports/child-labor/maldives.htm

4

Widows

"When a poor person dies of hunger, it has not happened because God did not take care of him or her. It has happened because neither you nor I wanted to give that person what he or she needed."

- Mother Teresa

Introduction

Old age consists of age nearing or surpassing the life expectancy of human beings, and the end of the human life cycle. Old people often have limited regenerative abilities and are more prone to disease, syndromes, and sickness than younger adults. The chronological age denoted as *"old age"* varies culturally and historically. Early old age is a pleasant time: children are grown, retirement from work, and is time to pursue interests. The rights of older persons are the entitlements and independence claimed for senior citizens (i.e. above 60 years of age). Elderly rights are one of the fundamental rights of India. The International Day of older persons is celebrated annually on October 1. The 2001 census of India demonstrated that aged people in India have crossed over 100 million. Many oldies in India are not alert about the human rights of older persons, due to high occurrence of illiteracy and lack of alertness. Elder illiteracy directly contributes to lack of knowledge regarding human rights for the older people in India, and contributes to the infringement of those rights. The government of India provides various concessions and facilities to its senior citizens.[1]

Who are Widows?

A woman who has lost her husband by death and has not remarried is called a widow. Widows are considered to be a marginalised group in India because they occupy a very low social status in society. Consequently they have to face severe social, economic and cultural deprivations.[2]

Widows in India

India has an estimated 40 million widows which is approximately 10 per cent of the country's female population. Thousands of widows have been making their way to one particular town in the north of India. Few places are as closely associated with the deity Krishna as is Vrindavan, on the banks of the Yamuna, a few hours' drive south-east of Delhi. Radha and Krishna, the two names bound together forever and in the minds of every pilgrim who arrives in town to walk the ritual circuit of temples and bathing *Ghats*. Widows in India no longer throw themselves on the funeral pyres of their husbands. But life for them can still be hard. Delhi-based non-governmental organisation Maitrial helps providing food and shelter for some of the widows.[3] The holy Indian city of Vrindavan has become a magnet for widows. After being abandoned by their families, the women flock to the town in their thousand. But most end up living a life of poverty and seclusion. This central pilgrimage town, believed to be birthplace of the Hindu deity *Krishna*, has more than 4,000 temples. With a population of nearly 60,000 thousand people, there are an estimated 20,000 widows living in the town. Over the years, Vrindavan has become a magnet for these women. The city is full of dingy guest houses, shelters, and cramped quarters where impoverished and neglected widows come to eke out an existence till death. Despite advanced age, many widows cook their own meals and clean their own clothes and utensils. Superstitious relatives claim the widows bring misfortune and blame them for their husbands' death.

Challenges before Widow

Widows were considered inauspicious and were not permitted to attend festive occasions, despite many of them being young girls whose marriage had not even been consummated. It was very common for the mother-in-law to taunt her as being responsible for her son's death. The death of the husband was the only beginning of a young woman's problems.[4] The treatment of widows around the world varies, but unequal benefits and treatment generally received by widows compared to those received by widowers globally has spurred an interest on the issue by human rights activists. It is often necessary for women to comply with the social customs of her area, because her fiscal stature depends on it, but this custom is also abused by others often as a way to keep money within the patriarchal family.[5] The widows in all communities carried the stigma of inauspiciousness and were required not to participate in religious or auspicious social functions such as marriage or other celebrations. A widow was not even allowed to perform the ritual ceremony to welcome her own daughter-in-law.

The problem of economic insecurity is faced by the elderly when they are unable to sustain themselves financially. Many older persons either lack from the opportunity and/or the capacity to be as productive as they were. Isolation or a deep sense of loneliness is a common complaint of many elderly is the feeling of being isolated. The elderly, especially those who are weak and/or dependent, require physical, mental and emotional care and support. When this is not provided, they suffer from neglect, a problem that occurs when a person is left uncared for and that is often linked with isolation. The elderly are highly vulnerable to abuse, where a person is willfully or inadvertently harmed, usually by someone who is part of the family or otherwise close to the victim. Many older persons live in fear. Whether rational or irrational, this is a relevant problem faced by the elderly that needs to be carefully and effectively addressed. Lowered self-esteem among older persons has a complex etiology that includes isolation, neglect, reduced responsibilities and decrease in value or worth by one-self, family and/or the society.[6]

Abolition of *Sati*

Sati is described as a Hindu custom in India wherein the widow was burnt to ashes on her dead husband's pyre. Basically, the custom of *Sati* was believed to be a voluntary Hindu act where the woman voluntary decides to end her life with husband after his death.[7] Literary evidence about the practice appears from the 4th century BCE, while archaeological evidence appears only from the 5th and 6th centuries CE. The Rajput practice of *Jauhar*, known from Rajasthan and Madhya Pradesh was the collective suicide of a community facing certain defeat in a battle against Muslims. It consisted of the mass immolation of women, children, the elderly and the sick, at the same time when their fighting men died in battle. Royal funerals sometimes have included the deaths of many wives and concubines. *Sati* is often described as voluntary, although in some cases it may have been forced. The practice of *Sati* originated from the Goddess *Sati* also known as *Dakshayani*, who sacrificed herself by fire because she could not bare the shame that was bestowed upon her husband *Shiva*, by her very own father, *Daksha*. It is hard to trace the original of the *Sati*. It does have its roots in ancient times; however historians disagree on the actual time-frame. Some will date back to the evidence written in the Vedas, around 5,500 thousand years ago. It was also estimated that certain areas such as Bengal and the region of Rajasthan had the highest incident of *Sati*. All in all, *Sati* occurred in about one per cent of the total Indian population affecting royal families and higher-level caste system women of the past.

The practice was outlawed by the British Raj in 1829 within their own territories in India, followed up by laws in the same direction by the authorities in the princely states of India in the ensuing decades, with a general ban for the whole of India issued by Queen Victoria in 1861. The Indian Sati Prevention Act from 1987 makes it criminal to aiding, abetting, and even only *"glorifying"* the act of *sati*, placing upon those who could prevent the act a legal duty to prevent it from happening.[8]

Widow Remarriage

Vidyasagar pressed on and urged the British to pass legislation that will allow Hindu widows to remarry. To support his request, Ishwar Chandra Vidyasagar collected almost 1,000 signatures and sent his petition to the Indian legislative council. The council received thousands of signatures for and against this measure, but the members finally decided to support the enlightened minority, The Hindu Widow Remarriage Act was passed in 1856. Vidyasagar lived in a world where the males among the Kulin Brahmins, an aristocratic caste with rigid marriage rules were highly sought after as bridegrooms and able to marry as many women as they wished. Arguing that the practice of Kulinism was inhuman, Ishwar Chandra Vidyasagar presented the government with a petition signed by 2,500 persons requesting the legislative prohibition of polygamy.[9]

Legal Perspectives

There is the 2007 Maintenance and Welfare of Parents and Senior Citizens Act that makes it an offense for children to abandon their parents, but many of India's 40 million widows are not aware of their rights, and the act provides for only relatively mild penalties (three months jail or a fine not exceeding $100). Women fear exercising their rights, because they do not want to be branded a bad woman, a bad mother.[10] India's Supreme Court has ordered government and civic agencies to improve the lives of women in Vrindavan after media reports of their deplorable living conditions. The Uttar Pradesh government has now appointed a panel to collect data on the socio-economic conditions.[11] Remarriage of widows was legalised in all cases by the Hindu Widows Remarriage Act, 1856. But, the Act provided that all rights and interest with a widow had in her deceased husband's estate would *"cases and determine"* on her remarriage, as if she had died. However, the Hindu Women's Right to Property Act, 1937 gave better right to Hindu women in respect of property, but gave a limited estate, which is held only during her life time and then reverts to her husband's heirs. But, in view of the limited right becoming an absolute right by virtue of the Hindu succession Act, 1956, the question of divesting the property on remarriage does not arise. Under section 14 (1), of the Act, the widow's limited interest gets automatically converted into an absolute right. Among Hindus, there are two kinds of property (1) self acquired and (ii) ancestral / joint family.[12]

Following the outcry after the *sati* of Roop Kanwar, the Indian government enacted the Rajasthan Sati Prevention Ordinance, 1987 on October 1, 1987 and later passed the Commission of Sati (Prevention) Act, 1987. The *Prevention of Sati Act* makes it illegal to support, glorify or attempt to commit *sati*. Support of *sati*, including coercing or forcing someone to commit *sati*, can be punished by death sentence or life imprisonment, while glorifying *sati* is punishable with one to seven years in prison. Enforcement of these measures is not always consistent. The National Council for Women has suggested amendments to the law to remove some of these flaws.[13]

Hindu Widows' Remarriage Act, 1856

The Hindu Widows' Remarriage Act, 1856, also Act XV, 1856, enacted on July 25, 1856, legalised the remarriage of Hindu widows in all jurisdictions of India under East India Company rule. In order to protect both, what it considered family honour and family property, upper-caste Hindu society had long disallowed the remarriage of widows, even child and adolescent ones, all of whom were expected to live a life of austerity and abnegation. The Hindu Widows' Remarriage Act of 1856, enacted in response to the campaign of Pandit Ishwar Chandra Vidyasagar, provided legal safeguards against loss of certain forms of inheritance for remarrying a Hindu widow, though, under the Act, the widow forsook any inheritance due from her deceased husband.[14]

Maintenance and Welfare of Parents and Senior Citizens Act, 2007 Prune the Herding!

Maintenance and Welfare of Parents and Senior Citizens Act, 2007 is a legislation enacted in 2007, initiated by Ministry, Government of India to provide more effective provision for maintenance and welfare of parents and senior citizens. This Act makes it legal obligation for children and heirs to provide maintenance to senior citizens and parents, by monthly allowance. This Act also provides simple, speedy and inexpensive mechanism for the protection of life and property of the older persons. Indian society lays high importance on providing care and protection for parents and elderly. Withering of joint family system has contributed to the challenges faced by elderly. Now-a-days, they are forced to live alone and are exposed to various kinds of problems such as lack of physical, social, emotional and financial support. This Act provides in-expensive and speedy procedure to claim monthly maintenance for parents and senior citizens. This Act casts obligations on children to maintain their parents/grandparents and also the relative of the senior citizen to maintain such senior citizens.[15]

Conclusion

For many traditionalists, this Hindu practice symbolizes the epitome of wifely devotion, especially among the Rajput caste of Northern India. Historically, *sati* is not unique to India. In the north Indian state of Rajasthan, it came to be associated with the people of the warrior Rajput caste, who viewed *sati* as the extreme expression of marital valor. The practice of *Sati* was banned in India in 1829 by the British Government. Indian leaders such as Rajaram Mohan Roy and his Brahmo Samaj organisation were one of the first Indian organisations to denounce and support the eradication of *Sati*. The Rajasthan Sati Prevention Ordinance of 1987 was passed to insure the end of this ancient ritual. The National Council of Women has suggested amendments to the law to eradicate some of its flaws. However, controversy about prohibition of shrines etc, still remains controversial and far from being solved. According to Indian feminists, it is this traditional ideology that continues to oppress women. According to them, the expectations placed on women to offer selfless nurturance are great and to be socialised to commit suicide for the benefit of others is ludicrous. Some feminists believe that women have also been targeted by fundamentalists, such as the Committee for the Defense of the Religion of *Sati*.

REFERENCES

1. *Elder law in India,* Retrieved from http://en.wikipedia.org/wiki/Elder_law_in_India
2. Varun Malik (2013). Problems Of Widow Remarriage In India: A Study, *Journal of Business Management & Social Sciences Research,* Retrieved from http://borjournals.com/Research_papers/feb_2013/1142M.pdf
3. Anthony Denselow (2013). *The Indian town with 6,000 widows,* Retrieved fromhttp://www.bbc.com/news/magazine-21859622
4. Varun Malik (2013). Problems Of Widow Remarriage In India: A Study, *Journal of Business Management & Social Sciences Research,* Retrieved from http://borjournals.com/Research_papers/feb_2013/1142M.pdf

5. Owen, Margaret. *A World of Widows. Illustrated.* Atlantic Highlands, NJ: Zed Books, 1996. 181-183. eBook.
6. *Problems of the elderly*, Retrieved from http://www.helpageindiaprogramme.org/Elderly%20Issues/problems_of_the_elderly/index.html
7. *Sati - The burning of the widow,* Retrieved from http://adaniel.tripod.com/sati.htm
8. *Sati (Practice).* Retrieved from http://en.wikipedia.org/wiki/Sati_(practice)
9. *Reforms : Widow remarriage,* Retrieved from http://indiansaga.com/history/reforms_vidyasagar1.html
10. See http://world.time.com/2013/10/07/if-youre-an-indian-widow-your-children-could-kick-you-out-and-take-everything/
11. *India's city of widows (2013).* Retrieved from http://www.dw.de/indias-city-of-widows/a-16992242
12. *Widow's Rights - How To Implement Them,* Retrieved from http://timesfoundation.indiatimes.com/articleshow/msid-47870463,curpg-2.cms
13. *Sati (Practice).* Retrieved from http://en.wikipedia.org/wiki/Sati_(practice)
14. *Hindu Widows' Remarriage Act, 1856*, Retrieved from http://en.wikipedia.org/wiki/Hindu_Widows'_Remarriage_Act,_1856
15. *Maintenance and Welfare of Parents and Senior Citizens Act, 2007,* Retrieved from http://en.wikipedia.org/wiki/Maintenance_and_Welfare_of_Parents_ and_Senior_Citizens_Act,_2007

5

Farmers' Suicide

"No one has yet fully realised the wealth of sympathy, kindness and generosity hidden in the soul of a child. The effort of every true education should be to unlock that treasure."

- Emma Goldman

Introduction

Agriculture is the science of farming, including cultivation of the soil for the growing of crops and the rearing of animals to provide food, wool, and other products. Agriculture and related products are the main economic drivers of thirds world countries as opposed to manufacturing in developed nations. Agriculture is very important as it is the backbone to socially and politically stable nation. Agriculture is the largest sector that provides food and employment to many people. It also appraises a country's development standard and contributed to the GDP of a country. A farmer is a person engaged in agriculture, raising living organisms for food or raw material. A farmer might own the farmed land or might work as a labourer on land owned by other. Farmers are often members of local, regional, or national farmers' Unions or agricultural producers' organisations and can exert significant political influence. Farmed products might be sold either to a market, in a farmers' market, or directly from a farm. In a subsistence economy, farm products might to some extent be either consumed by the farmer's family or pooled by the community.[1] India is an agrarian country with around 60 per cent of its people depending directly or indirectly upon agriculture. Agriculture in India is often attributed as gambling with monsoons, because of its almost exclusive dependency on precipitation from monsoons. India's small farmers, once the country's economic backbone and most reliable vote bank, are increasingly being left behind. With global competition and rising costs cutting into their lean profits, their ranks are dwindling, as is their contribution to the gross domestic product.[2]

Reasons of Farmers' Suicide

Farmers' suicides are the most tragic and dramatic symptom of the crisis of survival faced by Indian peasants. Rapid increase in indebtedness is at the root of farmers taking their lives. Debt is a reflection of a negative economy. Two factors have transformed agriculture from a positive economy into a negative economy for peasants: the rising of costs of production and the falling prices of farm commodities. Both factors are rooted in the policies of trade liberalisation and corporate globalisation. The region in India with the highest level of farmer's suicides is the Vidharbha region in Maharashtra (4000 suicides per year, 10 per day). The rigged prices of globally traded agriculture commodities steal from poor peasants of the South.[3] Distress in agriculture, compounded by the lack of water to save standing crops, resulted in the suicide of some farmers. One strand attributes the suicides to the agro-economic problems, namely crop failure, indebtedness and the macro-policy issues arising out of the WTO-led economic regime. The second strand attributes the suicides to the failure of the state and its politico economic policy.[4] Campaign group's claim the suicides have been caused by food speculators manipulating cereal prices, and GM companies who are selling expensive cotton seeds and fertilisers. In many times farmers takes loans from mahajans or money lenders for cultivation and if production falls then farmer's suicides.

After nationalisation of the banking system in 1969, there was an impressive expansion of credit to the agricultural sector. The share of agricultural credit in total bank lending nearly doubled from around 10 per cent in the mid-1970s to about 18 per cent in the late 1980s. Financial liberalisation, an important part of the neoliberal policy regime, reversed this trend. The share of agricultural credit in total bank lending declined from the peak of 18 percent in the late 1980s to about 11 per cent in 2005. The decline has continued since then.

Farmers' Suicide in India

After the independence, according to Gandhiji's vision of Gram-Swaraj, villages and specially farmers were to be the main focus of any development plan of India. As years passed by, agriculture as an industry lost its importance for policy makers of India. This over the time caused severe distress among the farmers leading to recent dramatic rise in the number of suicides among farmer community. Every day in national newspaper invariably there is news related to farmers' suicides.[5]

Since the 1990s, farmers' suicides in India have made headlines. The high number was first noticed in the state of Maharashtra and then the media began reporting it happening in other parts of India.[6] More than 270,000 Indian cotton farmers have killed themselves since 1995. As many as 38 farmers have committed suicide in the state in February 2014, after hailstorms and unseasonal rain, official figures show. North Maharashtra alone has reported 16 cases. Hailstorms have affected 28 of the 35 districts, destroying crop of over 19 lakh hectares and leaving farmers on the brink. The rabi wheat, jowar and sugarcane have been damaged, and fruit crops including pomegranate, mango, orange and grapes were affected. The state government has asked the Centre for Rs. 5,000-crore relief. It is facing flak for not acting before the model code came into force.[7] Nationwide; the farmers' suicide rate was 16.3 per 100,000 farmers in 2011. That's a lot higher than 11.1, which is the rate for the rest of the population. In Maharashtra, for instance, the rate is 29.1 suicides per 100,000 farmers. This is over 160 per cent higher than that for all Indians excluding farmers. Such gaps exist in other states, too. In as many as 16 of 22 major states, the farmer's suicide rate was higher than the rate among the rest of the population in 2011. Ten states show a higher farmer's suicide rate in 2011 than in 2001. That includes the major farming zones of Punjab and Haryana. At least 270,940 Indian farmers have taken their lives since 1995, NCRB records show. This occurred at an annual average of 14,462 in six years, from 1995 to 2000.[8] In 2006, the state of Maharashtra, with 4,453 farmers' suicides accounted for over a quarter of the all-India total of 17,060, according to the National Crime Records Bureau.

Agriculture is the main stay of the state of Maharashtra. Average annual profit from cultivation in the state of Maharashtra is the lowest of all Indian states. The reasons for such pathetic state of farmers include below average rainfall, heavy load-shedding, lack of small irrigation projects, poverty, pressure of private moneylenders and banks, ignorance of ancillary occupations for raising income, employment problem of the farmers' children, decreasing interest of the young generation in farming, rapid urbanisation, apathy and lack of political willpower toward welfare and development of the region, etc. Vidarbha is home for approximately 3.4 million cotton farmers and 95 per cent of these struggle with the massive debt. Most of the villages in Vidarbha are badly in need of basic social infrastructure like all-weather roads, drinking water, regular electricity, primary health care, and basic education. Majority of suicide cases are from cotton growing areas. The cotton farmers in India paying more prices for inputs like seeds, pesticides, fertilisers, electricity, water, and labour.[9] Vidarbha was in the media for a spate of farmer suicides in recent years ostensibly because of the falling Minimum Support Price for cotton. The problem is complex and root causes include lopsided policies of the World Trade Organisation and developed nations' subsidies to their cotton farmers which make Vidarbha's cotton uncompetitive in world markets.

A state government-commissioned study conducted by three prominent universities in Punjab laid bare the magnitude of the crisis. On an average estimate, three persons committed suicide every two days in the last decade in this grain bowl state of Punjab. The report says that more than 5,000 farmers and farm labourers, about 500 each year, committed suicide between 2000 to 2010. Sixty per cent of these suicides took place in the grain producing belts essentially in two districts of Bathinda and Sangrur. Heavy farm debts, reduced land holding and diminishing farm returns have been among the major escalators to the crisis. Till a few years ago, the farm debt in Punjab was at nearly

Rs. 31,000 crore, which today is sure to have increased sizeably. As per study, about 38 per cent of those who committed suicide in the last decade were in the prime of their life between 20 to 30 years. The failure to pay back the debt, among other reasons, drove many of them to suicide. The problem is more when it comes to small and marginal farmers. A study by the Punjab Agriculture University in Ludhiana states that 34 per cent of marginal farmers in the state are living below poverty line.[10]

A total of 2,639 farmers killed themselves in Orissa in the past ten years. The farmers killed themselves mostly due to personal problems and family disputes. Of the total deaths, 2,575 committed suicide between 2000 and 2008. The remaining 64 deaths took place from 2009 up to February 10, 2011.[11] Sambalpur became the epicenter of the crisis, where 600 villages lost most of their crops and five farmers committed suicide. Now that the uncertainties of monsoon have increased, this kind of pest attack has increased and they have also increased their investment by seven to eight times. So, their entire system has failed. As many as 3,509 farmers committed suicide in the past eleven years in Orissa. The highest number of 418 farmers committed suicide in 1998. A total of 48,631 people committed suicide in the state from 1997 to 2008. The number of farmers' suicide was 3,509 during the period. Stating that 73 per cent of the state's population earns livelihood from their cultivation, he said most of the farmers committed suicide had reasons like family disputes and other reasons.[12] Among other major states, Kerala saw 1,081 such farm deaths, a steep increase of 251 over its 2011 number of 830. Uttar Pradesh saw 745 farm suicides, up by 100 over its 2011 figure. Tamil Nadu reported a decline of 124 to log 499. Other states seem inspired by Chhattisgarh's methods. West Bengal sent in no data at all on farm suicides (or some other categories, too) in 2012. But its three-year average for 2009-2011 was 951.[13]

India is going through an agrarian crisis. The farmers who have been involved in one of the most meaningful livelihoods on earth are struggling to make ends meet. The Cauvery delta was once a place of prosperity, but has been facing many challenges now. The last two seasons have seen severe problems in agriculture with insufficient water due to truant monsoons and Cauvery water sharing issues. Most farmers in the delta region did not cultivate the Kuruvai crop as there was no water but had cultivated paddy in samba with the hope that water would be available through the season. There are farmers' suicides happening in the delta districts and very clearly distress in agriculture is a major/ important reason for all suicides. Apart from the government, other local associations and media did not report the deaths in an unbiased/impartial manner. However, they also played an active role in bringing the issue to the forefront. The opposition parties DMK and DMDK have offered relief to some of the families.[14]

The agrarian crisis and farmers' distress in Kerala are closely linked to the neo-liberal policy regime implemented in the country in the recent past. The association between the two is more in the regions of the state that are heavily dependent on export-oriented crops such as coffee and pepper. The worst affected are the small farmers, as they are more vulnerable to crop losses and price declines. Unless the plight of farmers is addressed in terms of changing the macro-policies regulating taxes, prices and imports, the condition of the farmers cannot be improved on sustainable basis, either by increasing the availability of institutional credit or providing some alleviatory sops to the victims of suicide families.[15] After a long time, farmers' suicides have become a burning issue with incidents being reported from Wayanad district. The hill regions of Wayanad are known for the long-gestation plantation crops like tea, coffee and pepper. Fluctuations in prices, climatic changes and disease-related problems have prompted many farmers to shift to annual crops like ginger and plantain. Lured by the good prices of these crops, many farmers started cultivation on leased land in Karnataka. Farmers go for intensive cultivation by investing heavily on land, fertilisers and pesticides. When crops fail or prices fall, they suffer huge losses. The demand for land in Karnataka has gone up so much that the lease rentals, which were in the range of Rs 2,000 per acre ten years ago, have touched Rs 70,000 per acre. In the case of plantains, the farmers are negotiating a price fall of nearly 40 per cent in season. Heavy rains have caused widespread damage to the crop.[16]

The farming sector in Karnataka has been going though painful phase since the last few years and a whopping 2,909 farmers committed suicide across the state during the last one decade (2003-04 to July 31, 2012). With farming becoming economically unviable owing to various factors, the data provided by the State Agriculture Department revealed that on an average 25 farmers committed suicide in Karnataka every month in the last ten years. As many as 1,077 farmers ended their lives since the BJP came to power in the state in 2008. The tragic incidents primarily occurred due to agrarian distress caused by crop loss on account of drought, floods and diseases; debts; high farming cost, particularly fertilizer; and low returns due to faulty policies of both state and central governments. The growth rate of the agriculture sector has been erratic during the last five years. According to Economic Survey, the sector recorded growth of 12.4 per cent of Gross State Domestic Product in 2007-08, 2.3 per cent in 2008-09, 3.6 per cent in 2009-10, and 13.3 per cent in 2010-11. The state faced three consecutive droughts during the S.M. Krishna regime (2001-04) and two consecutive droughts during the BJP rule (2011-12 and 2012-13). With declaration of 140 taluks as drought-hit in the current sowing season, the state is facing the worst drought in the last 40 years. ISEC research study (2011) noted that implementation of the prime minister's rehabilitation package (Rs. 2,689.64 crore) in six districts of Belgaum, Chikmagalur, Chitradurga, Hassan, Kodagu and Shimoga had not helped small and marginal farmers. In fact, better-off farmers were benefited from the package.[17]

The spate of suicides by farmers in Saurashtra and continuing agrarian distress give the lie to Narendra Modi's assertions of Gujarat being a developed state. Driving one past massive industrial unit after another on Gujarat's superfast highways in Saurashtra, it is hard to imagine that just a few kilometres off those roads lie villages ravaged by drought and untouched by development. Saurashtra appears to be on the brink of massive agrarian crisis, which from all accounts can only be addressed by the state. With the cotton crop failing owing to the lack of timely rains, farmers, steeped in debt and seeing no hope of relief are ending lives in tragic ways. From 2003 to 2007, there were 489 instances of suicide by farmers in Gujarat. The crops grown in this belt are largely cotton and groundnut, both of which have failed owing to the scanty rainfall. The National Disaster Management Authority clearly states that *"agriculture is the first sector to be affected by drought. Within the agricultural sector, marginal and small farmers are more vulnerable to drought because of their dependence on rain-fed agriculture. Pressure and fear of losing social status due to drought-induced poverty forces farmers to take drastic steps like suicide."*[18]

While Maharashtra has been in the news for its horrific farmer suicides, neither the regional nor national media has had much to say about the plight of farmers in the states of Madhya Pradesh and Chhatisgarh. There are occasional stories about drought-affected farmers being forced to migrate in search of work, but increasing instances of suicide among farmers in these states has gone almost unnoticed. A study by the Madras Institute of Development Studies, quoted by *The Hindu*s Rural Affairs Editor P Sainath in the November 14, 2007 issue puts the number of farmers' suicides in the two states at well over 2,000 a year from 1997 onwards when the Institute began documenting suicide figures. According to its data, 2,390 farmers committed suicide in the two states in 1997; 2,278 in 1998; 2,654 in 1999; 2,660 in 2000; 2,824 in 2001; 2,578 in 2002; 2,511 in 2003; 3,033 in 2004; and 2,660 in 2005. Higher input costs and declining market prices for crops have hit farmers. While the government's trade policies allow more and cheaper imports, thus reducing both price and demand for local products, input costs have gone up. The cost of diesel has risen from Rs 13 to Rs 38. Irrigation and power cost more. In 1999-2000, farmers were selling mustard at Rs. 2,200 per quintal. Today, they sell it at Rs 1,600 a quintal, because of the increase in imports of edible oils. The import of palmolein, for example, has gone up from four lakh tonnes in 1999-2000 to 60 lakh tonnes in 2007. In Madhya Pradesh, in 2001-02, 15,000 tonnes of gram from Kabul and Pakistan were dumped in the Indore market; in a single day.[19] The Madhya Pradesh government has taken a host of welfare measures that could help to curb farmers' suicides. The state has reported several farmers' suicides mainly because of damage to crops due to intense cold and untimely rainfall.[20]

Among the major states, only a few including Karnataka, Kerala and West Bengal avoided the sharp rise these six years and lowered the average by over 350 compared to the 1997-2003 period. Other states of higher farmers' suicides were Assam, Jharkhand, Chhatisgarh, Rajasthan, Jharkhand, Nagaland,

Odhisa, Sikkim and Delhi. Karnataka, Arunachal Pradesh, Bihar, Gujarat, Haryna, Himachal Pradesh, Jammu & Kashmir, Madhya Pradesh, Meghalaya, Mizoram, Punjab, Tamil Nadu, Tripura, Uttarakhand saw fewer number of farmers' suicides.[21] In all, 18 of 28 States reported higher farm suicide numbers in 2009. Some, like Jammu and Kashmir or Uttarakhand, saw a negligible rise. Rajasthan, Kerala and Jharkhand saw increases of 55, 76 and 93 respectively. Assam and West Bengal saw higher rises of 144 and 295.[22]

Effects of Suicide

Thousands of farmers have committed suicides in India in general. For many in Andhra Pradesh's Agrarian crisis, even death is not the end of the trouble. Instead, it is the beginning of a new burden for the surviving women such as mothers, wives and daughters of the immolating farmers. To begin with, they were doing the bulk of the work. Now, they have to face the banks and the money lenders. They have to bring up the children and send them to schools. Raising and spending money for the needs of the households becomes their job. And on top of it, they have to run the farm. Sometimes, the pressure becomes much. In this struggle against poverty and sudden death (suicides) by male members in the family, the stress on the widows is enormous.[23]

Government Assistance

India has been taking steps to address the higher number of farmers in India, who are immolating themselves. A series of government inquiries followed, looking into the causes of farmers' suicides. Former Agriculture minister Sharad Pawar said it was a serious issue with many factors responsible, and he said the government was increasing investment in agriculture and raising minimum prices of crops to increase farmers' income. The Maharashtra government announced Rs 4,000-crore package in March, 2014 for farmers affected by unseasonal rain and hailstorms. The state government has asked for Rs 5,000 crore from the Centre to help farmers. The state cabinet also decided to waive Rs 268 crore towards interest on crop loans and electricity bills of Rs 200 crore of farmers.[24]

Maharashtra had a programme for procurement of cotton since 1972-73. The purpose of the Monopoly Cotton Procurement Scheme (MCPS) was to ensure a stable price to farmers. However, with liberalisation and opening of trade, operation of the MCPS was curtailed. It is true that the Maharashtra government was incurring high losses due to these operations. Serious problems had emerged in the form of middlemen between the farmers and MCPS who appropriated parts of the subsidy that should have gone to farmers. But the losses of the MCPS seem to be a function of other policies as well (like the ones stated below), which depressed the open market price and inflated the subsidy bill, rather than the inefficiency of farmers. In 2004-05, cost of production of cotton in Maharashtra was Rs 2,216 per quintal according to CACP (Commission on Agricultural Cost and Price). The minimum support price offered by the MCPS was Rs 1,960. The minimum support price was below the cost of production. 2004-05 was a particularly bad year for Amaravati division in Maharashtra. There was deficient monsoon in a number of districts: Wardha has 22 per cent deficient rain, Washim 31 per cent, and Yavatmal 51 per cent. This meant that a part of the cotton crop withered on the field.[25]

Andhra Pradesh was the first state after the 2004 polls to appoint a commission to go into the agrarian crisis. Based on the commission's advice, it also took some steps towards handling that crisis. It restored compensation for the suicides that had been stopped by the previous regime in 1998. It persuaded creditors to accept one-time settlement of debt in several cases. This possibly helped see a decline after the terrible years of 2002-04. Kerala created a *"Debt Relief Commission"* soon after the change in government in 2005. The Commission held a case by case scrutiny, while the government halted aggressive loan recovery measures by banks and money lenders. On the Commission's advice, the government decided to declare the entire Wayanad revenue district distress-affected.[26]

Prime Minister Manmohan Singh on March 6, 2013 said stringent action would be taken if any irregularities are found in the Rs 52,000 crore farm loan waiver scheme of the United Progressive Alliance (UPA) government. *"The reference is to the CAG report on loan waiver scheme. This is a matter which would interest the PAC (Public Accounts Committee),"* Prime Minister Manmohan Singh said, when the issue was raised in the upper house. The Comptroller and Auditor General (CAG), in a report tabled in parliament, pointed out that several ineligible farmers were favoured and a large number of deserving small and marginal farmers left out on implementation of the United Progressive Alliance's much-touted Rs 52,000-crore farm loan waiver scheme. The Agricultural Debt Waiver and Debt Relief Scheme (ADWDRS) was launched in Vidarbha by Prime Minister Manmohan Singh in May 2008. Initially, it was launched in Maharashtra, Andhra Pradesh and Kerala, where suicides by farmers peaked in 2008. It was estimated that 3.69 crore small and marginal farmers and about 0.60 crore other farmers would benefit from the scheme and become eligible for fresh loan. According to the CAG, the monitoring of the scheme was deficient. There was even *prima facie* evidence of tampering with, overwriting and alteration of records. In certain cases, lending institutions such as banks claimed from the government charges such as interest in excess of the principal amount, unapplied interest, penal interest, legal charges, inspection charges and miscellaneous charges, all of which they themselves should have borne.

Besides, the Department of Financial Services (DFS) under the Ministry of Finance, which implemented the scheme, accepted the reimbursement claims of the RBI in respect of urban cooperative banks, amounting to Rs 335.62 crore, despite the fact that even the total number of beneficiaries' accounts was not indicated. The CAG observed that in the absence of monitoring of the scheme, lending institutions did not issue debt waiver/ relief certificates to eligible beneficiaries. Nor was acknowledgement sought from farmers making them eligible for fresh loans. The RBI and the National Bank for Agriculture and Rural Development were the nodal agencies for monitoring, but they themselves were relying on the data of lending institutions, without independently checking the veracity of claims by banks and cooperative societies. After the presentation of the draft report to the Government in January, 2013 the CAG noted that the DFS had asked the RBI and NABARD to take immediate corrective measures.

Conclusion

On average, one Indian farmer committed suicide every 32 minutes between 1997 and 2005. Since 2002, that has become one suicide every 30 minutes. Since long time, Indian farmers have been facing a number of socioeconomic problems, such as harassment by moneylenders, inability to repay debts following crop loss, inability to get medical treatment for the family, etc. The problem is compounded by lack of positive and cooperative support from banks especially in the face of inclement weather and market fluctuations. The number of suicides was 135,445 in 2012. Over the last 10 years (since 2002), the suicide rate has only increased marginally from around 10.5 to 11.2 now, probably because of more reporting. Number of states in this direction are 12.5 per cent of those 135,445 suicides occurred in Tamil Nadu, 11.9 per cent in Maharashtra, 11.0 per cent in West Bengal and 10.5 per cent in Andhra Pradesh. Gujarat's share was 5.2 per cent. Meanwhile, no satisfactory insurance system exists. The existing crop insurance scheme is not really a proper insurance mechanism. A farmer borrows, commercialises and diversifies.

REFERENCES

1. *Farmer (2014),* Retrieved from http://en.wikipedia.org/wiki/Farmer
2. *After Farmers Commit Suicide, Debts Fall on Families in India,* Retrieved from http://www.nytimes.com/2014/02/23/world/asia/after-farmers-commit-suicide-debts-fall-on-families-in-india.html?_r=0
3. Vandana Shiva (2009). *Why Are Indian Farmers Committing Suicide and How Can We Stop This Tragedy?*
4. *Causes of Farmer Suicides in Maharashtra: An enquiry (2005).* Retrieved from http://www.vnss-mission.gov.in/htmldocs/Farmers_suicide_TISS_ report.pdf
5. *Farmers' suicide in Vidarbha region of Maharashtra state: A myth or reality? (2008).* Retrieved from http://www.indianjpsychiatry.org/article.asp?issn=0019-5545;year=2008;volume=50;issue=2;spage=124;epage=127;aulast=Behere

6. See http://www.bbc.com/news/magazine-21077458
7. *The Hindu (March 20, 2014).* 38 Maharashtra farmers' suicides in a month, Retrieved from http://www.thehindu.com/news/cities/mumbai/38-maharashtra-farmer-suicides-in-a-month/article5806613.ece
8. *The Hindu (March 18, 2013).* Farmers' suicide rates soar above the rest
9. *Farmers' suicide in Vidarbha region of Maharashtra state: A myth or reality? (2008).* Retrieved from http://www.indianjpsychiatry.org/article.asp?issn=0019-5545;year=2008;volume=50;issue=2;spage=124;epage=127;aulast=Behere
10. *Farmers' suicides reflect the crisis in India's grain bowl (2014).* Retrieved from http://www.deccanherald.com/content/388199/farmers039-suicides-reflect-crisis-india039s.html
11. See http://zeenews.india.com/news/odisha/orissa-2-639-farmers-committed-suicide-in-ten-years_687557.html
12. *Outlook (Nov 21, 2009).* 3,509 Farmers Committed Suicide in Orissa in 11 Years, Retrieved from http://news.outlookindia.com/items.aspx?artid=669870
13. *The Hindu (June 29, 2013).* Farm suicide trends in 2012 remain dismal, Retrieved from http://www.thehindu.com/opinion/columns/sainath/farm-suicide-trends-in-2012-remain-dismal/article4860980.ece
14. S. Kannaiyan and Jayaram Venkatesan (2013). *A fact finding report on Farmer Suicides in the Delta Region of Tamil Nadu,* Retrieved from http://tnlabour.in/wp-content/uploads/2013/03/Farmer_suicide_report_English_fullreport.pdf
15. Analysis of Farmer Suicides in Kerala (2006). *Economic and political weekly*, Vol-XLI, No: 16, Retrieved from http://www.epw.in/special-articles/analysis-farmer-suicides-kerala.html
16. *The Economic Times (Nov 10, 2011).* Farmer suicides becomes a burning issue again in Kerala districts, Retrieved from http://articles.economictimes.indiatimes.com/2011-11-10/news/30382077_1_wayanad-crop-failure-farmer-suicides
17. *The Hindu (August 26, 2012).* 25 farmers committed suicide in Karnataka every month, Retrieved from http://www.thehindu.com/

news/national/karnataka/25-farmers-committed-suicide-in-karnataka-every-month/article3815181.ece

18. See http://www.hindu.com/thehindu/thscrip/print.pl?file=20130308300403800.htm&date=fl3004/&prd=fline&
19. Sushmita Malaviya and Jinendra Singh (2008). *Farmer suicides rampant in MP, Chhattisgarh too,* Retrieved from http://infochangeindia.org/trade-a-development/features/farmer-suicides-rampant-in-mp-chhattisgarh-too.html
20. *The Times of India (Jan 23, 2011).* Steps taken to curb farmer suicides in MP, says Shivraj Singh Chouhan, Retrieved from http://timesofindia.indiatimes.com/india/Steps-taken-to-curb-farmer-suicides-in-MP-says-Shivraj-Singh-Chouhan/articleshow/7349032.cms
21. *Business Line (Dec 13, 2013).* Fewer no of farmers' suicides in 2012: Govt, Retrieved from http://www.thehindubusinessline.com/economy/fewer-no-of-farmers-suicides-in-2012-govt/article5455861.ece
22. *The Hindu (Dec 28, 2010).* 17,368 farm suicides in 2009, Retrieved from http://www.thehindu.com/opinion/columns/sainath/17368-farm-suicides-in-2009/article995824.ece
23. B. Ratna Kumari, *Farmer's Suicides in India : Impact on Women,* Retrieved from http://www.easternbookcorporation.com/moreinfo.php?txt_searchstring=16925
24. See http://www.ndtv.com/article/india/farmer-suicides-maharashtra-government-announces-rs-4000-crore-package-497636
25. See http://sanhati.com/excerpted/4504/
26. *The Hindu (Nov 15, 2007).* One farmer's suicide every 30 minutes, Retrieved from http://www.hindu.com/2007/11/15/stories/2007111554771300.htm
27. *The Hindu (March 6, 2013),* Sloppy loan waiver edges out deserving farmers: CAG, Retrieved from http://www.thehindu.com/news/national/sloppy-loan-waiver-edges-out-deserving-farmers-cag/article4478433.ece

6

AIDS

"When we walk away from global warming, Kyoto, when we are irresponsibly slow in moving toward AIDS in Africa, when we don't advance and live up to our own rhetoric and standards, we set a terrible message of duplicity and hypocrisy."

- John F. Kerry

Introduction

Disease is an important aspect of interaction between humans and their environment i.e., both inanimate and biological. Human bodies function best when healthy. Diseases are caused by a variety of pathogens which have developed ways of infecting our bodies. Diseases affect humans in different ways, and they arise from different causes. While some diseases are caused by pathogenic organisms, such as bacteria, others seem to arise spontaneously, such as heart disease or cancer. The human body has a highly successful system of resistance infection, which has enabled the race to survive and develop over millions of years. Infectious diseases have always been an important part of human life. They have significantly influenced human biology and society, determining even the course of major historical events. There is compelling evidence that many of the risks leading to most frequent chronic diseases in adulthood originate in the earliest stages of life. Adverse environmental conditions during infancy can lead to negative health effects during subsequent lifetime of the exposed individual.

Disease is an abnormal condition that affects the body of an organism. Death due to disease is called death by natural cause.

There are four main types of disease: pathogenic disease, deficiency disease, hereditary disease, and physiological disease. Only some diseases such as influenza are contagious and commonly believed infectious. The micro-organisms that cause these diseases are known as pathogens and include varieties of bacteria, viruses, protozoa and fungi. Disease burden is the impact of health problem in an area measured by financial cost, mortality, morbidity, or other indicators.[1] While malaria is the best-understood example of an infectious disease that has driven human evolution, numerous infectious diseases have also acted in human population over generations, allowing thus resistance alleged to emerge and spread over time. West Africa has been identified as the location of the first known incidents of AIDS, but the occurrences of the disease were shrouded in secrecy. There are a number of hypotheses present in regard to the origins of HIV, including a linking the disease to the preparation of bushmeat (wild animals, including primates, hunted for food) in Cameroon and early to mid-20th-century medical practices. It is also inferred that since the virus transferred itself from chimpanzees (or other apes) to humans, this might have been the catalyst for origination of HIV among human population in this region around 1930.[2]

What is AIDS/HIV?

HIV/AIDS, which is known as Human immunodeficiency virus infection/acquired immunodeficiency syndrome, is a disease of the human immune system caused by infection with human immunodeficiency virus. There are three main stages of HIV infection: *acute infection, clinical latency* and *AIDS*. During the initial infection, a person may experience brief period of influenza-like illness. Human immunodeficiency virus (HIV) is transmitted primarily via unprotected sexual intercourse, contaminated blood transfusions, hypodermic needles, and from mother to child during pregnancy, delivery, or breastfeeding. HIV/AIDS has had a great impact on society, both as an illness and as a source of discrimination. The disease has also significant economic impact.

Reasons of AIDS

HIV is not as contagious as often believed. The virus does not survive long outside the body and can only be transmitted through the direct exchange of certain body fluids such as blood, semen and vaginal fluid. The virus can gain access to the body at its moist surfaces during sex, or through direct injection into the blood stream. Sex is the major mode of transmission of HIV worldwide. HIV can be transferred from one person to another (transmitted) through: (1) Unprotected vaginal or anal intercourse with an infected person; (2) A mother's infection passing on to her child during pregnancy, birth or breastfeeding; (3) Injection with contaminated needles, which may occur when intravenous drug users share needles, or when health care workers are involved in needle prick accidents; (4) Use of contaminated surgical instruments, for example during traditional circumcision; (5) Blood transfusion with infected blood; and (6) Contact of a mucous-membrane surface with infected blood or body fluid, for example with a splash in the eye.[3]

AIDS: Global Perspectives

HIV/AIDS in Africa is one of the most important global public health issues, and perhaps, in the history of mankind. In Africa, AIDS is one of the top causes of death. While only comprising slightly under 15 per cent of the total population of the world, Africans account for nearly 70 per cent of those who live with HIV and are dying of AIDS.[4] With only five per cent of the world's population, Eastern and Southern Africa is home to half the world's population living with HIV. Today, the region continues to be the epicentre of the HIV/AIDS epidemic, with 48 per cent of the world's new HIV infections among adults, 55 per cent among children, and 48 per cent of AIDS-related deaths. The Southern Africa sub-region, in particular, experiences the most severe HIV epidemic in the world. Nine countries i.e., Botswana, Lesotho, Malawi, Mozambique, Namibia, South Africa, Swaziland, Zambia and Zimbabwe have adult HIV prevalence rates of over 10 per cent. For many pregnant women living with HIV, such treatment remains out of reach, especially for those living in rural areas, and those fearful of stigma and discrimination if they are tested positive.[5]

North Africa has one of the lowest HIV prevalence rates worldwide. This low rate is usually attributed to the essential role that Islam plays in the region's societies. This strong influence on local values, morals, and government policies has sustained infection rates at negligible level. Horn of Africa has a fairly low infection rates like North Africa. HIV infection rates in East and Central Africa are generally moderate to high. Chad, Niger, and Mali have the lowest HIV prevalence in West Africa while Burkina Faso, Côte d'Ivoire and Nigeria have the highest. Southern Africa is the most affected area worldwide.[6] There are various reasons for high HIV incidences in Africa. Medical professionals site as being detrimental to HIV treatment such as male promiscuity and polygamy in some places. The most obvious challenge to the AIDS pandemic is the lack of funding for medical facilities and treatment distribution in developing countries, even with plenty of aid distributed throughout. Medical facilities in many African countries are lacking. There are also not enough health care workers available.[7] Although, HIV prevalence is stabilizing and declining in some countries, southern Africa remains the epicenter of the AIDS epidemic with 31 per cent of new infections and 34 per cent of AIDS deaths in 2009. In 2009, an estimated 2.6 million people were infected with HIV, of which an estimated 69 per cent occurred in Sub-Saharan Africa.[8]

For decades nobody knew the reasons behind the birth of the AIDS epidemic. But, it is now clear that the epidemic's birth and crucial early growth happened during Africa's colonial era, amid massive intrusion of new people and technology into a land, where ancient ways still prevailed. Many simians, such as gorillas and monkeys can carry virus that resembles HIV. But scientists now know that HIV-1 group M was born from virus circulating among community of chimpanzees concentrated in Cameroon, a sprawling country with bustling Atlantic Ocean ports, populous highlands, and lightly developed southern region, where relatively few people live even today. This was home to the chimps. Scientists had long known that a blood sample, preserved from 1959, showed that HIV had been circulating in Kinshasa, the capital of Congo for several decades before the virus first drew international attention in the 1980s. One scientist discovered, had traveled east from Kinshasa toward Lake Victoria. One went south to Zambia, Botswana and South Africa. One hopped all the way across the ocean to Haiti, then on to the United States and Europe.[9]

Some 131,000 people were newly infected with HIV in Europe and nearby countries in 2012, an eight per cent rise from a year earlier and a worrying reversal of a recent downward trend in AIDS cases in the West. Some 76,000 new HIV infections were reported in Russia alone, accounting for more than half the region's cases. While reported AIDS cases had been declining steadily in Western Europe dropping to 48 per cent between 2006 and 2012 in the east of the WHO's European region, which includes many Asian former Soviet republics, the number of people newly diagnosed with AIDS increased by 113 per cent. Experts said this increase was closely linked to lack of prevention measures for people at high risk of contracting the human immunodeficiency virus (HIV) that causes AIDS.[10]

The first recorded case of HIV/AIDS in Australia was in Sydney in October 1982, and the first Australian death from AIDS occurred in Melbourne in July 1983. The AIDS councils were formed in South Australia, Victoria and Western Australia in 1983 and in New South Wales, Queensland, Tasmania and the Australian Capital Territory in 1985. Non-governmental organisations formed swiftly and have remained prominent in addressing AIDS. The Australian health policy response to HIV/ AIDS has been characterised as emerging from the grassroots rather than top-down, and as involving a high degree of partnership between government and non-government stakeholders. Australian governments have made it illegal to discriminate against a person on the grounds of their health status, including having HIV/AIDS. Australia was one of the first countries to screen all blood donors for HIV antibodies, with screening in place for all transfused since March 1985.[11] There is a relatively low prevalence of HIV/AIDS in New Zealand. The rate of newly diagnosed HIV infections was stable at around 100 annually through the late 1980s and the 1990s, but rose sharply from 2000 to 2005. In 1985, Eve van Grafhorst was ostracised in Australia since she had contracted HIV/AIDS caused by a transfusion of infected blood.[12]

Major gains have been made in the fight against the spread of HIV and AIDS in Latin America and the Caribbean, where the infection rate was stable over the past decade. In 2009, some 58,000 died in Latin America of AIDS-related causes, according to UNAIDS data, up from 53,000 in 2001. In most of Latin America and the Caribbean countries, the HIV/AIDS epidemic is concentrated in certain key population, including men who have sex with men, sex workers, drug users and transgender women. Most countries in Latin America and the Caribbean fund their own HIV response programme. The boost in the availability of antiretroviral therapy has led to an increase in the number of people living with AIDS in the region, from 1.1 million to 1.4 million. According to the USAID study, the number of children acquiring the disease in Latin America and the Caribbean declined by 45 per cent between 2001 and 2010, from 9,200 to 5,100 cases. Child deaths from AIDS dropped from 6,300 to 3,700 during that same period.[13] There are numerous barriers to receiving treatment in Latin America, though this varies by country. Poverty, homophobia, and stigma prevent many people in Latin America from getting proper HIV/AIDS treatment. It is important to note that each country in Latin America faces different types of challenge in the fight against HIV/AIDS.

According to UNAIDs statistics, there were 83,000 new infections in 2011, which is lower than previous years. In 2011, AIDS related deaths were trending down. Men who have sex with men (MSM) are the largest percentage of people in Latin America infected with HIV. Countries like Bolivia and Ecuador have low infection rates among sex workers, because of condom use and STI testing check-ups. Argentina, Brazil, Uruguay, and Paraguay are countries, where intravenous drug use is a common cause of the spread of HIV. In Colombia, gay men are particularly affected by HIV/AIDS. Several political groups are responsible for creating HIV stigma in Columbia, which impedes the creation of prevention programmes and treatment. In Honduras, HIV is mainly spread through heterosexual. act. There is an extreme epidemic among the Garifuna, who are descendants of Nigerian slavery. Guatemala's Mayan community, considered to be a minority group is thought to be at an increased risk of HIV infection.[14]

Acquired Immune Deficiency Syndrome (AIDS) was first detected in Canada more than 30 years ago. Since then, thousands of Canadians continue to become infected with the Human

Immunodeficiency Virus (HIV) every year. HIV is a virus that attacks the immune system, resulting in a chronic, progressive illness that leaves people vulnerable to infections.[15] Since HIV reporting began in Canada in 1985, a cumulative total of 76,275 positive HIV test reports have been reported to PHAC. In 2012 alone, 2,062 HIV cases were reported up to December 31st, which represents a 7.8 per cent decrease from the 2011 reports (2,237 cases) and is the lowest number of annual HIV cases since reporting began in 1985. In 2012, as in previous years, Ontario accounted for the highest number of cases (843) followed by Quebec (450), Alberta (239), British Columbia (238) and Saskatchewan (184). Both Ontario and British Columbia noted a decrease in their annual number of cases from 2011 to 2012 – a 10.8 per cent decrease in Ontario and a 17.4 per cent decrease in British Columbia. In 2012, 23.1 per cent of all cases were females. The Canadian Perinatal HIV Surveillance Program is administered by the Canadian Pediatric AIDS Research Group (CPARG) and provides data on perinatal HIV to PHAC for national reporting.[16]

The first cases of what would later become known as AIDS were reported in the United States in June of 1981. Since then, more than 1.8 million people in the U.S. are estimated to have been infected with HIV, including over 650,000 who have already died; today, more than 1.1 million people are living with HIV. Despite advances in combating HIV, hundreds of thousands have already died from the disease, and cumulative deaths among people with AIDS reached 658,992 at the end of 2010. Ten states accounted for about two-thirds (65 per cent) of HIV diagnoses in 2011. Regionally, the South accounted for about half (48 per cent) of HIV diagnoses in 2011. More than 275,000 women are living with HIV in the U.S. Key programmes that provide health insurance coverage, care, and support to people with HIV in the U.S. include Medicaid, Medicare, the Ryan White Programme, and HOPWA, the Housing Opportunities for Persons with HIV/AIDS Programme. Social Security's income programmes for those who are disabled (SSI and SSDI) are also important sources of support.[17] Since 2007, HIV and AIDS rates have gone up throughout rural Mexican states, partly as a result of returning migrants, who have engaged in high-risk behaviours in the United States and not been able to receive diagnosis or treatment. Medical experts are shifting their attention to the particular dangers faced by Central American migrants i.e., human trafficking, sexual abuse, prostitution, isolation, depression, and drug use. Within the state, Tuxtla Guttierrez, Tonalá, Cintalapa and Tapachula were labeled *"red flags"* municipalities, where rates of infection and the presence of at-risk groups, like sex workers and increasingly migrants, are statistically higher than the rest of the state.[18]

After peaking at around 143,000 cases in 1991, the number of new HIV infections in Thailand declined to an estimated 19,000 in 2003. HIV prevalence among certain high risk groups, such as injecting drug users, is still high and overall prevalence in Thailand remains the highest in the region. Thailand was one of the first countries in Asia to offer both first- and second-line treatment regimens. Cambodia's HIV epidemic is concentrated among sex workers, MSM and injecting drug users. It has been suggested that Vietnam's HIV epidemic has shown signs of stabilizing. HIV prevalence among the most affected groups has declined. Myanmar is one of the least densely populated countries in Asia, with more than three-quarters of the population living in small villages.[19]

The first case of HIV in Bangladesh was detected in 1989. Even prior to this first case, the Government of Bangladesh (GoB) had become active and formed the National AIDS Committee (NAC) in 1985 in anticipation of an epidemic. The National AIDS/STD Programme (NASP), within the Directorate General of Health Services (DGHS) of the Ministry of Health and Family Welfare (MoHFW), acts as a nodal body responsible for programming to address HIV issues in the country. In Dhaka, data from research and from the surveillance showed that the HIV epidemic was localized in a specific neighbourhood which could be considered to be the epicentre of the epidemic.[20]

The country faces a concentrated epidemic, and its very low HIV-prevalence rate is partly due to prevention efforts, focusing on men, who have sex with men, female sex workers, and intravenous drug users. The overall prevalence of HIV in Bangladesh is less than one per cent, however, high levels of HIV infection have been found among injecting drug users (7 per cent in one part of the capital city, Dhaka). Due to the limited access to voluntary counseling and testing services, very few Bangladeshi's are aware of their HIV status. Men having sex with men are largely hidden due to the powerful stigma and discrimination they face in Bangladesh. Many men who have sex with men are bi-sexual and do not necessarily identify them as such. Men buying sex from other men rarely use condoms and many continue to have sex with their wives. Approximately 250,000 people leave Bangladesh for employment every year. The risk is that they will get infected during their stay abroad and return to Bangladesh, where they may transmit the virus to others, especially their wives who could in turn transmit infection to their babies. UNICEF has played significant role in maintaining the low HIV prevalence status of Bangladesh through management of the HIV/AIDS Prevention Project (HAPP) from 2004 to 2007 and the HIV/AIDS Targeted Interventions (HATI) project from January 2008 until it is handed over to the Government during 2009.[21]

The infection rate of HIV/AIDS in Nepal among the adult population is estimated to be below the 1 percent threshold which is considered *"generalized and severe"*. The first case of *AIDS in Nepal* was reported in 1988. As of December 2007; the Government of Nepal reported 1,610 cases of AIDS and 10,546 HIV infections, which has grown to 13,000 infections by World AIDS Day 2008. The Government of Nepal's National Center for AIDS and STD Control (NCASC) estimated that number to be closer to 70,000 in December 2007. Migrants have become so vulnerable to infection due to uncertainty about their immigration status. While India and Nepal have an open border policy, whereby Nepalese citizens have the same rights as Indians to live and work in India and vice-versa. NGOs operating in Nepal must be registered with the Social Welfare Council. The number of registered NGOs in Nepal is significant. The various NGOs provide a range of services within the communities served including Care and Support, Health Education, Advocacy, Income Generation etc.[22]

HIV/AIDS in Bhutan remains relatively a rare disease among its population. It has grown into an issue of national concern since Bhutan had first reported case in 1993. Despite preemptive education and counseling efforts, the number of reported HIV/

AIDS cases has climbed since the early 1990s. In 2011, there were 246 reported cases of HIV representing just over 0.3 per cent of the population. HIV/AIDS treatment and counseling are available exclusively under the Bhutanese universal health care system. Persons living with HIV/AIDS in Bhutan carry social stigma and often face discrimination, including disowning and unemployment, because it is a sexually-transmitted disease.[23] HIV is not currently dominant epidemic in Pakistan. However, the number of cases is growing. Moderately high drug use and lack of acceptance that non-marital sex is common in the society have allowed the AIDS epidemic to take hold in Pakistan. Pakistan enjoyed a low prevalence phase of epidemic from 1987 to 2003. A major factor that must be accounted for in the overall HIV transmission scenario is the rampant use of therapeutic injections, often with non-sterile injection equipment. Pakistan's response to HIV/AIDS began in 1987 with the establishment of a Federal Committee on AIDS by the Ministry of Health. The national AIDS control programme was then established.[24]

Between 1991 and 2011, 15 HIV cases were reported among Maldivians, compared to 168 among expatriate workers. Of the Maldivian cases, 13 were males, and two females, and all patients cited heterosexual transmission as the cause. Human trafficking for purposes including sexual entertainment has put more locals at risk. Further risk factors include falling rates of contraceptive use.[25] An estimated 4,200 people including young children are currently living with HIV in *Sri Lanka*. The first confirmed case of HIV/Aids appeared in Afghanistan in 1989. Instances of the disease remained negligible for the next 15 years, before a combination of circumstances including a rise in poppy cultivation, drug trafficking and drug use; unscreened blood being used in transfusion and conflict scattering refugees around the world began to push infection rates up.[26]

AIDS in India

The adult HIV prevalence in India is declining from estimated level of 0.41per cent in 2000 through 0.36 per cent in 2006 to 0.31 per cent in 2009. Adult HIV prevalence at a national level has declined notably in many states, but variations exist still across the states. Soon after the first case emerged in 1986, the

Government of India established the National AIDS Committee within the Ministry of Health and Family Welfare. This formed the basis for the current apex Government of India body for HIV surveillance, the National AIDS Control Organisation (NACO). The majority of HIV surveillance data collected by the NACO is done through annual unlinked anonymous testing of prenatal clinic (or antenatal clinics) and sexually transmitted infection clinic attendees. The first National AIDS Control Programme (NACP) was implemented over seven years (1992–99), focused on monitoring HIV infection rates among risk populations in selected urban areas. In 2009, India established a *"National HIV and AIDS Policy and the World of Work"*, which sought to end discrimination against workers on the basis of their real or perceived HIV status.[27]

The first case of HIV/AIDS was reported in India in Tamil Nadu in 1986. Since then, the virus has spread from the high-risk group to the general population very fast. Women and children are increasingly becoming vulnerable to HIV/AIDS. The new findings conclude that 38 per cent of the infected persons in India are women. This indicates the increasing feminisation of HIV/AIDS in India. Over 35 percent of AIDS cases reported are below 25 years of age and 50 per cent of new infections are between 15 and 24 years old. The current HIV/AIDS programmes are reaching only 15 per cent of young people and 17 per cent of high-risk groups such as sex workers, men who have sex with men and injecting drug users.[28]

According to the latest epidemiological report of HIV/AIDS in Manipur, brought out by the Manipur State AIDS Control Society (September 1986 to April 2003), 15,166 out of a total of 95,734 blood samples screened were HIV-positive. In a state which has an area of 22,327 sq km and a population of around 2.3 million (2001 census), this is the highest concentration of HIV/AIDS infection in India. The first HIV cases were reported from a study of random blood samples of injecting drug users (IDUs) during 1989-90. At 56.81 per cent of the total population of HIV-positive people in Manipur is IDUs, though the figure was as high as 80 per cent at one point. The geographical proximity of Manipur to Burma (Myanmar) and consequently the Golden Triangle drug trail has made it a major transit route for drug smuggling, with easily available drugs. During the early-'90s, the belief that people who are drug users would mend ways if they were married and made parents marry off their wards at very young age. Most of the men have now died, leaving behind acutely vulnerable wives and children. The women are pushed out of their marital homes because of property disputes while their own families do not want them back on account of young age and widowed status. Government/non-government agencies and organisations have been implementing intervention programmes (counseling, condom promotion, medical check-ups, needle and syringe exchange programmes) among vulnerable groups like IDUs, Men having Sex with Men (MSM), sex workers, truck drivers etc.[29]

Effects of AIDS

AIDS affects different segments of society in different ways. For example, children may have to care for an ill-parent. Schooling may suffer as a result. Other times, children become orphans as parents succumb to AIDS. AIDS is exacerbated by other conditions such as TB.[30] The impact of the disease is not only measured by the number of deaths. The social consequences are major. AIDS destroys the efforts made to enable the empowerment of women, destroys the slow progress in terms of education, impact people's health care (in South Africa today, 80 per cent of patients hospitalized in public hospitals are HIV positive.[31] The earliest symptoms of HIV can resemble the flu and they generally clear up within a month or two. These symptoms may include fever, headache, fatigue, and swelling in the lymph nodes, particularly those in the neck and groin. Several of the main skin conditions that affect people with HIV are caused by viruses most people already have in their bodies. However, these viruses typically do not cause disease in people whose immune systems are healthy. Some of the more common dermatological, or skin effects of HIV include Varicella zoster virus (VZV) infection, Herpes simplex virus, and Kaposi's sarcoma.[32]

HIV and AIDS affect economic growth by reducing the availability of human capital. People living with HIV/AIDS will not only be unable to work, but will also require significant medical care. The forecast is that this will probably cause a collapse of economies and societies in countries with a significant AIDS population. In some heavily infected areas, the epidemic has left behind many orphans cared for by elderly grandparents. By killing off mainly young adults, AIDS seriously weakens the taxable population, reducing the resources available for public expenditures such as education and health services not related to AIDS resulting in increasing pressure for the state's finances and slower growth of the economy. On the level of the household, AIDS results in both the loss of income and increased spending on healthcare by the household.[33]

Preventive Measures

Primary prevention among young people is the greatest hope to change the course of the epidemic in India. As a result, the Adolescent Education Programme was conceived by UNICEF, NACO, Ministry of Education, UNESCO and UNFPA. The programme was implemented in all states across the country through the Department of Education (DoE) in collaboration with the State AIDS Control Societies (SACS). The curriculum includes growing up, HIV/AIDS, life skills and extra-curricular activities. Already, 110,000 of the 150,000 high schools in India trained teachers and peer educators to pass on life skills and preventive messages.[34] HIV prevention refers to practices done to prevent the spread of HIV/AIDS. Early treatment of HIV-infected people with antiretrovirals protected 96 per cent of partners from infection. Programmes to prevent the transmission of HIV from mothers to children can reduce rates of transmission by 92-99 per cent. The use of the single agent zidovudine reduces the risk of subsequent HIV infection five-fold following a needle stick injury. Consistent condom use reduces the risk of heterosexual HIV transmission. For HIV positive mothers wishing to prevent the spread of HIV to their child during birth, antiretroviral drugs have been medically proven to reduce likely spread of the infection. Scientists worldwide are currently researching on other prevention systems.[35]

There is currently no cure or effective HIV vaccine. Measures to prevent opportunistic infections are effective among many people with HIV/AIDS. In addition to improving current disease, treatment with antiretrovirals reduces the risk of developing additional opportunistic infections. In the US, approximately 60 per cent of people with HIV use various forms of complementary or alternative medicine, even though the effectiveness of these therapies has not been established. HIV/AIDS has become a chronic rather than an acutely fatal disease in many areas of the world. The primary causes of death from HIV/AIDS are opportunistic infections and cancer, both of which are frequently the result of the progressive failure of the immune system.

Assistance to Victims

There are various non-governmental organizations are working for providing assistance to the HIV infected people. Some of them are;

1. *Global Fund to Fight AIDS, Tuberculosis and Malaria:* The Global Fund galvanises support for the fight against AIDS, TB and malaria, working with partners to support the most effective prevention and treatment. We have an historic opportunity to seize new advances in science and apply practical experience to defeat these diseases and remove them as threats to public health. Working together, we can do great things.[36]
2. *International AIDS Society:* The International AIDS Society is the world's leading independent association of HIV professionals, with over 14,000 members from more than 190 countries working at all levels of the global response to AIDS. Its members include researchers from all disciplines, clinicians, public health and community practitioners on the frontlines of the epidemic, as well as policy and program planners.
3. *Kaiser Family Foundation:* The Kaiser Family Foundation is a non-profit, private operating foundation focusing on the major health care issues facing the U.S., as well as the U.S. role in global health policy. The foundation serves as a non-partisan source of facts, information, and analysis for policymakers, the media, the health care community, and the public.
4. *UNAIDS:* UNAIDS is the Joint United Nations Programme on HIV/AIDS, is an innovative partnership that leads and inspires the world in achieving universal access to HIV prevention, treatment, care and support. Established in 1994

by a resolution of the UN Economic and Social Council and launched in January 1996, UNAIDS is guided by a Programme Coordinating Board with representatives of 22 governments from all geographic regions, the UNAIDS cosponsors, and five representatives of non-governmental organisations, including associations of people living with HIV. With its headquarters in Geneva, Switzerland, the UNAIDS Secretariat works on the ground in more than 80 countries.[37]

National AIDS Control Organisation

The National AIDS Control Organisation (NACO), established in 1992, is a division of India's Ministry of Health and Family Welfare that provides leadership to HIV/AIDS control programme in India through 35 HIV/AIDS Prevention and Control Societies, and is *"the nodal organisation for formulation of policy and implementation of programs for prevention and control of HIV / AIDS in India."* In 2010, NACO approved the Teach AIDS curriculum for use in India, an innovation which represented the first time that HIV/AIDS education could be provided in a curriculum which need not be coupled with sex education.[38]

Conclusion

AIDS is a global phenomenon. It is more serious problem in southern African countries. The transmission of the virus from the mother-to-child during pregnancy, labour and delivery or breastfeeding is called parent-to-child-transmission to emphasise the role of the father in both the transmission of virus and management of the infected mother and child. It is estimated that 70,000 children below the age of 15 are living with HIV in India and 21,000 children are infected every year through parent-to-child transmission. A small proportion are also infected by unsafe injections and infected by blood transfusions. The areas of impact considered are: economic and demographic; labour productivity; agricultural production and development; pressures on the health sector; the role of families and households; children; women; HIV/AIDS discrimination; and the impact of HIV/AIDS on the individual.[39] The National AIDS Control Programme (NACP) III 2007-2012 has the overall goal of halting and reversing the epidemic in India. Over 99 per cent of the population in the country is free from infection. NACP III places highest priority on prevention while seeking to integrate care, support and treatment for those affected by HIV/AIDS.

REFERENCES

1. *Disease (2014).* Retrieved from http://en.wikipedia.org/wiki/Disease
2. AIDS in Africa - Statistics and facts about HIV in Africa, Retrieved from http://www.medwiser.org/hiv-aids/around-the-world/aids-in-africa/
3. *What are the causes of HIV/AIDs?* Retrieved from http://www.health24.com/Medical/HIV-AIDS/Overview/What-are-the-causes-of-HIVAids-20130205
4. *AIDS in Africa - Statistics and facts about HIV in Africa*, Retrieved from http://www.medwiser.org/hiv-aids/around-the-world/aids-in-africa/
5. *Eastern and Southern Africa-AIDS: Overview,* Retrieved from http://www.unicef.org/esaro/5482_HIV_AIDS.html
6. *AIDS in Africa - Statistics and facts about HIV in Africa,* Retrieved from http://www.medwiser.org/hiv-aids/around-the-world/aids-in-africa/
7. *AIDS in Africa - Statistics and facts about HIV in Africa*, Retrieved from http://www.medwiser.org/hiv-aids/around-the-world/aids-in-africa/
8. *HIV/AIDS Regional Update – Africa,* Retrieved from http://web.worldbank.org/WBSITE/EXTERNAL/COUNTRIES/AFRICAEXT/EXTAFRHEANUTPOP/EXTAFRREGTOPHIVAIDS 0,,contentMDK:20415756~menuPK:1830800~pageP K:34004173~piPK:34003707~theSitePK:717148,00.html
9. *Co-lo-ni-al-ism in Africa helped launch the HIV epidemic a century ago,* Retrieved from http://www.washingtonpost.com/national/health-science/colonialism-in-africa-helped-launch-the-hiv-epidemic-a-century-ago/2012/02/21/gIQAyJ9aeR_story.html

10. *AIDS proves stubborn in Europe as new HIV infections rise,* Retrieved from http://www.reuters.com/article/2013/11/27/us-aids-europe-idUSBRE9AQ07R20131127
11. *HIV / AIDS in Australia*, Retrieved from http://en.wikipedia.org/wiki/HIV/AIDS_in_Australia
12. *HIV / AIDS in New Zealand,* Retrieved from http://en.wikipedia.org/wiki/HIV/AIDS_in_New_Zealand
13. *AIDS in Latin America: Epidemic stable, but still deadly*, Retrieved from http://www.globalpost.com/dispatch/news/health/121204/hiv-aids-latin-america-caribbean-global-health
14. *AIDS in Latin America*, Retrieved from http://www.medwiser.org/hiv-aids/around-the-world/aids-latin-america/
15. See http://www.healthycanadians.gc.ca/health-sante/disease-maladie/hiv-vih-eng.php?utm_source=aids_13&utm_medium=banner_link&utm_ campaign=hpfeaturebox
16. *At a Glance - HIV and AIDS in Canada: Surveillance Report to December 31st, 2012,* Retrieved from http://www.phac-aspc.gc.ca/aids-sida/publication/survreport/2012/dec/index-eng.php
17. *The HIV / AIDS Epidemic in the United States,* Retrieved from http://kff.org/hivaids/fact-sheet/the-hivaids-epidemic-in-the-united-states/
18. *Mexico: Efforts to Provide HIV-AIDS and Other Health Services to Migrants Face Major Obstacles (2013).* Retrieved from http://upsidedownworld.org /main/mexico-archives-79/4318mexico-efforts-to-provide-hiv-aids-and-other-health-services-to-migrants-face-major-obstacles
19. See http://www.avert.org/south-east-asia-hiv-aids-statistics.htm
20. See http://www.ncbi.nlm.nih.gov/pmc/articles/PMC2740703/
21. *HIV and AIDS in Bangladesh, UNICEF,* Retrieved from http://www.unicef.org/bangladesh/HIV_AIDS(1).pdf
22. *HIV / AIDS in Nepal*, Retrieved from http://en.wikipedia.org/wiki/HIV/AIDS_in_Nepal
23. *HIV / AIDS in Bhutan*, Retrieved from http://en.wikipedia.org/wiki/HIV/AIDS_in_Bhutan
24. *HIV / AIDS in Pakistan,* Retrieved from http://en.wikipedia.org/wiki/HIV/AIDS_in_Pakistan

25. *High-risk behaviour leaves Maldives at risk of HIV/AIDS "explosion,* Retrieved from http://minivannews.com/society/high-risk-behaviour-leaves-maldives-at-risk-of-hivaids-explosion-31116
26. *Afghanistan's new crisis: the spread of HIV/Aids,* Retrieved from http://www.thenational.ae/news/world/south-asia/afghanistans-new-crisis-the-spread-of-hiv-aids
27. *HIV/AIDS in India,* Retrieved from http://en.wikipedia.org/wiki/HIV/AIDS_in_India
28. *UNICEF-HIV/AIDS-India,* Retrieved from http://www.unicef.org/india/children_2358.htm
29. Chitra Ahanthem, *HIV/AIDS in Manipur: The need to focus on women*, Retrieved from http://infochangeindia.org/public-health/analysis/hivaids-in-manipur-the-need-to-focus-on-women.html
30. Anup Shah, *AIDS in Africa,* Retrieved from http://www.globalissues.org/article/90/aids-in-africa
31. *HIV/AIDS in Africa*, Retrieved from http://www.africaalive.org/
32. Elizabeth Connor, *The Effects of HIV on the Body,* Retrieved from http://www.everydayhealth.com/hiv-aids/effects-of-hiv-on-body.aspx
33. *Economic impact on HIV/AIDS*, Retrieved from http://en.wikipedia.org/wiki/Economic_impact_of_HIV/AIDS
34. *UNICEF-HIV/AIDS-India,* Retrieved from http://www.unicef.org/india/children_2358.htm
35. *Prevention of HIV/AIDS,* Retrieved from http://en.wikipedia.org/wiki/Prevention_of_HIV/AIDS
36. *The Global Fund galvanizes support for the fight against AIDS, TB and malaria,* Retrieved from http://www.theglobalfund.org/en/
37. See http://aids.gov/federal-resources/around-the-world/global-hiv-aids-organizations/
38. *National AIDS Control Organisation,* Retrieved from http://en.wikipedia.org/wiki/National_AIDS_Control_Organisation
39. *The social impact of HIV/AIDS in developing countries,* Retrieved from http://www.ncbi.nlm.nih.gov/pubmed/7992124

7

Urbanisation

"All over the world, social innovation is tackling some of the most pressing problems facing society today - from fair trade, distance learning, hospices, urban farming and waste reduction to restorative justice and zero-carbon housing. But most of these are growing despite, not because of, help from Governments."

- Geoff Mulgan

Introduction

Human evolution is the evolutionary process leading up to the appearance of modern humans. In early days, human life was very hard. They spent their life in caves, wrap animal skin and tree leaves over their body and hunt animals for food. With time, they discovered many things like fire, tools, farming etc. that made their life better than earlier. But these changes in early human life had taken a very long time. Early humans lived in jungle and were afraid of bigger and stronger wild animals. Earlier they had no house to live in and spend their time on the trees or hide themselves behind bushes.[1] There are different information about early mankind. The early man lived a very simple life. They hunted for food and didn't need much. They owned very little material items and knew how to survive in the wilderness. About 50 human footprints almost one million year old were discovered in England. The footprints were discovered in the village of Happisburgh, Norfolk, by a team of experts from the British Museum, the Natural History Museum and Queen Mary University of London. In addition to the footprints, archaeologists also found the remains of at least a hundred animal species, including 15 types of mammals and 160 different species of insects, and more than 100 types of plants. As human developed their needs are changed. Population is increasing very rapidly and human lives in society where they have scarcity of various essential things. Housing, food, cloth, shelter are among on them.

What is Urban Area?

An urban area is characterised by higher population density and vast human features in comparison to the surrounding areas. Urban areas may be cities, towns or conurbations, but the term is not commonly extended to rural settlements such as villages and hamlets. There are about 7.1 billion people living on the planet. In 2009, the number of people living in urban areas (3.42 billion) surpassed the number living in rural areas (3.41 billion).[2] Urban areas can refer to towns, cities, and suburbs. An urban area includes the city, as well as the surrounding areas. Many urban areas are called *metropolitan areas*. Rural areas are the opposite of urban areas. Rural areas, often called *"the country,"* have low population density and large amounts of undeveloped land.[3]

Urbanisation is an index of transformation from traditional rural economies to modern industrial one. It can be measured by two ways: First, level and growth of urban share of total population and its distribution by size, classes of cities and towns. This is called *demographic approach*. Second, changes in number and growth of urban centers and an expansion of geographical boundaries of existing urban areas. This is called *geographical approach*.[4] Urbanisation denotes a diffusion of the influence of urban centres to a rural hinterland. It can also be defined as a process of concentration of population in a particular territory. According to Mitchell, urbanisation is a process of becoming urban; moving to cities, changing from agriculture to other pursuits common to cities.[5] It refers to the increasing number of people that live in urban areas.

Global perspectives

The onset of modern and universal process of urbanisation is relatively a recent phenomenon and is closely related with industrial revolution and associated economic development. As industrial revolution started in Western Europe, United Kingdom was the initiator of industrial revolution. Historical evidence suggests that urbanisation process is inevitable and universal. Currently developed countries are characterised by high level of urbanisation and some are in final stage of urbanisation process and experiencing slows down of urbanisation due to host of factors. Urban agglomeration is a continuous urban spread constituting a town and its adjoining urban outgrowth or two or more physical contiguous town together and any adjoining urban outgrowth of such towns.[6]

Urban growth, which is mostly due to natural increase, is inevitable. However, the speed and size of the growth are not fixed, and vary widely among regions. The most effective way to slow rates of urban growth is to reduce unwanted fertility in both rural and urban areas. Lowering poverty, empowering women and providing quality reproductive health services influence fertility preferences and ability to meet them. Fertility rates are lower in urban than in rural areas throughout the world. However, the fact that such large per centage of people in many developing countries are young means that urban population growth will continue rapidly for years to come. Poverty is now growing faster in urban than in rural areas. One billion people live in urban slums, which are typically overcrowded, polluted and dangerous, and lack from basic services such as clean from water and sanitation.[7]

By 2050, it is predicted that 64.1 per cent and 85.9 per cent of the developing and developed world respectively will be urbanised. Urbanisation is closely linked to modernisation, industrialisation, and the sociological process of rationalisation. It is not merely a modern phenomenon, but a rapid and historic transformation of human social roots on a global scale, whereby predominantly rural culture is being rapidly replaced by predominantly urban culture.[8] Asian cities are growing rapidly. Another 1.1 billion people will live in the region's cities in the next 20 years. By 2030, more than 55 per cent of population of Asia will be urban. In many places, cities will merge together to create urban settlements on a scale never seen before. These new configurations will take the form of mega-regions, urban corridors and city-regions. The prosperity of nations is intimately linked to the prosperity of cities. No country has ever achieved sustained economic growth or rapid social development without urbanising. Climate change may threaten the sustainability of water use in urban centers by reducing water availability and quality from surface and groundwater sources, while water demand for household and industrial use may simultaneously increase as temperatures rise. Between the years 2000 and 2010, Asia showed the greatest gains in moving people out of slum conditions, with the People Republic of China (PRC) and India together lifting around 125 million people. The Gaobei Dian Wastewater Treatment Plan in Beijing is one of the biggest sewage treatment plants in the PRC, taking care of about 40 per cent of the city's daily untreated wastewater. There is an inequitable distribution of health threats within urban areas. Families with lowest income are at risk of their children being malnourished and dying early, have less access to health services such as skilled birth attendance, and are disadvantaged in terms of living conditions, such as access to piped water.[9]

In 2010, the Asia-Pacific region's urban population amounted to 754 million people, which is more than the combined population of the United States of America and the European Union. Now, almost half of the population, namely 45.5 per cent in the region, is living in urban areas. Urbanisation rates in Asia and the Pacific vary widely by sub-region. While the Pacific has more than 70 per cent of its population living in urban areas (mainly driven by Australia and New Zealand with urbanisation rates above 85 per cent), in South and South-West Asia only 34 per cent of the population lives in urban areas. Seven of the 10 most populous cities of the world are in the Asia Pacific region, namely Tokyo, Delhi, Shanghai, Mumbai, Beijing, Dhaka and Kolkata. Overall, megacities (with population over 10 million) and metropolitan areas (with population between one and ten million) are home to 11 and 29 per cent of Asia's urban population, respectively.[10]

With its stunning urban landscapes, historical cities and cultural treasures, Europe remains one of the world's most desirable and healthy places to live and the most frequently visited world-travel destination. From 72 per cent today, around 80 per cent of Europeans will be living in urban areas by 2020; in several countries the proportion will be 90 per cent or more. Over the past 50 years, European cities have expanded on average by 78 per cent, whereas the population has grown by only 33 per cent. Managing cities is certainly a complex and interrelated task which highlights the potential dangers of ad-hoc decision making: the solution to one problem, at one scale, often is the cause of another, at a similar or different scale.[11]

Over the past forty years, Latin American cities have boomed. In 1950, 40 per cent of the region's population was urban, but by 1990 it was up to 70 per cent. Today, about 80 per cent of the region's population lives in cities, making Latin America the world's most urbanised region. As the world's most urbanised region, Latin America is a critical platform from which to launch a global dialogue on urban trends. Nearly nine out of 10 Latin Americans will live in cities by the year 2050, and the region should use this moment of economic stability and slower population growth to make those cities more equitable.

Urbanisation in India

Urbanisation in India has been relatively slow compared to many developing countries. The per centage of annual exponential growth rate of urban population reveals it grew at faster pace from the decade 1921-31 to until 1951. Thereafter, it registered a sharp drop during the decade 1951-61. The decades 1961-71 and 1971-81 have showed significant improvement in the growth which thereafter has steadily dropped to the present level 2.7. The decline in rural population growth was within small range during 1981-91 and 1991-2001. Tempo of urbanisation refers to speed of urbanisation and is measured as change registered in the level or degree of urbanisation over the years.[12] One of the most recent phenomena observed in India is the formation of urban agglomerations, which is defined as geographic concentration of urban population and economic activities. Urban economic growth is measured by the growth rate of urban GDP.[13] Urbanisation in India has occurred more slowly than in other developing countries and the proportion of the population in urban areas has been only 28 per cent based on the 2001 census.

The pace of urbanisation is now set to accelerate as the country sets to more rapid growth. India needs to work on several areas to manage its urbanisation. The following are perhaps the most important: inclusive cities, urban governance, funding, planning, capacity building and low-income housing. India also needs to start a political process, where the urban issues are debated with evolution of meaningful solutions.[14] Urbanisation has become a common feature of Indian society. Growth of industries has contributed to the growth of cities. As a result of industrialisation people have started moving towards the industrial areas in search of employment.

Most Indian cities are very densely populated. New Delhi, for example, had 6,352 people per square kilometer in 1991. Congestion, noise, traffic jams, air pollution, and major shortages of key necessities characterise urban life. Every major city of India faces similar proliferating problems of grossly inadequate housing, transportation, sewerage, electric power, water supplies, schools, and hospitals. Increasingly conspicuous in India's cities are the growing ranks of the middle class. About one in six Indian city residents lives in an urban slum with unsanitary conditions that are "unfit for human habitation," according to the first complete census of India's vast slum population. More than 40 per cent of households in Mumbai, India's financial capital and largest city with 19 million people, are located in overcrowded shanty town where most residents are squatting illegally and many have little access to basic sanitation. New Delhi, the Indian capital, had a relatively low 15 per cent of households in slums, while major cities Kolkata and Chennai had 30 per cent and 29 per cent respectively. High-tech center Bangalore had only nine per cent of its households in slums.

Like other developing countries, India has undergone rapid urbanisation over the past fifty years. As per the 2001 Census, 28 per cent of the population of India was living in urban areas. From 1951 to 2001, India's urban population grew almost five-fold, from around 62 million in 1951 to around 286 million in 2001. After China, India has the largest urban population in the world. In the post-independence period, the growth rate of the urban population in India has always remained higher than the growth rate of the rural population. The size of the country's urban population is projected to increase to nearly 586 million by 2030. By 2015, more than 50 cities in India are expected to have a population of more than one million. It is estimated that urban population growth will account for over two-thirds of total population growth in India in the first quarter of the 21st century, as elsewhere in the world, the increasing concentration of population in slums in urban areas in India is seen as an indication of increasing urban poverty.

Problems of Urbanisation

Problem of urbanisation is manifestation of lopsided urbanisation, faulty urban planning, urbanisation with poor economic base and without having functional categories. Hence India's urbanisation is followed by some basic problems in the field of: (1) housing, (2) slums, (3) transport, (4) water supply and sanitation, (5) water pollution and air pollution, (6) inadequate provision for social infrastructure (school, hospital, etc). Class I cities such as Calcutta, Bombay, Delhi, Madras etc have reached saturation level of employment generating capacity.[15]

Today, an estimated 828 million people live in slum conditions, representing around one-third of the world's urban population. Slum dwellers experience difficult social and economic conditions that manifest in different forms of deprivation i.e., material, physical, social, and political. They live in overcrowded, poorly constructed housing, often with insecure land possession. Housing in these settings ranges from high-rise tenements to shacks to plastic sheet tents on sidewalks, often located in undesirable parts of the city such as steep hillsides, riverbanks subject to flooding, or industrial areas. Slum dwellers' health is further affected by reduced access to safe food and water, poor sanitation, a breakdown of traditional family structures, high crime, and high unemployment rates. Due to the high population density, overcrowding, and lack of safe water and sanitation systems, slums are productive breeding grounds for tuberculosis, hepatitis, dengue, pneumonia, cholera, and diarrheal disease.[16]

Government Policies/Programmes

Although a variety of livelihood programmes and projects for women exists in India, access is generally restricted to married women. The few nascent experiments involving unmarried adolescent girls are limited in scale and have not been evaluated. When adolescent girls are involved in income-generating activities, they generally assist their mothers in home-based work for which they may or may not be remunerated. Moreover, adolescent girls are not participant in savings and credit programmes. Programmatic initiatives that prepare girls in India for future livelihood and foster their mobility are rare, and evaluation of such programmes are even less common.[17]

Ministry of Urban Development, Government of India, is the apex body for formulation and administration of the rules and regulations and laws relating to the housing and urban development in India. The ministry also published the National city rating, which ranked the cleanest cities in India. Urban Development Department adopted a Citizen's Charter in 1999 city rating, which set out objectives and activities and spell out the commitment towards the people, who had dealings with the Department. The Urban development department formulates policy, provides funds, monitors and coordinates with the activities, of the urban local bodies.[18] In the federal structure of the Indian polity, the matters pertaining to the housing and urban development have been assigned by the Constitution of India to the state governments. The Constitutions (74th Amendment) Act have further delegated many of these functions to the urban local bodies. The constitutional and legal authority of the Government of India is limited only to Delhi and other Union Territories and to the subject which state legislatures authorise the Union Parliament to legislate.[19] Ministry of Urban Development has prepared model building bye-laws, which contain provisions for improving access to various public buildings by disabled and elderly persons. These building bye-laws have been sent to the state governments, union territories, Delhi Development Authority, Municipal Corporation of Delhi, New Delhi Municipal Committee etc. for adoption. 16 states/UTs have already notified the amended building bye-laws and six states/UTs are in process of amending the building byelaws. Rests of the States/UTs are being pursued. All the state governments have been requested to designate an official in each district for bringing cases of non-compliance to the notice of the concerned authorities.[20]

Jawaharlal Nehru National Urban Renewal Mission (JNNURM) is a massive city-modernisation scheme launched by the Government of India under Ministry of Urban Development. It envisages a total investment of over $20 billion over seven years. Named after Jawaharlal Nehru, the first prime minister of India, the scheme was officially inaugurated by Prime Minister Manmohan Singh on December 3rd, 2005 as a programme meant to improve the quality of life and infrastructure in the cities. JNNURM is a huge mission which relates primarily to development in the context of urban conglomerates focusing to the Indian cities. As of 2012 Gujarat led the tally for the state-level reforms, being the only state to have achieved ten reforms required by the mission. Five states have achieved nine out of ten reforms: Andhra Pradesh, Maharashtra, Madhya Pradesh, Orissa and Uttar Pradesh.[21]

Urban Renewal is one of the thrust areas in the National Common Minimum Programme of the government and accordingly Jawaharlal Nehru National Urban Renewal Mission was launched on December 3rd, 2005 with an investment of Rs 1,00,000.00 crores in mission period of seven years beginning 2005-06. Urban Infrastructure Development Scheme for Small and Medium Towns (UIDSSMT) is one of the components of JNNURM. The mission is the single largest initiative of the Government of India for planned development of cities and towns. The objectives of the scheme are: (a) Improve infrastructural facilities and help create durable public assets and quality oriented services in cities and towns; (b) Enhance public-private-partnership in infrastructural development; and (c) Promote planned integrated development of towns and cities. Urban infrastructure Development Scheme for Small and Medium Towns was launched on 3.12.2005 for improvement in urban infrastructure in towns and cities in a planned manner. It subsumed the erstwhile schemes of Integrated Development of Small and Medium Towns (IDSMT) and Accelerated Urban Water Supply Programme (AUWSP). The scheme will apply to all cities/towns as per 2001 census, excepting cities/towns covered under Jawaharlal Nehru National Urban Renewal Mission. The components for assistance under the scheme include all urban infrastructure development projects including water supply and sewerage. The sharing of funds would be in the ratio of 80:10 between central government and state government and the balance 10 per cent could be raised by the nodal/implementing agencies from the financial institutions. Central assistance (grant) released will go directly to the nodal agencies identified by the State government as Additional Central Assistance. The grant from Government of India and state government will flow to the nodal agency designated by state government. Urban local bodies and implementing agencies including parastatal agencies, will submit detailed project reports to the designated state level nodal agencies for appraisal.[22]

The majority of urban infrastructure projects currently being undertaken by the urban local bodies (ULBs) depends mostly on funds from state governments, the government of India-sponsored JNNURM (including the UIDSSMT), and other governmental agencies. Besides, most of the local bodies lack from requisite capacities/expertise to prepare bankable urban infrastructure projects. Ongoing programmes of both the central and state governments may not be adequate to fill the resource gap, in light of the extent of the resourcc gap. To enable ULBs to bridge this gap through accessing market funds for their infrastructure projects, the Government of India has decided to launch, in the current fiscal year, the pooled finance development scheme (PFDS). The scheme is meant to provide credit enhancement grants to enable ULBs to access market borrowing through pooled finance municipal bonds for investment in urban infrastructure projects. The main objectives of the PFDS are to: (i) facilitate ULBs to access capital and the financial market for investment in essential municipal infrastructure; (ii) facilitate development of bankable (structured with appropriate credit enhancements in such manner a way that they demonstrate the capacity for servicing market debt to the satisfaction of the rating agencies and potential investors) urban infrastructure projects; (iii) reduce the cost of borrowing to local bodies with appropriate credit enhancement measures; and (iv) facilitate development/ strengthening of the municipal bond market.[23]

The Centrally sponsored scheme of Integrated Development of Small & Medium Towns (IDSMT) was initiated in the year 1979-80 and is continued with timely amendments and modifications upto 2004-2005 and in December 2005 it was subsumed in UIDSSMT Scheme. Investment in the development of small urban centres would help in reducing migration to large cities and support the growth of surrounding rural areas as well. IDSMT scheme will be applicable to towns/cities with population upto five lakh. Towns are to be identified and prioritised by the state governments and UTs according to their urban strategy within the framework of guidelines of the schemes. The IDSMT scheme will be applicable to only those towns, where elections to the local bodies have been held and elected bodies are in position.[24] Prime Minister's Award for Excellence in Urban Planning and Design comprises following two categories: (i) implemented urban planning and design projects signifying built environment of exceptional quality; and (ii) innovative ideas/concepts and plans in Urban Planning and Design, where the projects were still in the pipeline or at implementation stage. These awards are open to all Indian architects, town planners and allied professionals, their firms and government, public and private sector institutions/organisations who planned/implemented projects anywhere in India.[25]

Central government has set up a pooled finance development fund (PFDF) to provide credit enhancement to ULBs to access market borrowings based on their credit worthiness through state-level-pooled finance mechanism. For implementing pooled finance mechanism, a state pooled finance entity (SPFE) shall be required to be set up in each state. Each SPFE is to be primarily state designed and could either be a Trust or a Special Purpose Entity, provided that the entity is only a pass through vehicle. The basic advantage of setting up of SPFE would be that it would enable the ULBs to enter the bond market on a regular basis and take advantage of scaled up operations. Further, efficient SPFEs can generate fair degree of goodwill in the bond market and may be able to achieve much higher levels of efficiency in operations than individual ULBs.[26]

In pursuance of the joint statement towards Japan–India strategic and global partnership announced by the Prime Ministers of Japan and India in December, 2006, inter-alia, referring to the launching of working groups by the two countries in the field of urban development, a Memorandum of Understanding (MoU) between India and Japan on cooperation in the field of urban development was signed on 1.5.2007 at New Delhi. It was signed by Minister of Urban Development on behalf of Government of India and Minister of Land, Infrastructure and Transport, Government of Japan on behalf of Government of Japan. As per the MoU, the Working group will meet once a year and the first meeting will be held in Japan, and the second and subsequent meetings will be held alternately in India and Japan.[27]

Housing and Urban Development Corporation Limited

The Housing and Urban Development Corporation Limited (HUDCO) is a government-owned corporation in India. One of the public sector undertakings, it is wholly owned by the Union Government and is under the administrative control of the Ministry of Housing and Urban Poverty Alleviation. It is mandated with building affordable housing and carrying out urban development.[28]

Urban Slum

Slum is a heavily populated urban informal settlement characterised by substandard housing and squalor. Slums were common in the nineteenth and early twentieth centuries in the United States and Europe. According to UN-HABITAT, around 33 per cent of the urban population in the developing world in 2012, or about 863 million people, lived in slums. Slums form and grow in many different parts of the world for many different reasons. Some causes include rapid rural-to-urban migration, economic stagnation and depression, high unemployment, poverty, informal economy, poor planning, politics, natural disasters and social conflicts. Rural-urban migration is one of the causes attributed to the formation and expansion of slums. Many people move to urban areas primarily because cities promise more jobs, better schools for poor's children, and diverse income opportunities than subsistence farming in rural areas. Lack of affordable low cost housing and poor planning encourages the supply side of slums. Insufficient financial resources and lack of coordination in government bureaucracy are two main causes of poor housing planning. Some of the slums in today's world are a product of urbanisation brought by colonialism.

Others were created because of segregation imposed by the colonialists. Poor families that cannot afford transportation, or those who simply lack any form of affordable public transportation, generally end up in squat settlements within walking distance or close enough to the place of their formal or informal employment.[29]

It has been observed that the most disadvantaged section of society or the rural population which migrate to urban areas in search of employment or better conditions of living find no place to live in and end up in squatter settlements or in the unhygienic housing clusters in cities. These clusters having insufficient facilities of hygiene, toilets, drinking water, sanitation etc. are termed as slums. During the last few years the growth of slums in the urban areas specially the big cities has become a major problem for the planners and policy makers. As per the Census of India, 2001, 640 towns spread over 26 states/UTs have reported existence of slums. It is reported that 42.6 million people consisting of 8.2 million households are living in slums of these towns. Nine States/UTs have not identified any slums. It is a coincidence that both NSSO in 2002 and Census of India, 2001 found that every seventh person in the urban India is a slum dweller. The census of India has also identified that 17.4 per cent (7.4 million) scheduled castes and 2.4 per cent (1.00 million) scheduled tribes live in the identified slums in India.[30]

Slums have risen dramatically since 1947. There were two main reasons for slum development. One is partition of India and the other is Industrial revolution after independence. Before 1950, slums were predominantly found around the mills, factories etc. They were mostly industrial workers in one room tenements. Health and services provisions to these areas rose as main issues. Instead of going farther, the density of the slums started growing in and around the cities. From 1950 to1968 the number of slums increased to 18 per cent, in the 1970s there was a huge surge and by 1980 slum dwellers were half of the entire city's population. Although, there was the level of urbanisation has been rising gradually, and the decadal increase in urban population remains quite high, there is still enormous potential for increase in India's urban population.[31]

Rural-Urban Migration

Human migration is the movement by people from one place to another with the intention of settling in the new location. The movement is typically over long distances and from one country to another, but internal migration is also possible. Migration has continued under the form of both voluntary migration within one's region, country, or beyond and involuntary migration. According to the International Organisation for Migration's World Migration Report 2010, the number of international migrants was estimated at 220 million in 2013. Historic migration of human population begins with the movement of *Homo erectus* out of Africa across Eurasia about a million years ago. Early humans migrated due to many factors such as changing climate and landscape and inadequate food supply. While the pace of migration had accelerated since the eighteenth century already (including the involuntary slave trade), it would increase further in the nineteenth century. Industrialisation encouraged migration wherever it appeared. The First and Second World Wars, and civil wars, genocides, and crises sparked by them, had an enormous impact on migration. In modern India, estimates based on industry sectors mainly employing migrants suggest that there are around 100 million circular migrants in India. Caste, social networks and historical precedents play a powerful role in shaping patterns of migration. Migration for work in the 21st century has become a popular way for individuals from impoverished developing countries to obtain sufficient income for survival.[32]

Rural-urban migration usually leads to loss of necessary manpower in the rural areas to work on the farm lands. It also leads to congestion in the urban centres, it lends to a high unemployment level, poor housing situations and an increase in crime levels. On the other hand, increased man power in urban centres provides cheap labour to the industries in these areas. Rural-urban migration has long been associated with economic development and growth in the economic literature. In particular, Todaro and Harris-Todaro-type probabilistic models that examine migration have concentrated on the expected wage disparities between rural and urban (formal) labor markets as a driving force behind migration decision. These models, which are static and partial equilibrium in nature, have virtually ignored the cost-of-living differentials across regions that arise from the presence of regional non-traded (home) goods.[33]

Migration is a strategy adopted by rural population to improve household livelihood and benefit from better services in urban areas. It also enables rural residents to fund investment in rural housing and economic activities. Rural-urban migrants benefit generally from access to better opportunities in urban areas and financial transfers for relatives back home. At the same time, cities also benefit from the steady supply of labour that comes from rural areas. Many people migrate to cities due to natural disasters. Cities near disaster-affected areas are usually receivers of the displaced persons and their number is expected to increase in the future due to environmental change.[34] Rural-urban migration has negative consequences. It leads to overpopulation of the urban areas thus poliferating crime in the society. Those who engage in crime prefer the urban areas being relation with wealthy individuals. Rural-urban migration slows down the rate of development of the rural areas. In view of the negative consequences, government of each country in the world should strive to provide social amenities and facilities in the rural areas and also provide jobs for the citizens in the rural areas.[35]

United Nations Human Settlement Programme

The United Nations Human Settlement Programme UN-Habitat is the United Nations agency that has been mandated by the UN General Assembly to promote socially and environmentally sustainable towns and cities to provide adequate shelter for all. The United Nations Human Settlement Programme (UN–Habitat) is the United Nations agency for human settlements and sustainable urban development. It was established in 1978 in Vancouver in Habitat I meeting and has its headquarters at the United Nations Office at Nairobi, Kenya. It is mandated by the United Nations General Assembly to promote socially and environmentally sustainable towns and cities with the goal of providing adequate shelter for all. The governing council of UN-Habitat is the inter-governmental decision-making body for the Programme. Every two years, the governing council examines the UN-Habitat's work and relationship with its partners. The World Urban Forum is an international conference dedicated to urban issues, organised by UN-Habitat. The United Nations has designated the first Monday of October every year as World Habitat Day. The UN-Habitat Scroll of Honour Award is an award given by the United Nations Human Settlement Programme in recognition of the work carried out in the field of human settlements development.[36]

Conclusion

Urbanisation is closely linked to modernisation, industrialisation, and the sociological process of rationalisation. It is not merely a modern phenomenon, but a rapid and historic transformation of human social roots on a global scale, whereby predominantly rural culture is being rapidly replaced by predominantly urban culture. It occurs as individual, commercial, social and Governmental efforts reduce time and expense in commuting and transportation and improve opportunities for jobs, education, housing, and transportation. Living in cities permits the advantages of the opportunities of proximity, diversity, and marketplace competition. Economic opportunities are just one reason people move into cities. Cities offer a larger variety of services, such as specialist services that aren't found in rural areas. People located in cities are more productive than those working outside dense agglomerations. The dominant conurbation(s) of a country also benefit from even more intense concentrations of the very same things cities offer, making them magnets for not just the non-urban population, but urban and suburban population from other conurbation.

REFERENCES

1. *Early Human's Life,* Retrieved from http://www.studyvillage.com/resources/3366-essay-on-early-human-s-life.aspx
2. *Urban* area (2014). Retrieved from http://en.wikipedia.org/wiki/Urban_area
3. *Urban area (2014).* Retrieved from http://education.nationalgeographic.com/education/encyclopedia/urban-area/?ar_a=1
4. Sabyasachi Tripathi (2013), An overview of India's Urbanisation, *Urban Economic Growth and Urban Equity,* Retrieved from http://mpra.ub.uni-muenchen.de/45537/1/MPRA_paper_45537.pdf

5. *Urbanisation: Causes and Effects of Urbanisation in India,* Retrieved from http://www.yourarticlelibrary.com/india-2/urbanisation-causes-and-effects-of-urbanisation-in-india-766-words/4659/
6. Pranati Datta, *Urbanisation in India,* Retrieved from http://www.infostat.sk/vdc/epc2006/papers/epc2006s60134.pdf
7. *Urbanisation: A Majority in Cities (2014).* Retrieved from http://www.unfpa.org/pds/urbanisation.htm
8. *Urbanisation*, Retrieved from http://www.sciencedaily.com/articles/u/urbanisation.htm
9. *Facts and Data about Cities and Urbanisation in Asia*, Retrieved from http://www.adb.org/features/12-things-know-2012-urbanisation-asia
10. *Urbanisation trends in Asia and the Pacific*, Retrieved from http://www.unescapsdd.org/files/documents/SPPS-Factsheet-urbanisation-v5.pdf
11. *Urbanisation in Europe: limits to spatial growth*, Retrieved from http://www.eea.europa.eu/media/speeches/urbanisation-in-europe-limits-to-spatial-growth
12. Pranati Datta, *Urbanisation in India*, Retrieved from http://www.infostat.sk/vdc/epc2006/papers/epc2006s60134.pdf
13. Sabyasachi Tripathi (2013). *An overview of India's Urbanisation, Urban Economic Growth and Urban Equity,* Retrieved from http://mpra.ub.uni-muenchen.de/45537/1/MPRA_paper_45537.pdf
14. *The Challenges of Urbanisation in India,* Retrieved from http://12thplan.gov.in/12fyp_docs/17.pdf
15. Pranati Datta, *Urbanisation in India*, Retrieved from http://www.infostat.sk/vdc/epc2006/papers/epc2006s60134.pdf
16. *Slum residence: Situation and trends-WHO,* Retrieved from http://www.who.int/gho/urban_health/determinants/slum_residence_text/en/
17. See http://www.popcouncil.org/uploads/pdfs/wp/194.pdf
18. See http://delhi.gov.in/wps/wcm/connect/doit_udd/Urban+Development/Home
19. See http://mhupa.gov.in/ministry/index2.htm
20. See http://urbanindia.nic.in/programme/ud/promotionofnon.htm

21. *Jawaharlal Nehru National Urban Renewal Mission*, Retrieved from http://en.wikipedia.org/wiki/Jawaharlal_Nehru_National_Urban_Renewal_Mission
22. *Urban Infrastructure Development Scheme for Small and Medium Towns,* Retrieved from http://urbanindia.nic.in/programme/ud/uidssmt_pdf/overview.pdf
23. *Pooled Finance Development Scheme*, Retrieved from http://urbanindia.nic.in/programme/ud/toolkit_pfds.pdf
24. *Integrated Development of Small & Medium Towns,* Retrieved from http://urbanindia.nic.in/programme/ud/integrateddevelopment.pdf
25. *Prime Minister's Award for Excellency in Urban Planning and Design*, Retrieved from http://urbanindia.nic.in/programme/ud/primeministers.htm
26. *Pooled Finance Development Fund Scheme,* Retrieved from http://urbanindia.nic.in/programme/ud/overview_pooled.pdf
27. Indo-Japan working group on Urban development, Retrieved from http://urbanindia.nic.in/programme/ud/indo_japan.pdf
28. *Housing and Urban Development Corporation Limited* , Retrieved from http://en.wikipedia.org/wiki/Housing_and_Urban_Development_Corporation
29. *Slum (2014).* Retrieved from http://en.wikipedia.org/wiki/Slum
30. *Urban Slums – Overview, Chapter VIII,* Section B, Retrieved from http://mhupa.gov.in/ministry/housing/11thplanChapter-VIII.pdf
31. Dr. Abir Bandyopadhyay & Vandana Agrawal (2013). Slums In India: From Past To Present, *International Refereed Journal of Engineering and Science,* Volume 2, Issue 4, Retrieved from http://www.irjes.com/Papers/vol2-issue4/Version%20%201/I245559.pdf
32. *Migration (2014).* Retrieved from http://en.wikipedia.org/wiki/Human_migration
33. *Rural-urban Migration and Economic Growth in Developing Countries*, Retrieved from http://ideas.repec.org/p/red/sed004/241.html
34. *Urbanisation trends in Asia and the Pacific,* Retrieved from http://www.unescapsdd.org/files/documents/SPPS-Factsheet-urbanisation-v5.pdf

35. *Causes and effects of rural urban migration (2009).* Retrieved from http://voices.yahoo.com/causes-effects-rural-urban-migration-4933406.html?cat=6
36. *United Nations Human Settlements Programme, Retrieved* from http://en.wikipedia.org/wiki/United_Nations_Human_Settlements_Programme

8

Arms Trafficking

"I'm no longer just a candidate. I'm the President. I know what it means to send young Americans into battle, for I have held in my arms the mothers and fathers of those who didn't return. I've shared the pain of families who've lost their homes, and the frustration of workers who've lost their jobs."

- Barack Obama

Introduction

Arm is any device used in order to inflict damage or harm to living beings, structures, or systems. Weapons are used to increase the efficacy and efficiency of activities such as hunting, crime, law enforcement, self-defense, and warfare. Ancient weapons were evolutionary improvements of late neolithic implements, but then significant improvements in materials and crafting techniques created a series of revolutions in military technology. The European Renaissance marked the beginning of the implementation of firearms in western warfare. Guns and rockets were introduced to the battlefield.[1] On April 2, 2013; the General Assembly adopted the landmark Arms Trade Treaty, regulating the international trade in conventional arms, from small arms to battle tanks, combat aircraft and warships. The treaty will foster peace and security by thwarting uncontrolled destabilising arms flows to conflict regions. It will prevent human rights abusers and violators of the law of war from being supplied with arms.[2]

Despite the economic downturn it has been business as usual for the world's biggest arms companies who have seen sales of weapons and military services rise during 2010 and exceed \$400bn (£250bn). The highly-concentrated industry is also highlighted by the report, which states that the top 10 arms producing companies account for 56 per cent of the total top 100 arms sales. This amounts to \$230 bn of the total arms sales.[3] Every day, millions of people suffer from the direct and indirect consequences of the irresponsible arms trade: thousands are killed, others are maimed, many are raped, and/or forced to flee from homes, while many others live under constant threat of weapons. The poorly regulated global trade in conventional arms and ammunition fuels conflict, poverty and human rights abuses.[4]

What is Arms Trafficking?

Arms trafficking are the illegal trafficking or smuggling of contraband weapons or ammunition. Legal trade in firearms varies widely, depending on local and national laws.[5] Illegal arms availability has become a global threat to the sovereignty of states at macro and micro levels. Such trade can best be described as unlawful procurement, trade and trafficking of small arms, light weapons and ammunition. It is a persistent, widespread and dangerous problem which causes havoc in many parts of the world.

Reasons of Arms Trafficking

Reasons for arm trade are various. Drivers of small arms demand include social, economic, and political insecurity; demographics; governance problems; weak and corrupt law enforcement; inadequate opportunities for education and economic development; failure of states to protect the vulnerable; social and economic disparities; inadequate post-conflict disarmament; and embedded cultures of violence.[6]

Global Perspectives

The arms industry is a global business, which manufactures weapons and military technology and equipment. It consists of commercial industry involved in research, development, production, and service of military material, equipment and facilities.[7] Hundreds of thousands of small arms in leaky Government arsenals are vulnerable to theft, loss and diversion.[8] Developing nations have slowly become host to illicit small arms markets. The increasing number of internal conflicts and the high rate of violence and crime in post-conflict situations are closely connected to destabilising accumulations and transfers of small arms and light weapons (SALW).[9] Illegal weapons smuggling between the U.S. and Mexico threatens the overall safety and security of both countries. Weapons smuggled into Mexico from the United States often end up in the hands of the drug cartels or other smuggling organisations, where they can be employed against law enforcement officers and citizens in either country.[10]

Nigeria in particular may seem like an ideal arms trading partner for Russia. Both countries are major oil producers. They have a strong diplomatic relationship and are energy partners. But in Nigeria, legal trade in small arms and light weapons, or SALW, isn't exactly booming. That's because the Economic Community of West African States or ECOWASs has taken steps to curtail the proliferation of SALW in the region. Nigeria is its member. A 1998 moratorium on the import and exports of these weapons, dating from the Sierra Leone and Liberia civil wars, was made legally binding in 2006.[11]

Small arms trafficking in the 21st century is nothing if not a global operation. In 2002, traffickers acquired 5,000 AK-47s from Yugoslavian army stocks and moved them from Serbia to Liberia under the guise of a legal transaction with Nigeria. One of the planes used in shipment came from Ukraine and made a refueling stop in Libya while en route. In particular, small arms fuel regional instability. These persistent weapons often remain behind at the end of conflicts, thus enabling disputes to reignite or spread to neighboring countries. Even when further war is avoided, small arms become instruments for criminal violence and the disruption of development efforts. The vast majority of small arms on the black market were produced and traded legally before being diverted into an illicit network. Arms trafficking networks rely on many different actors in many different countries. Pilots flying planes originating in Belgium, Ukraine, or South Africa traffic weapons originating in Eastern Europe and deliver them to clients from Africa to Afghanistan.[12]

Libya has been named as the primary source of illegal weapons trade that is fueling conflicts in at least 14 countries around the world, a final report from the UN's independent panel on Libya's sanctions announced. The UN arms embargo was enacted on Libya at the start of the unrest, which eventually ousted former leader Muammar Gaddafi. Non-lethal equipment was allowed to enter Libya when the UNSC eased its sanctions as the UN cautioned Tripoli against the spread of weapons to nearby states.[13]

Arms Trafficking in West Africa

Arms and Conflict in Africa Arms transfers and trafficking remain one of sub-Saharan Africa's major security problems. Africa continues to have the greatest number of armed conflicts of any continent. There are about nine opposition groups in Sudan, which include Beja Congress, Darfur Liberation Front (DLF), Democratic Unionist Party (DUP), Janjaweed, Justice and Equality Movement (JEM), National Alliance Forces (SAF), Sudan Liberation Army (SLA), Sudan Liberation Movement (SLM), and Sudan People's Liberation Army (SPLA). Two main rebel groups in Sudan, the JEM and the Sudan Liberation Movement/Army (SLM/A), flared up a conflict with the Government in 2003 over marginalization and distribution of wealth and power. This conflict has resulted in fighting between splinter rebel groups, increased banditry and ethnic clashes. The Darfur conflict pits mostly non-Arab rebels against the Arab-dominated government. The SPLM governs in South Sudan.[14]

In mid-2001, latent or open hostilities affected Angola, Burundi, Chad, Cote d'Ivoire, Democratic Republic of Congo (DROC), Djibouti, Eritrea-Ethiopia, Guinea, Guinea-Bissau, Kenya, Liberia, Nigeria-Cameroon, Republic of Congo, Rwanda, Senegal, Sierra Leone, Somalia, Sudan, Tanzania-Zanzibar, Uganda, and Zimbabwe. The influx of light weapons financed by cash, diamonds, or other commodities did not cause Africa's wars but it has prolonged and made them more lethal.[15] Every year millions of pistols, light machine guns and revolvers are manufactured and exported all over the world. In Africa the abundance of small arms, such as simple pistols, rifles and machine guns are fuels the continent's conflicts. In some parts of Africa an AK-47 automatic rifle can be bought for as little as $6.[16] Illegal arms trade in Africa has been the central focus of the United Nations in the past years.[17] According to available statistics, out of the estimated 500 million small arms and light weapons in circulation worldwide, 100 million are found in Africa.[18] In Africa, and elsewhere, the illicit trade in small arms and light weapons is opaque, amorphous and dynamic. Arms trade is also a global enterprise with illicit weapons across Africa coming virtually from every major arms producing country in the world.[19]

Male has become an established transit route for weapons heading from West Africa's increasingly peaceful coastal states to active conflicts in West and Central Africa. On the demand side, some of the weapons stay in Mali and are used for criminality. Others go to active conflicts in the north of Mali, in Niger, Chad and even as far away as Sudan.[20] In Mali and close to 20 other countries, poorly regulated international arms transfers continue to contribute to the recruitment and use of boys and girls under the age of 18 in hostilities by armed groups and, in some cases, government forces.[21] The United Nations says conflict in Central Africa is fueled by an illegal-weapons trade that increases cross-border crime and threatens national reconciliation. Organised crime involved in drug trafficking and the illegal exploitation of mineral resources provides steady flow of weapons that is making conflict in Central Africa more violent and more difficult to contain. Weapons trafficking in Central Africa have complex links, not only to conflict, but also to a number of other criminal activities, which undermine efforts to engender social justice, foster the rule of law and, ultimately, achieve the Millennium Development Goals.[22] Uganda has taken a number of steps to combat the illicit trade and use of small arms and light weapons. The Ugandan parliament is looking at improving the national law to better deal with weapons given to civic defense forces, among other items.[23]

The African Union (AU) is an inter-governmental organisation consisting of states from the African Continent. The AU was established on July 9, 2002, to replace the amalgamated African Economic Community (AEC) and the Organisation of African Unity (OAU). Its headquarters is located in Addis Ababa, Ethiopia. The OAU Council of Ministers endorsed the Bamako Declaration (by Decision CM/Dec.599 (LXXIV of the 74th Ordinary Session) in July 2001, just prior to the United Nations Conference on the Illicit Trade in Small Arms and Light Weapons in All Its Aspects (July 9 to 20, 2001). In December 2005, the AU convened a meeting of governmental experts from member states, to adopt an African Common Position for the Conference to Review the UN Programme of Action to Prevent, Combat and Eradicate the Illicit Trade in Small Arms and Light Weapons in All Its Aspects (PoA) that was due to be held in June 2006.[24]

The UN has imposed arms embargoes against Liberia and Somalia and against various insurgent groups, including the Revolutionary United Front (Sierra Leone), National Union for the Total Independence of Angola (UNITA), and Hutu and ex-far extremists in Central Africa. The United Nations has perhaps made greatest effort to enforce its arms embargo against UNITA by essentially freezing its bank accounts, restricting the travel of UNITA officials, and limiting UNITA's ability to market diamonds. In collaboration with the Pretoria-based Institute for Security Studies, the OAU devised the Initiative on Small Arms Proliferation and Africa, designed to raise awareness of the small arms proliferation problem and to facilitate an in-depth discussion of the menace it poses. Mali, working through the Economic Community of West African States (ECOWAS—Benin, Burkina Faso, Cape Verde, Cote d'Ivoire, Gambia, Ghana, Guinea, Guinea-Bissau, Liberia, Mali, Mauritania, Niger, Nigeria, Senegal, Sierra Leone, and Togo) devised the West African Small Arms Moratorium that imposed renewable three-year (1998-2001) voluntary ban on the manufacture, import, and export of weapons throughout member states.[25]

Home made guns have been bought and sold across India for decade. According to International Action Network on Small Arms, there are 40 million illegal small arms in circulation across the country, for more than half the 75 million illegal small arms currently in circulation globally.[26]

Arms Trafficking in India

India has been an active participant in the Arms Trade Treaty (ATT) negotiations. Underlying participation in such extended negotiations was the principle that member states have a legitimate right for self-defence and belief that there is no conflict between the pursuit of national security objectives and the aspiration that the Arms Trade Treaty be strong, balanced and effective.[27] India is likely to spend approximately USD 100 billion for the import of weapons and defence equipment over the next 10 years. The DPP stipulates an offset commitment of 30 per cent of the total value of a contract, if it exceeds USD 66 million (Rs 300.00 crore). In fact, the offset obligation specified for the multi-mission, medium-range combat aircraft (MMRCA) is 50 per cent of the total value, which is estimated to exceed USD 12 billion. South Asia is arguably the second most dangerous global hotspot after West Asia and radical extremism in the Af-Pak area is making the region further dangerous. One of the major reasons for this is the large-scale proliferation and easy availability of small arms and light weapons (SALW). India has witnessed around 152 militant movements since independence, of which 65 are believed to be still active in one form or the other.[28] Today India is second only to the U.S. in the proportion of civilians who own guns, and the number is growing. The Control Arms Federation of India estimates that 5000 people are killed each year in small arms violence unrelated to the country's domestic insurgencies.

The United States has already made *"tremendous progress"* in expanding weapons sales to India since 2008, and U.S. companies could see *"billions of dollars"* in additional sales in coming years. U.S. sales of military equipment to India had grown from zero in 2008 to around $8 billion, despite a decision by India to choose a French-built plane in a closely-watched fighter plane competition.[29] The UN General Assembly has overwhelmingly approved the first ever arms treaty regulating the $70 billion global arms trade, even as India abstained from saying that the draft was weak on terrorism and non-state actors. The resolution got 154 votes in favour, while three nations voted against in the 193-member General Assembly. There were 23 abstentions, including that of India. Iran, North Korea and Syria had blocked the adoption of the treaty saying it failed to ban sales of weapons to groups that commit *"acts of aggression"*. The three countries voted against the resolution. From the beginning of the ATT (Arms Trade Treaty) process, India has maintained that such treaty should make a real impact on illicit trafficking in conventional arms and their illicit use especially by terrorists and other unauthorised and unlawful non-state actors. However, the draft treaty that is annexed to the resolution is weak on terrorism and non-state actors and these concerns find no mention in the specific prohibitions of the Treaty.[30]

Arms Trafficking and Terrorism

The terrorists are engaged in illegal arms trade and threaten the innocent people. Every nation is currently facing the crisis of small arms. Even though no civilian is issued a license for small arms, administrative measures have failed to control illegal arms trade. Terrorists routinely recruit children and youths for combat and often forced to become fighters, human shields, and sex slaves. Many children are abducted and more than a half of the armed groups are under 12.[31] Insurgents, armed gang members, pirates, terrorists can multiply their force through the use of unlawfully acquired firepower.[32] Illicit arms trafficking fuels civil wars, contributes to sky-rocketing crime rates and feeds the arsenals of world's worst terrorists. Particularly troubling is the illicit trade in small arms and light weapon. Unlike weapons of mass destruction, small arms and many light weapons have legitimate military, law enforcement, and/or sporting and recreational uses. Hundreds of thousands of small arms in leaky government arsenals are vulnerable to theft, loss and diversion. Once acquired by traffickers, these weapons are smuggled across national borders in every conceivable way. They are hidden under sacks of vegetables in the back of pick up trucks, packed into household appliances that are then loaded onto cargo ships, even air-dropped out of old Soviet military transport planes. In the hands of terrorists and other criminals, these weapons have the capacity to kill dozens, even hundreds, of innocent civilians.[33]

The illicit circulation of small arms, light weapons and their ammunition destabilises communities, and impacts security and development in all regions of the world. The illicit trade in small arms, light weapons and ammunition wreaks havouc everywhere. Small arms are cheap, light, and easy to handle, transport and conceal. A build-up of small arms may not alone create conflicts in which they are used, but their excessive accumulation and wide availability gravates the tension. Most present-day conflicts are fought mainly with small arms, which are broadly used in inter-state conflict. They are the weapons of choice in civil wars and terrorism, organised crime and gang warfare.[34]

One of the most destructive aspects of illegal arms trade is the trafficking of small arms (such as pistols and rifles), which are responsible for more than 1,300 deaths every day. Because, they are small and portable, small arms have been purchased illegally by rebel groups, terrorists and warring factions across Asia, Africa and South America.[35] Small arms are responsible for armed violence in many different contexts, from urban violence to conflict and crisis zones, from organised crime to piracy and terrorism. There are an estimated 875 million of them in circulation worldwide, produced by more than 1,000 companies from nearly 100 countries, with an estimated annual authorised trade that exceeds $8.5 billion. The transition from the legal to the illegal realm can occur at any stage of a weapon's life cycle: manufacture, first delivery, domestic or international transfer, possession, storage or final disposal.[36]

In June 2010, the representatives of United Nations (UN) member states came together at the biennial meeting of states in New York to consider the implementation of the 2001 Programme of Action (POA) on the illicit trade in small arms. The programme was initiated in July 2001 to keep a check on the ever-growing illicit trade on Small Arms and Light Weapons (SALW) and to help countries, combat this pernicious problem. While most of the issues relating to the illicit trade of SALW are highlighted in the media, few talks about ways and methods through which globalisation have spurred the black market of SALW. The global illegitimate business in small arms is valued approximately around US$ 1 billion. The structure of the small arms black market today is a complex network stretching across the globe, siphoning the gains of globalisation. At heart, it's essential to map out the structure of illicit arms trade which not only includes black market, but also grey market and craft production.[37]

Effects of Arms Trafficking

The majority of conflict deaths are caused by the use of small arms, and civilian population bear the brunt of armed conflict more than ever. Small arms are the dominant tools of criminal violence. It facilitates a vast spectrum of human rights violations, including killing, maiming, rape and other forms of sexual violence, enforced disappearance, torture, and forced recruitment of children by armed groups.[38] Armed conflicts facilitated by illicit trade of small arms not only lead to direct costs such as medical costs, military expenditure, the destruction of infrastructure, and the care for displaced people which divert money from more productive uses but has far more impinging consequences. The indirect costs indicate that each nation has a huge price to pay. The economy of nation comes to almost standstill, especially industries like tourism which are capable of contributing heavily to a country's gross domestic product. The country suffers from inflation, debt, and reduced investment, while people suffer from unemployment, lack of public services, and trauma.[39] The ease of access to light weaponry is the main problem for many afflicted regions.[40]

Controlling Arms Trafficking

Arms control treaties and agreements are often seen as a way to avoid costly arms races which could prove counter-productive to national aims and future peace.[41] Small arms and light weapons are used to cause many deaths in conflicts around the world. Small arms control was first broached by UN Resolution A/RES/46/36 (December 1991), which was expanded upon by A/RES/50/70 (January 1996).[42] Control of firearms trafficking is crucial in the fight against insecurity and criminality. Several EU-level measures have been adopted to complement EU States' initiatives to reinforce controls on the legal sale and holding of firearms in the EU.[43] The United States will announce a $3.43 million assistance programme to combat illicit trafficking in firearms as part of the Caribbean Basin Security Initiative (CBSI). The U.S. Department of State has also provided $1 million to the United Nations Regional Center for Peace, Disarmament and Development in Latin America and the Caribbean (UNLIREC) to assist fourteen Caribbean states in the development of National Action Plans on Stockpile Management and Firearms Destruction, specialised training for law enforcement officials, and recommendations on legal reforms, and updates to national firearms acts.[44]

The Arms Trade Treaty is a multilateral treaty to regulate the international trade in conventional arms. The Treaty was adopted by the United Nations General Assembly on April 2, 2013 and opened for signature on June 3, 2013. On September 25, the United States became the 91st state to sign the Treaty. As of October, 113 states have signed and 7 states have ratified it. The Arms Trade Treaty will enter into force following ratification by 50 states. The United States worked closely with international partners during the negotiations to secure a treaty that advances global security and respects national sovereignty and the legitimate arms trade. The United States is prepared to work for strong international standards in the international arms trade, provided that the Conference on the Arms Trade Treaty at the United Nations operates under the rule of consensus decision-making. Consensus is needed to ensure that all countries can be held to standards that will actually improve the global situation by denying arms to those who would abuse them and to avoid loopholes in the Treaty that can be exploited by those wishing to export arms irresponsibly.

The treaty aims to reduce human suffering caused by illegal and irresponsible arms transfers, improve regional security and stability, as well as to promote accountability and transparency by state parties concerning transfers of conventional arms. The ATT is the product of nearly two decades of advocacy and diplomacy. After years of preparation, a UN diplomatic conference was formally convened in July 2012, but fell short of reaching consensus on a final text and another two week-long diplomatic conference was convened in March 2013 to complete work on the treaty. The Arms Trade Treaty requires all states-parties to adopt basic regulations and approval processes for the flow of weapons across international borders, establishes common international standards that must be met before arms exports are authorised, and requires annual reporting of imports and exports to a treaty secretariat.

Gun politics addresses safety issues and ideologies related to firearms through criminal and noncriminal use. Gun politics deals with rules, regulations, and restrictions on the use, ownership, as well as distribution of firearms.[45] Amid growing concerns about the proliferation of weapons in the Arab world, a landmark United Nations' treaty designed to control the international flow of arms was signed. The treaty also prohibits sales where there is suspicion the arms could be illegally trafficked or used in genocide or crimes against humanity.[46] The United Nations Office for Disarmament

Affairs (UNODA) launched the International Small Arms Control Standards (ISACS) to ensure UN support to Member States on putting in place effective controls over the full life-cycle of small arms and light weapons from manufacture, marking and recordkeeping to storage, transport and international transfer to the tracing, collection and destruction of illicit weapons.[47] Some countries in Africa have already made significant efforts to prevent irresponsible transfers of weapons.[48] Some African regions have adopted regional policies to fight the proliferation of small arms. These instruments contain very strong references to the need not to transfer arms where they risk being used in breach of international humanitarian law (IHL). These instruments are also legally-binding: (a) The Bamako Declaration; (b) The Nairobi Declaration and the Nairobi Protocol on Small Arms and Light Weapons; (c) The ECOWAS Convention on Small Arms and Light Weapons; and (4) The Southern African Development Community (SADC) Protocol on the Control of Firearms, Ammunition and Related Materials (2001).[49] Ninety per cent of the casualties among civilians comes from illicit arms, Lebanon, in compliance with the United Nation Security Council resolution 1701 agreed to take further measures against the illicit trade and shipment of small arms. The United Nations is working around the world trying to stop the illegal trade and trafficking of small arms.[50]

Conclusion

Arms trafficking is the illegal trafficking or smuggling of contraband weapons or ammunition. Legal trade in firearms varies widely, depending on local and national laws. The illicit trade in small arms and light weapons occurs in all parts of the globe but is concentrated in areas afflicted by armed conflict, violence, and organised crime, where the demand for illicit weapons is often highest. Every day, thousands of people are killed, injured or forced to flee from their homes as a result of violence and conflict involving weapons. Millions of people have been forced to flee homes in fear of their lives due to armed conflict. This often pushes people further into poverty by restricting access to clean water and shelter, while increasing the likelihood of deadly diseases. Insurgents, armed gang members, pirates, terrorists can multiply their force through the use of unlawfully acquired firepower. The illicit circulation of small arms, light weapons and their ammunition destabilises communities, and impacts on the security and development in all regions of the world.

REFERENCES

1. *Weapon (2014),* Retrieved from http://en.wikipedia.org/wiki/Weapon
2. *The arms trade treaty,* Retrieved from http://www.un.org/disarmament/ATT/
3. *Arms sales: who are the world's 100 top arms producers?* Retrieved from http://www.theguardian.com/news/datablog/2012/mar/02/arms-sales-top-100-producers
4. *Why do we need a global Arms Trade Treaty?* Retrieved from http://www.oxfam.org/en/campaigns/conflict/controlarms/why-we-need-global-arms-trade-treaty
5. *Arms trafficking (2013),* Retrieved from http://en.wikipedia.org/wiki/Arms_trafficking
6. Mridulya Narasimhan (2013), *Arms for Alms: Africa and its story of illicit trade in small arms,* Retrieved from http://www.consultancyafrica.com/index.php?option=com_content&view=article&id=1242:arms-for-alms-africa-and-its-story-of-illicit-trade-in-small-arms&catid=87:african-finance-a-economy&Itemid=294
7. *Arms industry (2013),* Retrieved from http://en.wikipedia.org/wiki/Arms_industry
8. The illicit arms trade, Retrieved from http://www.fas.org/asmp/campaigns/smallarms/IssueBrief3ArmsTrafficking.html
9. *Small Arms and Light Weapons,* Retrieved from http://www.bmeia.gv.at/en/foreign-ministry/foreign-policy/disarmament/conventional-weapons/small-arms-and-light-weapons.html
10. *Firearms / Explosives Smuggling (2013),* Retrieved from http://www.ice.gov/firearms-explosives-smuggling/
11. Jacey Fortin (2013), *Nigeria Battles Illicit Small Arms, With Russians in The Cross-Hairs,* Retrieved from http://www.ibtimes.com/nigeria-battles-illicit-small-arms-russians-cross-hairs-1099962

12. Rachel Stohl, *The Tangled Web of Illicit Arms Traûcking,* See http: //www.americanprogress.org/kf/TerrorinShadows-Stohl.pdf
13. *Libya is epicenter of illicit arms trade – UN (March 11, 2014).* Retrieved from http://rt.com/news/libya-illegal-arms-trade-986/
14. *Question of Illicit Arms Trafficking in Africa,* Retrieved from http: //www.daimun.org/pdf/disec2012_02.pdf
15. *Arms Transfers and Trafficking In Africa*, Retrieved from http:// www.defense-aerospace.com/article-view/verbatim/16134/arms-transfers-and-trafficking-in-africa.html
16. *Small arms: Keeping Africa at war? (2001),* Retrieved from http:// news.bbc.co.uk/2/hi/talking_point/debates/african_debates/ 1441537.stm
17. *Disarmament and International Security Committee*, Retrieved from http://gsis-gmun.org/wp-content/uploads/2012/12/DISEC-TOPIC-A.pdf
18. *Small arms and light weapons,* Retrieved from http://www.africa-union.org/root/au/AUC/Departments/PSC/Small_Arms.htm
19. Konye Obaji Ori (2013), *New UN arms trade treaty and Africa,* Retrieved from http://www.theafricareport.com/North-Africa/new-un-arms-trade-treaty-and-africa.html
20. *Mali: Gun running worsening,* Retrieved from http:// www.irinnews.org/report/78701/mali-gun-running-worsening
21. *Global arms trade contributes to use of child soldiers*, Retrieved from https:/www.amnesty.org/en/news/global-arms-trade-contributes-use-child-soldiers-2013-02-11
22. *UN: Illegal Arms Trade Fuels Central African Conflicts,* Retrieved from http://www.voanews.com/content/illegal-arms-trade-fuels-central-african-conflicts-88828077/153799.html
23. *7-8 March, 2013 | National Assembly of Namibia, Windhoek,* Retrieved from http://www.pgaction.org/activity/2013/addressing-illegal-trade-in-salw-namibia-workshop-2013.html
24. *African Union (AU),* Retrieved from http://www.poa-iss.org/ RegionalOrganizations/19.aspx
25. *Arms Transfers and Trafficking In Africa,* Retrieved from http:// www.defense-aerospace.com/article-view/verbatim/16134/arms-transfers-and-trafficking-in-africa.html

26. Nilanjana Bhowmick (2012), *At Gunpoint: India Tackles an Upsurge in Illegal Arms,* Retrieved from http://world.time.com/2012/11/28/at-gunpoint-india-tackles-an-upsurge-in-illegal-arms/
27. *The Hindu (April 3, 2013).* Why India abstained on Arms Trade Treaty, Retrieved from http://www.thehindu.com/opinion/op-ed/why-india-abstained-on-arms-trade-treaty/article4573882.ece
28. *India abstains and exposes the Arms Trade Treaty,* Retrieved from http://idsa.in/idsacomments/IndiaabstainsandexposestheArmsTradeTreaty _gkanwal_080413
29. *U.S. aims to expand India arms trade by "billions of dollars",* Retrieved from http://www.reuters.com/article/2013/04/18/us-usa-india-weapons-idUSBRE93H10B20130418
30. *UN adopts global arms trade treaty, India abstains,* Retrieved from http://www.rediff.com/news/report/un-adopts-global-arms-trade-treaty-india-abstains/20130402.htm
31. *Terrorists are increasing because of Small Arms,* Retrieved from http://www.worldsecuritynetwork.com/Terrorism/Sarup-Kamala/Terrorists-are-increasing-because-of-Small-Arms
32. *Small arms (2013),* Retrieved from http://www.un.org/disarmament/convarms/SALW/
33. *The Illicit Arms Trade*, Retrieved from http://www.fas.org/asmp/campaigns/smallarms/IssueBrief3ArmsTrafficking.html
34. See http://www.un.org/disarmament/convarms/SALW/
35. *Ending the illegal arms trade – securing an international Arms Trade Treaty,* Retrieved from http://www.clarionevents.com/about-us/clarion-and-defencearmstradetreaty
36. *Illegal small arms trade requires a global response*, Retrieved from http://theconversation.com/illegal-small-arms-trade-requires-a-global-response-22560
37. *The Illicit Trade Of Small Arms*, Retrieved from http://www.geopoliticalmonitor.com/the-illicit-trade-of-small-arms-4273/
38. *Ending the illegal arms trade – securing an international Arms Trade Treaty,* Retrieved from http://www.clarionevents.com/about-us/clarion-and-defencearmstradetreaty

39. Mridulya Narasimhan (2013), *Arms for Alms: Africa and its story of illicit trade in small arms,* Retrieved from http://www.consultancyafrica.com/index.php?option=com_content&view=article&id=1242:arms-for-alms-africa-and-its-story-of-illicit-trade-in-small-arms&catid=87:african-finance-a-economy&Itemid=294
40. Paul Quirkc (2012), *The arms trade in Africa: Would an Arms Trade Treaty have a real impact?,* Retrieved from http://www.consultancyafrica.com/index.php?option=com_content&view=article&id=1149:the-arms-trade-in-africa-would-an-arms-trade-treaty-have-a-real-impact&catid=57:africa-watch-discussion-papers&Itemid=263
41. *Arms control (2013),* Retrieved from http://en.wikipedia.org/wiki/Arms_control
42. *Small Arms and Light Weapons (SALW),* Retrieved from http://en.wikipedia.org/wiki/SALW
43. *Trafficking in firearms (2013),* Retrieved from http://ec.europa.eu/dgs/home-affairs/what-we-do/policies/organized-crime-and-human-trafficking/trafficking-in-firearms/index_en.htm
44. United States Launches Initiative to Combat Illicit Firearms Trafficking in Caribbean Region.
45. *Gun politics (2013),* Retrieved from http://en.wikipedia.org/wiki/Gun_politics
46. *UN treaty is first step toward curbing arms trade (2013),* Retrieved firm http://www.thenational.ae/news/world/middle-east/un-treaty-is-first-step-toward-curbing-arms-trade
47. *United Nations takes action against the illicit trade in small arms and light weapons,* Retrieved from http://www.un-ngls.org/spip.php?page=article_s&id_article =4082
48. Mridulya Narasimhan (2013), *Arms for Alms: Africa and its story of illicit trade in small arms,* Retrieved from http://www.consultancyafrica.com/index.php?option=com_content&view=article&id=1242:arms-for-alms-africa-and-its-story-of-illicit-trade-in-small-arms&catid=87:african-finance-a-economy&Itemid=294

49. *Africa fight against Small Arms and Light Weapons,* Retrieved from http://www.aefjn.org/index.php/366/articles/africa-fight-against-small-arms-and-light-weapons.html
50. *Illicit Trade in Small Arms (2009),* Retrieved from http://www.glica.org/topics/show/57

9

Poverty in India

"Gender equality is more than a goal in itself. It is a precondition for meeting the challenge of reducing poverty, promoting sustainable development and building good governance."

- Kofi Annan

Introduction

Poverty can be defined as a social phenomenon in which a section of the society is unable to fulfill even basic necessities of life.[1] This is also referred to as absolute poverty or destitution. Relative poverty is the condition of having fewer resources or less income than others within a society or country or compared to worldwide averages.[2] Poverty is a denial of choices and opportunities for living a tolerable life. This is the concept of human poverty.[3] According to the Human Development Report, *"Someone can enjoy good health and live but be illiterate and thus cut off from learning, from communication and from interactions with others. Another person may be literate and quite well educated but prone to premature death because of epidemiological characteristics or physical disposition. Yet a third way be excluded from participating in the important decision-making processes affecting his / her life."*[4] Poverty and unemployment are the two most serious problems from which the country has been suffering from the beginning of the present century. Three precepts are often used to define poverty: (i) the amount of money required by a person to subsist, (ii) the life below a *'minimum subsistence level'* and *'living standard'* prevalent at a given time in a given place, and (iii) the comparative state of well-being of a few and the deprivation and destitution of the majority in society.[5] In India, the broadly accepted definition of poverty emphasised more on minimum level of living rather than on reasonable level of living. Accordingly, it is broadly agreed that poverty can be termed as a situation, where a section of the population fails to reach a certain minimum consumption standard.[6] Poverty and environment seemingly have been interrelated since time immemorial.[7] The relationship among population, poverty and environmental degradation in developing countries has been the subject matter of discussion at the global level.[8] The poor are thought to be both victims and agents of environmental damage.[9] The Planning Commission has adopted definition of poverty provided by the *'Task Force on Projections of Minimum Needs and Effective Consumption Demand.*[10] On this basis the cut-off points turn out to be Rs 49.09 for the rural areas and Rs 56.64 for urban areas at 1973-74 prices.[11]

Urban Poverty

The phenomenal increase in the city population is one of the main reasons for poverty in the urban areas of India. The massive and relatively recent increase is a result of major migration of rural families to cities. This migration is mainly caused by poor employment opportunities in villages and is exacerbated by the fact that there are few job opportunities in the cities as well.[12] At the national level, the percentage of the poor in rural areas is significantly higher than that in urban areas, only a few of the larger states conform to this pattern. States such as Andhra Pradesh, Goa, Gujarat, Haryana, Kerala, Madhya Pradesh, Maharashtra, Rajasthan, Tamil Nadu, Delhi and Union territory of Pondicherry have reported levels of urban population that are higher than rural poverty. States where rural poverty is higher than urban poverty are Arunachal Pradesh, Assam, Bihar, Himachal Pradesh and West Bengal.[13]

Rural Poverty

The rural poor live in a world that is changing rapidly. A globalised economy offers new opportunities and risks for developing countries, regional economic and political groupings are emerging and a number of middle-income developing countries have an ever-more important political and economic role in the world.[14] In India, rural poverty largely emanates from the semi-feudal relations of production in the agriculture. The land reform measures which were undertaken after Independence did not make substantial changes in the agrarian relations.[15] The number of poor people in India, according to the country's Eleventh National Development Plan, amounts to more than 300 million.[16] According to the Integrated Rural Development Programme definition, approved by the Ministry of Rural Development, as revised in May 1991, a rural household with an annual income of less than Rs 11000 is described as a poor household is described as a poor household.[17]

The following causes of Poverty in rural areas may be identified: (a) Low agricultural productivity resulting from dependence on traditional methods of cultivation and inadequate knowledge of modern skills; (b) Imperfect and exploited credit market; (c) Inter-caste conflicts and rivalries; (4) Poor quality of livestock; (5) Inadequate and ineffective implementation of anti-poverty programmes; (6) Political instability and civil strife; (7) Systemic discrimination on the basis of gender, race, ethnicity, religion, or caste; (8) External shocks owing to changes in the state of nature and conditions in the international economy; (9) Market imperfections owing to high concentration of land and other assets and distortionary public policies; (10) Large and rapidly growing families with high dependency ratios; (11) Economic policies that discriminate against or exclude that rural poor from the development process and accentuate the effects of other poverty-creating processes; and (12) High concentration of land ownership and asymmetrical tenancy arrangements.[18] Since 1970, the Indian government has implemented a number of programmes designed to eradicate poverty, and has had some success with these programmes.[19] The international economic environment directly influences the well-being of the Indian poor.[20]

Human Poverty Index (HPI)

Poverty is not just a financial state.[21] The highest human poverty index scores are in Central Africa, the lowest are in Japan.[22] The Human Poverty Index is an indication of the standard of living in a country, developed by the United Nations.[23]

The United Nations Development Programme has devised a Human Poverty Index in the 1997 report to redefine poverty, since it felt the income measure of poverty was inadequate. While the reports draw attention to human deprivation to complement income measures of poverty, their focus is on the percentage of poor that lacks basic capabilities as well as access to minimal facilities. The Human Poverty Index includes three indicators: (a) Vulnerability to death at a relatively early age as quantified in the percentage of people expected to die before the age of 40 years; (b) Deprivation in respect of reading and communication, measured by the percentage of illiterate adults; and (c) Deprivation in overall economic provisioning which is a combined index of three variables; (i) Percentage of people without access to safe drinking water; (ii) Percentage of people without access to health services; and (iii) Percentage of moderately and severely underweight children under five.[24]

Measurement

The most common measure of poverty is to count the number of persons below poverty line and express it as a percentage of total population in the country. This is known as the head-count measure of poverty or head count ratio (HCR). While this measure is simple and readily understandable, its weakness is that it gives equal weight to all the poor irrespective of their distance from the poverty line. Poverty can be measure by using the following ways,

1. ***Poverty Line:*** Below Poverty Line is an economic benchmark and poverty threshold used by the Government of India to indicate economic disadvantage and to identify individuals and households in need of government assistance and aid. It is determined using various parameters which vary from state to state and within states. The poverty line is the minimum level of income deemed necessary to achieve an adequate standard of living in a given country. The common international poverty line has in the past been roughly $1 a day. In 2008, the World Bank came out with a revised figure of $1.25 at 2005 purchasing-power parity (PPP).[25]

2. ***Head Count Ratio:*** The simplest measure of poverty is the Head Count Ratio, which is calculated by dividing the number of people below poverty line by the total population. Simply speaking, this is the proportion of poor in the total population.[26] The commonly known measurement of poverty is in terms of the so-called Head Count Rato (H).[27]
3. ***Income-Gap Ratio:*** The Income Gap Ratio (IGR) is another index that gives a superior idea of the extent of poverty. IGR is calculated by dividing the number of population below the poverty line by the total expenditure of the poor. Thus, it measures how far below the poverty line poor people actually are. Unlike the HCR policy of poverty alleviation which targets the *'least poor'*, the IGR policy will target the average poor.[28]
4. ***Poverty Gap Ratio:*** The HCR does not distinguish between people below the poverty line with dissimilar incomes or consumption levels. A circumstance, where spending of each person below the poverty line increases but still remains below the poverty line, the HCR would not alter any record even though the income/consumption of the poor is better. This can be captured by the Poverty Gap Ratio (PGR) which indicates the deepness of poverty. PGR can be calculated by multiplying Income Gap Ratio by the HCR.[29]

Types of Poverty

Different people think about poverty in different ways. Various ideas have been put forward to explain the classification of poverty, which are as follows,

1. ***Income Poverty and Non-Income Poverty:*** Income poverty happens when a household takes in less than one US dollar per day. It is due to people not having access to money or other assets. Non-income poverty happens when people may have a little bit of money but otherwise the quality of their life is not good. They do not have access to affordable social and physical services (schooling, health care, medicines, safe water, good sanitation, good transport) and may not feel safe in their homes they cannot either trust the authorities or belong to some particularly vulnerable group.[30]

2. ***Absolute Poverty and Relative Poverty:*** Absolute poverty is deliberate against pre-determined level of living that families should be able to afford. Consumption of food grains, vegetables, milk products and other substances, essential for a better living and access to other non-food things, included in the absolute minimum consumption basket. These standards are then transformed into monetary units and defined as the poverty line. Relative poverty considers the overall income distribution and the position of household within that distribution. The relative position of one group of people is compared with another group. The concept of relative poverty can be extended to other countries as well. Relative poverty is more closely associated with the issues of inequality.[31]

Indian Experience

The World Bank estimates that 456 million Indians (41.6 per cent of the total Indian population) now live under the global poverty line of $1.25 per day (PPP). This means that a third of the global poor now reside in India.[32] In order to ascertain the determinants of poverty, it is imperative to explain how poverty is measured. In estimating poverty levels, defining a poverty line is the first step. A poverty line demarcates the poor from the non-poor. It is identified as the minimum required consumption level of food, clothing, shelter, transport and healthcare. Poverty estimation in India is based on (a) the concept of poverty time, which is the prescribed minimum calorie intake necessary for a normal human being to survive and (b) size and distribution of population by expenditure obtained from household consumption surveys conducted by national sample survey.[33] Poverty can not be removed by only increasing wealth.

Maharashtra's image as progressive state has taken a beating with recent figures rating it third amongst major states following Uttar Pradesh and Bihar, as regards population below the poverty line.[34] In Madhya Pradesh, a population of 249.68 lakh (38.3 per cent) is bound to go to bedhungry, as they are poor and marginalised.[35] Rajasthan had the highest maternal mortality ratio, the third highest total fertility rate and the fourth highest infant mortality rate among the major states in India in 2001.[36] Poverty in Orissa is on the decline, but it is still a major issue. Rural Indians depend on unpredictable agriculture income, while urban Indians on jobs really are at best scarce.[37] Poverty and migration have always been interrelated in Orissa. The poverty profile shows income poverty as higher than in the rest of India. Although poverty has been falling over time, data sources indicate the gap in incomes and between Orissa and the rest of India has widened over the last twenty years.[38] Uttar Pradesh has suffered from regional disparities and inequality and even six decades after independence, some of its regions are very backward and the abode of largest proportion of poor in the country. The challenges rose by intra-regional disparities and their compounding implications on living conditions and governance are enormous.[39]

Amartya Sen has argued, '*The poor is not an economic class, nor convenient category to use for analyzing social and economic movements. Poverty is the common outcome of a variety of disparate economic circumstances and a policy to tackle poverty must, of necessary, go beyond the concept of poverty. The need for discrimination is essential.*'[40] The trickle down hypothesis in the simplest form states that rapid growth of per capita income will be associated with reduction in poverty. In the context of agricultural development in India, the trickle-down theory has been interpreted to suggest that growth in the agricultural output without radical institutional reform will reduce the incidence of poverty. Montek S. Ahluwalia has argued that an India trickle-down mechanism exists and therefore a rise in agricultural production and income levels per head could lead to some decline in rural poverty. This argument assumes that the distribution of income has remained constant over time and there were no adverse terms of trade effects on agriculture.[41] T.N.Srinivasan has asserted that there simply was not enough growth for trickle-down mechanism to make any significant impact on poverty.[42]

Causes of Poverty

Different thinkers have pointed out to different causes of poverty. The principal causes of poverty in India are as follows:

1. *Underdevelopment:* Due to the underdevelopment, '*a big segment of the population has to go without even the most necessary needs of daily life, because total national income,*

and hence aggregate consumption is too small relatived to the enormous size of the population'.

2. *Unemployment:* The continuously expanding army of unemployed is another cause of poverty. The job seekers are increasing in number at higher rate than the expansion in employment opportunity.
3. *Low productivity in Agriculture:* The level of productivity in agriculture is low due to subdivided and fragmented holdings, lack of irrigation facility, high population growth in rural areas, lack of capital, use of traditional methods of cultivation , illiteracy etc. This is the main cause of poverty in India.
4. *Regional Disparities:* It is not that poverty is equally spread in the country. There are extreme regional disparities accounting for the poverty of people of certain regions against the prosperity of others.
5. *Inadequate Growth Rate:* One reason for the failure of planning to make major knock on poverty has been the inadequate growth rate. During 1951-2000, the growth rate of NNP at constant prices was not more than one per cent per annum on the average.
6. *Scarcity of Capital and Able Entrepreneurship:* Capital and able entrepreneurship have important role in economic development of any nation. But these are in little supply making it hard to boost production significantly.
7. *Low Technology:* Low-level of technology is also responsible for the poverty in India. Developing countries are not only using old technology in agriculture but also in manufacturing sector.
8. *Inequality:* Poverty and inequality are interdependent i.e., if inequality increases then it also extends poverty.
9. *Low per capita Income:* Poverty is reflected in India by the low per capita income. If per capita income decreases then it also hampers standard of living of the common people.[43]
10. *Culture or subculture of poverty:* Culture sometime blocks attempts of the people to alter the ethics, norms, idea and daily life of the poor. The 'culture of poverty' thought suggests that in spite of financial changes, the poor have remained so because of their culture or sub-culture.[44]

Inequality, Growth and Income Poverty

Many people still think first of *'economic growth'* in relative to poverty reduction. Indeed, their relationship is one of the most discussing issues of hostile poverty. The relationship is of great importance because if there is a clear causal dependency, reducing poverty could fundamentally be limited to measures that promote growth. However, if there was little growth or stagnation, it would not promise to cut poverty decisively.[45] The links between poverty, economic growth, and income distribution have been studied quite extensively in recent literature on economic development. Absolute poverty can be alleviated if at least two conditions are met: economic growth must occur or mean income must rise on sustained basis; and economic growth must be neutral with respect to income distribution or reduce income inequality.

Effective Measures in Poverty Alleviation

The following measures for economic reforms in India:

1. *Distribution of income:* Not only income has to be increased by stimulating policies of economic growth by the government but distribution of income has to be given importance in the country.
2. *Containing Inflation:* Inflation may be contained by increasing production, when output increase then price will decrease. Inflation effects socio-economic life of people.
3. *Reframing of disinvestment policy:* The policy pertaining to disinvestment in public sector needs to be framed in such manner that if the unit is incurring losses, the government must get out. But there are units which are making huge profits. Selling the shares of such units is quite like selling the assets. It is a bad policy.
4. *Creating independent banking institutions:* In a market-based system, people must have institutions which are independent. They must work for more autonomy of the Reserve Bank. But the interest rates and the foreign exchange rate should not be entirely deregulated. The fundamental rates should be stable.
5. *Encouraging private investment:* Investment of capital in private industries has lagged behind in our country. It can

come if there is a belief that profitability will increase over a period of time. Adopting liberalisation can assure such beliefs.

6. *Land Reforms:* Land reforms have the slogan, *"land belongs to the tiller"*. Thus legislative measures were undertaken to eliminate zamindari structure. Intermediaries and ceiling on holdings was fixed. But it is a bad luck, these land reforms lack correct implementation. Even then, it is anticipated that if these reforms are implemented acutely, it would yield superior results which will be helpful to decrease the earnings of the affluent section.
7. *More Employment Opportunity:* Poverty can be eliminated by providing additional employment opportunities so that people may be able. For this reason, labour intensive rather than capital intensive techniques can assist to solve the problem to a greater extent. During the Sixth and Seventh Five Year Plans, the programmes like Integrated Rural Development Programme, Jawahar Rozgar Yojana, Rural Landless Employment Guarantee Programme etc have started with a view to eliminate poverty in the rural sector.

Conclusion

Poverty in India is widespread. Poverty increases the risk of homelessness. One cause is high population growth rate, although demographers generally agree it as symptom rather than cause of poverty. Poverty may also be understood as an aspect of unequal social status and inequitable social relationships, experienced as social exclusion, dependency, and diminished capacity to participate, or to develop meaningful connections with other people in society. Economic aspects of poverty focus on material needs, typically including the necessities of daily living, such as food, clothing, shelter, or safe drinking water. Poverty in this sense may be understood as a condition in which a person or community is lacking in the basic needs for minimum standard of well-being and life, particularly as a result of a persistent lack of income. The presence of a massive parallel economy in the form of black (hidden) money derived from foreign aid has contributed to the slow pace of poverty alleviation in India.

REFERENCES

1. Ruddar Datt & K.P.M. Sundharam, *Indian Economy*, Forty-Ninth Revised Edition, (New Delhi: S. Chand & Company Ltd. 2004) at 357.
2. *Poverty (2014).* Retrieved from http://en.wikipedia.org/wiki/Poverty
3. S.K.Misra & V.K. Puri, *Indian Economy,* 24th Revised Edition, (Mumbai: Himalaya Publishing House, 2006) at 247.
4. United Nations Development Programme, *Human Development Report, 1997,* (New York, 1997), p.16.
5. Ram Ahuja, *Social Problems in India*, 1st edition, (Jaipur: Rawat Publications, 2007) at 27.
6. P.K.Dhar, *Indian Economy its growing dimensions,* Eleventh Edition, (Ludhiana: Kalyani Publishers, 2003) at 669.
7. World Bank, *The Poverty and Hunger: Issues and Options for Food Security in Developing Countries,* Washington DC 1986.
8. *Ibid.*
9. Amrita Chakraborty, *Poverty and Environment an Introduction,* First Edition, (Hyderabad: The ICFAI University Press, 2006) at 96.
10. *Planning Commission, Sixth Five Year Plan,* 1980-85 (New Delhi, 1981), p. 51
11. S.K.Misra & V.K. Puri, *Indian Economy*, 24th Revised Edition, (Mumbai: Himalaya Publishing House, 2006) at 239.
12. *Poverty in India,* Retrieved from http://ezinearticles.com/?Poverty-in-India&id=2142554
13. Kalpana Rajaram, *Indian Economy*, Sixth Edition, (New Delhi: Spectrum Books (P) Ltd., 2006), at 176.
14. *Rural poverty report 2011,* Retrieved from http://www.ifad.org/rural/rpr2010/
15. John W. Mellor, *'Determinants of Rural Poverty: The Dynamics of Production, Technology and Price',* in John W.Mellor and Gunvant M.Desai (Eds), *Agricultural Change and Rural Poverty* (Delhi, 1986), p. 21.
16. http://www.ruralpovertyportal.org/web/guest/country/home/tags/india

17. Ram Ahuja, *Social Problems in India*, 1st edition, (Jaipur: Rawat Publications, 2007) at 44.
18. Venkata Seshaiah Sakaalya, *Poverty Issues in Economic Development,* First Edition (Hyderabad: Icfai University press, 2004) at 8.
19. *Poverty in India*, Retrieved from http://www.economywatch.com/indianeconomy/poverty-in-india.html
20. M.L. Narasaiah, Microcredit and Agricultural Development, First Publication, (New Delhi: Discovery Publishing House, 2007) at 129.
21. *Human Poverty*, Retrieved from http://www.worldmapper.org/posters/worldmapper_map174_ver5.pdf
22. *Human Poverty,* Retrieved from http://www.worldmapper.org/display.php?selected=174
23. *Human Poverty* Index (2014). Retrieved from http://en.wikipedia.org/wiki/Human_Poverty_Index
24. Venkata Seshaiah Sakaalya, *Poverty Issues in Economic Development*, First Edition (Hyderabad: Icfai University press, 2004) at 155.
25. *Poverty threshold*, Retrieved from http://en.wikipedia.org/wiki/Poverty_threshold
26. Kalpana Rajaram, *Indian Economy,* (New Delhi: Spectrum Books Pvt. Ltd, 2006) at 174.
27. R.K. Lekhi, *The Economics of Development and Planning*, Eight Revised & Enlarged Edition, (Ludhina: Kalyani Publishers, 2003-2004) at 79/VII.
28. Kalpana Rajaram, *Indian Economy,* (New Delhi: Spectrum Books Pvt. Ltd, 2006) at 174.
29. *Rural Development: Indian Context: Rural Society and Economy*, IGNOU, 2005, P. 89.
30. *Types of Poverty, Retrieved from* http://www.hakikazi.org/zwp/types_of_poverty.htm
31. *Rural Development: Indian Context: Rural Society and Economy,* IGNOU, 2005, P. 87.
32. *On the first position,* see e.g. Bhalla (2000a), Bhagwati (2001), Das (2000). On the other side, see Mehta (2001), Sainath (2001a, 2001b), Shiva (2001a), among others.

33. http://upgov.nic.in/upinfo/up_eco.html
34. *Problems in Orissa*, Retrieved from http://www.merinews.com/article/poverty-in-madhya-pradesh-what-statistics-dont-tell/126332.shtml
35. *Problems in Orissa,* Retrieved from http://www.merinews.com/article/scrutinising-the-poverty-line-in-madhya-pradesh/15772806.shtml
36. *Poverty still grips millions in India*, Retrieved from http://news.bbc.co.uk/2/hi/south_asia/7556489.stm
37. *Problems in Orissa,* Retrieved from http://www.merinews.com/article/problems-in-orissa/15772284.shtml
38. *Labour Migration: A shadow of poverty in Orissa,* Retrieved from http://ezinearticles.com/?Labour-Migration:-A-Shadow-of-Poverty-in-Orissa&id=115270
39. *Intra-regional disparities, inequality and poverty in Uttar Pradesh,* Retrieved from http://www.indiaenvironmentportal.org.in/content/intra-regional-disparities-inequality-and-poverty-uttar-pradesh
40. Amertya Sen, *'Poverty and Economic Development'*, in Charan D. Wadhva (Ed), Some Problems of India's Economic Policy (New Delhi, 1977), p.246.
41. Montek S. Ahluwalia, *'Rural Poverty, Agricultural Production and Prices: A Re-examination'*, in John. W. Mellor and Gunvant M. Desai (eds.), op. cit., pp.69-72.
42. T.N.Srinivasan, *'Agricultural Production, Relative Prices, Entitlements and Poverty'*, John W.Mellor and Gunvant M.Desai (Eds), op. cit., p. 50.
43. M.L.Jhingan, *The Economics of Development and Planning,* 36th revised & enlarged edition, (Delhi: Vrinda Publications (P) Ltd., 2003), at740.
44. Ram Ahuja, *Social Problems in India,* 2nd edition, (Jaipur: Rawat Publications, 2007) at 37.
45. M.L. Narasaiah, *Micro credit and Agricultural Development*, 1st edition (New Delhi: Discovery Publishing House, 2007) at 130.
46. Dr. Sukanta Sarkar and Dr. Md. Alam (2014), *Microfinance and Women Empowerment*, New Delhi: Global Vision Publishing House.

10

Violence against Women

"When women love us, they forgive us everything, even our crimes; when they do not love us, they give us credit for nothing, not even our virtues."

- Honore de Balzac

Introduction

Adam and Eve, according to the creation myth of Abrahamic religion were the first man and woman. The story of Adam and Eve is central to the belief that God created human beings to live in a paradise on earth, although they fell apart and formed the present world full of suffering and injustice. It provides the basis for the belief that humanity is in essence a single family, with everyone descended from a single pair of original ancestors. Women are important in the society. Every woman has her own job or duty in this modern society in which men are still the *'stronger gender'*. The role of women in society has been greatly overseen in the last few decades but now it is coming to a more positive perspective. In the early days women were seen only as wives who were intended to cook, clean and take care of the kids. They were not allowed to vote while men took care of having jobs and paying any bills that had to be paid. Violence against women is a real fact in modern life. The United Nations General Assembly defines *"violence against women"* as *"any act of gender-based violence that results in, or is likely to result in, physical, sexual or mental harm or suffering to women, including threats of such acts, coercion or arbitrary deprivation of liberty, whether occurring in public or in private life."* The UN Declaration on the Elimination of Violence against Women (1993) states that *"violence against women is a manifestation of historically unequal power relations between men and women, which have led to domination over and discrimination against women by men and to the prevention of the full advancement of women, and that violence against women is one of the crucial social mechanisms by which women are forced into subordinate position compared with men."* Let discuss various types of violence against women:

Rape

Rape is a type of sexual assault usually involving sexual intercourse, which is initiated by one or more persons against another person without that person's consent. The act may be carried out by physical force, coercion, abuse of authority or against a person who is incapable of valid consent, such as one who is unconscious, incapacitated, or below the legal age of consent. Different types of rape include date rape, gang rape, marital rape, incestual rape, child sexual abuse, prison rape, acquaintance rape, war rape and statutory rape. Date rape refers to rape committed by a person, who could be a friend, acquaintance or stranger, against a victim. Commonly, it is referring to drug facilitated sexual assault. Marital rape is non-consensual sex in which the perpetrator is the victim's spouse. It is a form of partner rape, of domestic violence, and of sexual abuse. Child molestation is a form of child abuse in which an adult or older adolescent uses a child for sexual stimulation. Prison rape refers to rape occurring in prison. It has come into common usage to refer to rape of inmates by other inmates, and less commonly to the rape of inmates by staff, and even less commonly rape of staff by inmates. The term statutory rape is used in some common law jurisdictions to refer to sexual activities in which one person is below the age required to legally consent to the behavior. In statutory rape, overt force or threat need not be present. The term statutory rape generally refers to sex between an adult and a sexually mature minor past the age of puberty. In many jurisdictions, the age of consent is interpreted to mean mental or functional age. As a result, victims can be of any chronological age, if their mental age makes them unable to consent to sexual act. War rapes are rapes committed by soldiers, other combatants or civilians during armed conflict or war, or during military occupation.

Marital Rape

Marital rape is a serious form of violence that can have life-shattering effects for its victims. It is non-consensual sex in which the perpetrator is the victim's spouse. It is a form of partner rape, of domestic violence, and of sexual abuse. Still, in many countries, spousal rape either remains legal, or is illegal but widely tolerated, with the laws being rarely enforced against it. As the concept of human rights has developed, the belief of a marital right to sexual intercourse has become less widely held. Increasing criminalisation of spousal rape is part of a worldwide re-classification of sexual crimes *"from offenses against morality, the family, good customs, honor, or chastity ... to offenses against liberty, self-determination, or physical integrity."* In December 1993, the United Nations High Commissioner for Human Rights published the *Declaration on the Elimination of Violence against Women*. This establishes marital rape as a human rights violation. Despite these trends and international moves, criminalisation has not occurred in all UN member states. Determining the criminal status of marital rape may be challenging because while some countries explicitly criminalise the act and others explicitly exempt spouses. In many countries, the ordinary rape laws are silent on the issue, and it remains unclear whether it can be prosecuted or not.

Honour Killing

Honour killing is the homicide of a member of the family or social group by other members due to the belief of perpetrators that the victim has brought dishonor or shame upon the family or community. Victims of honour killings are killed for reasons such as refusing to enter an arranged marriage, being in relationship that is disapproved by relatives, having sex outside marriage, becoming the victim of rape, dressing in ways which are deemed inappropriate, or engaging in homosexual relations. Honour killings are one of the most psychologically complex, sociologically complicated, morally distressing and legally challenging violent crimes against humanity. Such crimes have been happening throughout history all over the world in many communities, countries and cultures. In honour killings, victims are mostly women and murderers are mostly men like fathers, brothers, husbands or sons. Honour killings are directed mostly against women and girls.

The number of honour killings has been increasing rather than decreasing in many parts of the world. Honour killings have been reported in northern regions of India, mainly in the Indian states of Punjab, Rajasthan, Haryana, Uttar Pradesh, as a result of people marrying without their family's acceptance, and sometimes for marrying outside their caste or religion.The practice of honour killings has absolutely no sanction in the Qur'an, the Prophetic practice, or in the evolved systems of Islamic law. It is a cultural practice that predates Islam. It is something that has been practiced by all in Asia and Middle East, Muslim or non-Muslim. The overwhelming majority of Muslim societies are free from the practice. More than 1,000 young people in India have been done to death every year owing to *'Honour Killings'* linked to forced marriages and the country needs to introduce stringent legislation to deal firmly with the heinous crime.

Acid Throwing

Acid throwing is a form of violent assault defined as the pre-meditated act of throwing acid or a similarly corrosive substance onto the body of another *"with the intention to disfigure, maim, torture, or kill."* According to researchers and activists, countries typically associated with acid assault include Bangladesh, India, Pakistan, Nepal, Cambodia, Vietnam, Laos, Hong Kong, China, the United Kingdom, Kenya, South Africa, Uganda, and Ethiopia. The offenders throw acid to destroy the bodies of women and shatter their dreams for not allowing criminals to abuse them physically, or for the women's inability to bring handsome dowries from their parents. Anyone who throws acid on someone's face intends to scar them for life. The idea is to damage the face, because that will hurt a woman and her honour. It is a crime with a marked gender skew. The most notable effects of an acid attack are the lifelong bodily disfigurement. Consequently, the victim is faced with physical challenges, which require long term surgical treatment, as well as psychological challenges. An unmarried woman attacked with acid will never likely marry. In Bangladesh, reported attacks have fallen since the government tightened up the rules on the sale of acid and introduced the death penalty for attackers. Acid attacks against women and girls are continuing despite legal campaigns to halt their spread. India's Supreme Court has ordered federal and state governments to regulate the sale of acid in an attempt to reduce attacks on women.

Bride Burning

Bride burning is a form of domestic violence, most common in India, in which a bride is killed at home by her husband or husband's family due to his dissatisfaction over the dowry provided by her family. The act is often a result of demands for more or prolonged dowry after the marriage. Kerosene is most often used as the fuel. It is just one form of dowry death. Others include acid throwing and eve teasing. Because dowry typically depends on class or socio-economic status, women are often subjected to the dowry pressures of their future husband or his relatives. Burning normally occurs in India, where the majority of cases are reported. Dowry first originated in the upper class families as wedding gift to the bride from the family. Then the dowry was meant as help with marriage expenses and became insurance in case if the in-laws terrorised her. The groom often demands dowry consisting of a large sum of money, farm animals, land, furniture or electronics. According to statistics recently released by the National Crime Records Bureau, in 2010, 8,391 dowry death cases were reported across India, meaning a bride was burned every 90 minutes. In 1961, India enacted the Dowry Prohibition Act, to halt dowry murders. It was amended in the early 1980s to *"rectify several inherent weaknesses and loopholes"* in order to make it a criminal offense if the husband or his relatives causes a woman to *"die of burns or bodily injury or unnatural circumstances within seven years of marriage and where there is evidence that she suffered cruelty and harassment in connection with the dowry."* Another major Indian law, the 1983 *"Anti-Cruelty Statute,"* prohibits cruelty towards a wife and subjects the husband and/or in-laws to fines or imprisonment, if they inflict cruelty upon the wife.

Dating Abuse

Dating abuse is defined as the perpetration or threat of an act of violence by at least one member of an unmarried couple on the other member within the context of dating or courtship. This abuse/violence can take a number of forms: sexual assault, sexual harassment, threats, physical violence, verbal, mental, or emotional abuse, social sabotage, and stalking. Date rape is the modern version of dating abuse. It refers to rape committed by a person, who could be a friend, acquaintance or stranger, against a victim. Commonly, date rape is referring to drug facilitated sexual assault or an acquaintance rape. The alcohol or drugs may be knowingly or unknowingly consumed by the victim. The drugs can be any substance that affect the central nervous system (CNS). This includes street drugs (e.g. cocaine, marijuana, ecstasy, GHB), prescription drugs (e.g. anti-depressants, tranquilizers), and over-the-counter medications (e.g. cough syrup).

Domestic Violence

The Convention on preventing and combating violence against women and domestic violence states that: *"domestic violence" shall mean all acts of physical, sexual, psychological or economic violence that occur within the family or domestic unit or between former or current spouses or partners, whether or not the perpetrator shares or has shared the same residence with the victim."* There are five types of domestic violence: physical, sexual, psychological, emotional and economic. Domestic violence may start when one partner feels the need to control and dominate the other. Abusers may feel this need to control their partner because of low self-esteem, extreme jealousy, difficulties in regulating anger and other strong emotions, or when they feel inferior to other partner in education and the socio-economic background. National Crime Records Bureau reveal that a crime against a woman is committed every three minutes, a woman is raped every 29 minutes, a dowry death occurs every 77 minutes and one case of cruelty committed by either the husband or relative of the victim occurs every nine minutes.

According to Janet E. Jackson, the former deputy representative of the United Nations Population Fund (UNFPA) to Bangladesh, Bangladesh ranks fourth among the world's nations with respect to violence against women. Jackson observed that *'sixty-five per cent of Bangladeshi males think it is justifiable to beat up their wives, 38 per cent have no clear idea what constitutes physical violence and 40 per cent support keeping women socially dormant'*. Serious health problems often result from physical, emotional, and sexual forms of domestic violence. Physical injury is the most visible form of domestic violence. The scope of physical domestic/intimate partner violence includes slapping, pushing, kicking, biting, hitting, throwing objects, strangling, beating, threatening with any form of weapon, or using a weapon. Emotional abuse has been gaining more and more recognition in recent years as an incredibly common form of domestic violence. Women who experience domestic violence overwhelmingly tends to have greater overall emotional distress, as well as disturbingly high occurrences of suicidal thoughts and attempts. Sexual assault is another common form of domestic violence in India. The Domestic Violence Act of 2005 provides victims of abuse with a means for practical remedy through prosecution. According to Section 3 of the Act, *"any act, omission or commission or conduct of the respondent shall constitute domestic violence in case it - (a) harms or injures or endangers the health, safety, life, limb or well-being, whether mental or physical, of the aggrieved person or tends to do so and includes causing physical abuse, sexual abuse, verbal and emotional abuse and economic abuse; or (b) harasses, harms, injures or endangers the aggrieved person with a view to coerce her or any other person related to her to meet any unlawful demand for any dowry or other property or valuable security; or (c) has the effect of threatening the aggrieved person or any person related to her by any conduct mentioned in clause (a) or clause (b); or (d) otherwise injures or causes harm, whether physical or mental, to the aggrieved person."*

Female Genital Mutilation

Female genital mutilation (FGM) is defined by the World Health Organization (WHO) as *"all procedures that involve partial or total removal of the external female genitalia, or other injury to the female genital organs for non-medical reasons."* The WHO estimates that 140 million women and girls around the world have experienced the procedure, including 101 million in Africa. It may take place in a hospital, but is usually performed without anaesthesia by a traditional circumciser using a knife, razor or scissors. Although genital cutting is on the decline, the practice remains *"almost universal"* in some countries. Africa has the greatest amount of FGM, as the World Health Organisation believes that somewhere between 100 million and 140 million women and girls about have undergone the surgery throughout the world, 92 million of them over the age of ten living in Africa. FGM has immediate and late complications. Immediate complications are enhanced when FGM is performed in traditional ways, and without access to medical resources: the procedure is extremely painful and a bleeding complication can be fatal. Other immediate complications include acute urinary retention, urinary infection, wound infection, septicemia, tetanus, and in case of unsterile and reused instruments, hepatitis and HIV. FGM has no health benefits and it harms girls and women in many ways. It involves removing and damaging healthy and normal female genital tissue, and interferes with the natural functions of girls' and women's bodies. Immediate complications can include severe pain, shock, haemorrhage (bleeding), tetanus or sepsis (bacterial infection), urine retention, open sores in the genital region and injury to nearby genital tissue.

Femicide

Femicide is broadly defined as the killing of women but definitions vary depending on the cultural context. Feminist author, Diana Russell, narrows the definition of femicide to *"the killing of females by males because they are female."* Russell believes her definition of femicide applies to all forms of sexist killing, whether they be motivated by misogyny (the hatred of females), by a sense of superiority over females, by sexual pleasure, or by assumption of ownership over women. The manifestations of femicide vary greatly. Intimate partner femicide, sometimes called intimate femicide, refers to *"the killing of a woman by her intimate partner or her former intimate partner."* These include former or current boyfriends, husbands and common-law husbands. Globally, South Africa with the highest female murder rate, experiences intimate partner femicide every 6 hours. Spain, on the other hand, reports an intimate partner femicide rate of one woman every two days. Yearly, India's government reports the deaths of 5,000 women to this cause, but this number is believed to be grossly underestimated due to the under-reported prevalence of honor killings and dowry-related murders. One of the main motives that cause men to kill their intimate partners is jealousy.

Foot Binding

Foot binding is the custom of applying painfully tight binding to the feet of young girls to prevent further growth. Foot binding eventually became very popular because men found it to be highly attractive, and therefore became Chinese women's way of being beautiful and to show that they were worthy of a husband. The foot binding process begins with a young girl (4-7 years old) soaking her feet in warm water or animal blood with herbs. After soaking the feet, her toe nails were to be clipped short and given a foot massage. Feet-binding is a cruel practice that disregards the pain and torture inflicted on women. The trend of feet binding is thought to have started among dancers in the ninth century, and in time spread to the general population. The foot binding custom was used as a way for men to keep women completely helpless. Every walking movement was filled with pain and suffering. Men used foot binding as a way to control women, to keep them at home at their immediate disposal. Women could never enjoy a walk, let alone run away. Though banned in 1912 after the Qing dynasty fell and the Nationalists established a republic, the practice lingered, especially in remote areas of China.

Forced Abortion

A forced abortion or coerced abortion occurs when a woman undergoes an abortion against her own wishes. Forced abortion may occur when the perpetrator causes abortion by force, threat or coercion, or by taking advantage of woman's incapability to give her consent. This may include the instances when the conduct was neither justified by medical or hospital treatment. Over one hundred potential complications have been associated with induced abortion. *Minor* complications include: minor infections, bleeding, fevers, chronic abdominal pain, gastro-intestinal disturbances, vomiting, and Rh sensitisation. The nine most common *major* complications are infection, excessive bleeding, embolism, ripping or perforation of the uterus, anesthesia complications, convulsions, hemorrhage, cervical injury, and endotoxic shock. A growing body of evidence indicates that most abortions involve coercion. Coercion may be direct, indirect or both, often happening at once during narrow windows of vulnerability or duress. It may involve deceptive, conflicted or profit-driven counseling. It may include pressure from one's support network or authorities; negligent medical and professional practices; or abuses of power in various sectors of society. Coercion may happen in schools, medical offices, or even in the helping professions. In other cases, it may involve personal, emotional, financial or other forms of blackmail, threats, abuse or violence.

Forced Pregnancy

Forced pregnancy is the practice of forcing a woman to become pregnant, often as part of a forced marriage, or as part of a programme of breeding slaves, or as part of a programme of genocide. Rape, sexual slavery, and related actions including forced pregnancy and sexual slavery are now recognised under the Geneva Convention as crimes against humanity and war crimes; in particular from 1949, Article 27 of the Fourth Geneva Convention, and later the 1977 Additional Protocols to the 1949 Geneva Conventions, explicitly prohibit wartime rape and enforced prostitution.

Human Trafficking

Human trafficking is the trade in humans, most commonly for the purpose of sexual slavery, forced labour or for the extraction of organs or tissues, including surrogacy and ova removal. Tens of thousands of people are vulnerable to being trafficked in Southeast Asia. A 2012 UN Office on Drugs and Crime report on human trafficking recorded more than 10,000 cases of trafficking in persons in South Asia, East Asia and the Pacific between 2007-2010. International pressure to address trafficking in women and children became a growing part of the social reform movement in the United States and Europe during the late nineteenth century. International legislation against the trafficking of women and children began with the conclusion of an international convention in 1901, followed by conclusion of the International Agreement for the suppression of the White Slave Traffic in 1904. The League of Nations, formed in 1919, took over as the international coordinator of legislation intended to end the trafficking of women and children. In 1949, the first international protocol dealing with sex slavery was the 1949 UN Convention for the Suppression of the Traffic in Persons and Exploitation of Prostitution of Others.

Bride Purchasing

Bride-purchasing is the illegal industry or tradeoff *"purchasing a bride"* to become property and at times as property that can be resold or repurchased for reselling. A cultural preference for sons over daughters has skewed India's sex ratio in places like Haryana. As a result of female foeticide, there are about 861 women for every 1,000 men in Haryana, according to the last census. The national average is 927 women to 1,000 men. Since there aren't enough local women to marry, Haryana's men pay touts to bring women for them to marry and to work on their farms. Social activists reckon most of these women end up being used as sex slaves and then resold to other men in what looks like a flourishing market in trafficking of women. Decades of unchecked sex-selective abortions have made the once fertile states of Punjab and Haryana suffer a drought of brides, making human-trafficking a lucrative and expanding trade. Often projected as a voluntary marriage, every year, thousands of young women and girls are lured into the idea of a happy married life with a rich man in Punjab or Haryana. Sadly most *'purchased brides'* are exploited, denied basic rights, duplicated as maids, and eventually abandoned.

Murder of Pregnant Women

Murder of pregnant women is a type of homicide often resulting from domestic violence. Domestic violence is suffered by many people and in the majority of cases where the victim comes forward the victim is a woman. For many of these women, the fear of harm includes not just themselves but their unborn child as well. Pregnancy-associated death has become more commonly termed as pregnancy-associated homicide. The killing of a pregnant woman is horrifying enough. When a woman gets pregnant, she generally worries about the health of herself and the baby. She may recollect things like preeclampsia, gestational diabetes or ectopic pregnancy.

Forced Prostitution

Forced prostitution is the act of performing non-voluntary sexual activity due to coercion by a third party. Due to the illegal nature of prostitution and the different methodologies used in separating forced prostitution from voluntary prostitution, the extent of this phenomenon is difficult to estimate accurately. All forms of involuntary prostitution are regarded as an offence under customary law in all countries. While the legality of adult prostitution varies between different parts of the world, the prostitution of children is illegal nearly everywhere in the world. In 1949, the UN General Assembly adopted the Convention for the Suppression of the Traffic in Persons and of the Exploitation of the Prostitution of Others. This Convention supersedes a number of earlier conventions that covered some aspects of forced prostitution. It penalises the procurement and enticement to prostitution as well as the maintenance of brothels.

Genocidal Rape

Genocidal rape is a term used to describe the actions of a group who have carried out acts of mass rape during wartime against their perceived enemy as part of genocidal campaign. During the Yugoslav civil war and the Rwandan genocide, mass rapes that had been an integral part of those conflicts brought the concept of genocidal rape to international prominence. Instances of mass rape during wartime which have been defined as genocidal rape were the mass rapes during the Bangladesh liberation war, the civil wars in the former Yugoslavia and during the Rwandan Genocide.

Pregnancy from Rape

Pregnancy is a potential result of rape. It has been studied in the context of war, particularly as a tool for genocide, as well as other unrelated contexts, such as rape by a stranger, statutory rape, incest, and underage pregnancy. Rape has been used as a weapon of psychological warfare for centuries, to terrorize, humiliate, and undermine the morale of the enemy. Rape during war is recognised under United Nations Security Council Resolution 1820 as a war crime and a crime against humanity. Immediate post-rape treatment protocols call for medical professionals to assess the likelihood that a victim will become pregnant in their assessment of the physical damage done to the woman. Protocol calls for gaining history of the use of contraceptives, as a woman's use of birth control pills or other contraceptives before a rape affect her chance of becoming pregnant. Decisions of whether to end rape-related pregnancy or carry it to term, and whether to keep the child or give it up for adoption can be severely traumatising for a woman.

Sexual Violence

Sexual violence is a serious public health and human rights problem with both short and long term consequences on women's physical, mental, and sexual and reproductive health. In India, rape, sexual harassment and the abuse of women are common occurrences that go unspoken due to social stigma or... fear of retribution. Sexual violence has profound impact on physical and mental health. As well as causing physical injury, it is associated with an increased risk of a range of sexual and reproductive health problems, with both immediate and long-term consequences. Apart from physical force, it may involve psychological intimidation, blackmail or other threats. In armed conflicts, the breakdown of social infrastructures, the disintegration of families and communities and the disruption of responses leave women and girls vulnerable to sexual and other forms of gender-based violence, including rape by combatants and intimate partners or acquaintances and at times, sexual exploitation by humanitarian actors.

Violence against Prostitutes

Violence against prostitutes is very common. They are at high risk of violent crime, probably at higher risk of occupational mortality than other group of women ever studied. Perpetrators include violent clients, pimps, and corrupt law-enforcement officers. While women who work on the streets are the most likely to be victimised, attacks and even murders on prostitutes have occurred in licensed brothels. Prostitutes are sometimes targeted by serial killers, who may consider them easy pickings and less likely to be missed, or who use the religious and social stigma associated with prostitutes as justification for their murder.

Sati

Sati is described as a Hindu custom in India. *Sati* as per Hinduism is a woman who is fully dedicated to her husband. The *Sati* system was a long run evil prevailing in Indian society up to the British rule. It was a social funeral practice among some Indian communities in which a recently widowed woman would immolate herself on husband's funeral pyre. Those who jump out of fire were stopped by stoning and hitting. It was believed that if the woman get alive then it was regarded as bad woman so people tried to kill her. A few rulers of India tried to ban this custom. The Mughals tried to ban it. The British, due to the efforts of Hindu reformers like Raja Ram Mohan Roy outlawed this custom in 1829. From about 1812, the Bengali reformer Raja Rammohan Roy started his own campaign against the practice. He was motivated by the experience of seeing his own sister-in-law commit *Sati.* Among his actions, he visited Calcutta cremation grounds to persuade widows not to so die, formed watch groups to do the same, and wrote and disseminated articles to show that it was not required by Scripture. He not only abolished this practice, but also did many works for the uplift of women; he set up Brahmo Samaj in 1828 etc.

Sexual Slavery

Sexual slavery is the slavery of unwilling people for sexual exploitation. It is particular form of enslavement which includes limitations on one's autonomy, freedom of movement and power to decide matters relating to one's sexual activity. The crime includes forced marriages, domestic servitude or other forced labor that ultimately involves forced sexual activity. Sex trafficking is a type of human trafficking involving recruitment, transportation, transfer, harbour or receipt of persons, by coercive or abusive means for the purpose of sexual exploitation. Official estimates of individuals in sexual slavery worldwide vary. In 2001 the International Organisation for Migration estimated 400,000, the Federal Bureau of Investigation estimated 700,000 and UNICEF estimated 1.75 million.

Conclusion

Violence against women is a manifestation of historically unequal power relations between men and women and that violence against women is one of the crucial social mechanisms by which women are forced into subordinate position compared with men. Some of the forms of violence perpetrated by individuals are rape; domestic violence; sexual harassment; coercive use of contraceptives; female infanticide; pre-natal sex selection; obstetric violence and mob violence; as well as harmful customary or traditional practices such as honour killings, dowry violence, female genital mutilation, marriage by abduction and forced marriage. Some forms of violence are perpetrated or condoned by the state such as war rape; violence and sexual slavery during conflict; forced sterilisation; forced abortion; violence by the police and authoritative personnel; stoning and flogging. The World Health Organisation reports that violence against women puts undue burden on health care services, as women who have suffered violence are more likely to need health services at higher cost, compared to women who have not.

REFERENCES

1. *Acid Survivors Trust International (2013),* Retrieved from http://www.acidviolence.org/
2. *Abortion Emotional Side Effects,* See http://americanpregnancy.org/unplannedpregnancy/abortionemotionaleffects.html
3. *Abdullah Panniyankara, Honor killing in India*, See http://www.civilserviceindia.com/subject/Essay/honor-killing-in-india2.html
4. Chapter 7, *crime against women,* Retrieved from http://www.tnpolice.gov.in/pdfs/CIT2011/WRITEUPS_11/WRITEUP7_11.pdf

5. *Expert group meeting on 'Prevention of violence against women and girls' Bangkok,* Thailand17— 20 September 2012
6. *Foot binding (2013),* Retrieved from http://www.china-tour.cn/People-And-Customs/Chinese-Feet-binding.htm
7. *Female genital mutilation (2013),* Retrieved from http://www.who.int/mediacentre/factsheets/fs241/en/
8. *Millions at risk of female genital mutilation (2013),* Retrieved from http://www.aljazeera.com/news/africa/2013/07/2013722194844853494.html
9. *Olga Khazan and Rama Lakshmi (2012),* 10 reasons why India has a sexual violence problem, Retrieved from http://www.washingtonpost.com/blogs/worldviews/wp/2012/12/29/india-rape-victim-dies-sexual-violence-proble/
10. *Parveen Azam Ali (2013),* Violence against Women in Pakistan: A Framework for Analysis, Retrieved from http://www.refworld.org/docid/403dd1e40.html
11. Renu Agal (2006), *India's 'bride buying' country*, Retrieved from http://news.bbc.co.uk/2/hi/south_asia/4862434.stm
12. Ritika Chawla (2011). *Bride-Buying in Punjab and Haryana: A Disgrace For The Entire Country,* Retrieved from http://www.youthkiawaaz.com/2011/12/bride-buying-in-punjab-and-haryana-a-disgrace-for-the-entire-country/
13. *Sexual assault in India (2013),* Retrieved from https://crowdvoice.org/sexual-assault-in-india
14. *Sexual and reproductive health (2013),* Retrieved from http://www.who.int/reproductivehealth/topics/violence/sexual_violence/en/index.html
15. *The after effects of abortion,* See http://www.abortionfacts.com/reardon/the-after-effects-of-abortion
16. The Times of India (July 17, 2010), *More than 1000 honour killings in India every year: Experts*, Retrieved from http://articles.timesofindia.indiatimes.com/2010-07-04/india/28273812_1_honour-killings-marriages-heinous-crime
17. Tom de Castella (2013), *How many acid attacks are there?,* Retrieved from http://www.bbc.co.uk/news/magazine-23631395

18. *The Sati: The burning of widow*, See http://adaniel.tripod.com/sati.htm
19. The Times of India (Jun 23, 2013). *Girl dies after forced abortion*, Retrieved from http://articles.timesofindia.indiatimes.com/2013-06-23/varanasi/40146271_1_babulal-cartridges-police-station
20. *The atrocity of acid attracts (2013),* See http://www2.webster.edu/~woolflm/acidattacks.html
21. The Hindu (Aug 26, 2011), *Brides purchased, then exploited in Haryana, Punjab,* Retrieved from http://www.thehindu.com/news/national/brides-purchased-then-exploited-in-haryana-punjab/article2400857.ece
22. The Telegraph (Feb 27, 2012). *Indian dowry deaths on the rise*, Retrieved from http://www.telegraph.co.uk/news/worldnews/asia/india/9108642/Indian-dowry-deaths-on-the-rise.html
23. *Violence against women (2013),* Retrieved from http://www.womenshealth.gov/violence-against-women/
24. *What causes domestic violence?,* See http://psychcentral.com/lib/what-causes-domestic-violence/000344
25. *Women in a insecure world (2005),* Retrieved from http://www.womensdirectorate.gov.yk.ca/pdf/dcaf_report.pdf
26. Facts on violence against women in Nepal, Retrieved from http://www.worecnepal.org/blog/rameshbhandari/facts-violence-against-women-nepal
27. Sati-system, Retrieved from http://amplifyyourvoice.org/u/deepak_ghimire/2013/03/21/sati-system
28. http://www.publicserviceeurope.com/article/2205/chinese-forced-abortion-inhuman-and-degrading
29. Unwanted, coerced or forced abortions in America, Retrieved from http://www.theunchoice.com/coerced.htm
30. http://online.wsj.com/article/SB125800116737444883.html
31. Honor killing of women, Retrieved from http://www.drsohail.com/new_creations.aspx/creations/honour_killing_of_women
32. Islam and 'Honor Killings', Retrieved from http://www.netmuslims.com/index.php/islamic-articles/social-issues/129-honor-killings

33. Love Burns: Bride burning, Retrieved from http://my.telegraph.co.uk/hatefsvoiceofpeace/hatefsvoice/461/love-burns-bride-burning/
34. Female Genital Mutilation: History and Facts, Retrieved from http://www.mtholyoke.edu/~mcbri20s/classweb/worldpolitics/page1.html
35. Rape (2013), retrieved from http://en.wikipedia.org/wiki/Rape
36. Women in Society, Retrieved from http://www.gsl.k12.tr/socialexclusion/main.php?subj=woman
37. Breast Ironing, Retrieved from http://en.wikipedia.org/wiki/Breast_ironing
38. Genocidal rape, Retrieved from http://en.wikipedia.org/wiki/Genocidal_rape
39. Various sources from Wikipedia of human trafficking in India, Nepal, Bhutan, Sri Lanka, Pakistan, Afghanistan, Burma, Thailand, Vietnam, Malaysia, Indonesia, Cambodia, East Timor, Brunei etc.
40. Wikipedia of various types of rapes like, *date rape, gang rape, marital rape, incestual rape, child sexual abuse, prison rape, acquaintance rape, war rape, statutory rape, acid throwing, bride burning, bride-buying, domestic violence in India, dating abuse, date rape, violence against prostitutes, violence against women, sexual violence, sexual slavery, marital rape, pregnancy from rape, femicide, foot binding, murder of pregnant women, forced pregnancy, forced abortion, forced prostitution, female genital mutilation,*

11

Human Trafficking

"Crimes against children are the most heinous crime. That, for me, would be a reason for capital punishment because children are innocent and need the guidance of an adult society."

- Clint Eastwood

Introduction

Trafficking is a multifaceted problem which calls for comprehensive approaches. Trafficking in human beings is a sensitive and complex issue. No country is immune from it.[1] It is almost always a form of organised crime.[2] Member states of the European Union have not yet formulated harmonised notions either of trafficking or of the fight against it. Only those countries which have developed structural policies to address the issue of trafficking have government-organised protection and assistance programmes.[3] Under international law, trafficking is a crime involving the movement of persons and their exploitation.[4] Around the world, most trafficked people are women and children of low socio-economic status, and the primary trafficking.[5] Cases of human trafficking have increased rapidly within the last decade.[6] Generally, the flow of trafficking is from less developed countries to industrialised nations, including the United States[7], or toward neighboring countries with marginally higher standards of living.[8] Victims are often trafficked domestically or abroad in response to the specific demands of others.[9] Human trafficking is a form of modern-day slavery.[10] In terms of race and ethnicity, all subgroups of adolescents are at risk for prostitution.[11] The most trafficked areas are Africa, Asia, South America and Eastern Europe.[12] Trafficking in human beings causes great suffering not only to the victims, but also to persons close to them.[13]

In 1994, the UN General Assembly defined trafficking as the ... *illicit and clandestine movement of persons across national and international borders, largely from developing countries and some countries with economies in transition, with the end goal of forcing women and girl children into sexually or economically oppressive and exploitative situations for the profit of recruiters, traffickers and crime syndicates, as well as other illegal activities related to trafficking, such as forced domestic labour, false marriages, clandestine employment and false adoption.* Hughes defines sex trafficking as: *"Any practice that involves moving people within and across local or national borders for the purpose of sexual exploitation. Trafficking may be the result of force, coercion, manipulation, deception, abuse of authority, initial consent, family pressure, past and present family and community violence, economic deprivation, or other conditions of inequality for women and children."* As this definition implies, there are multiple phases, connections and areas associated with this process. The 2006 United Nations report on human trafficking highlights this complexity and identifies *"127 countries of origin, 98 transit countries and 137 destination countries."*[14]

Global Perspectives

Human trafficking has developed into a highly profitable business for organised crime that generates an estimated $30 billion a year around the world.[15] The trafficking of women and children for sexual exploitation is a low-risk trade for those who organise it, but it is detrimental to the millions of women and children exploited in slavery-like conditions in the global sex industry. Though people often associate with Eastern Europe or Asia, there is mounting evidence that the trafficking of women and children for sexual exploitation with its concomitant human rights abuses and health consequences is a significant problem in the Americas.[16] Africa is predominantly an origin for victims of trafficking. Western Europe and Western Africa are reported to be the main destination (sub-) regions for African victims. This points to intra-regional human trafficking in Africa in general and Western Africa in particular as an identified trend. Asia is mainly an origin as well as a destination for trafficking in persons. Asian victims are reported to be trafficked from Asia to Asian countries, in particular to Thailand, Japan, India, Taiwan and Pakistan. Trafficking can be internal, within state borders, or external, meaning that the victim crosses the national boundaries of his/her origin country and into a destination country. Exploitation of the victim can also take place in what is referred to as transit countries; countries that the victim enters *en route* to the intended destination. Human trafficking is a dehumanising crime which turns people into mere commodities.[17] The root causes of migration and vulnerability to trafficking include not only the weak economic situation of women, but also increasing trends such as discrimination against women in their countries of origin, violence against women, the contradiction between the lower position in the family and the responsibility for the family well-being, their virtual lack of influence in public/political life and their exclusion from decision-making processes.[18]

Traffickers commit the following crimes in the process of trafficking: assault and battery, rape, torture, abduction, sale of human beings, unlawful detention, murder and fraud. Most women enter prostitution because of lack of choice and many are coerced by pimps or traffickers. It is the men who buy sex who are exercising free choice. The UN estimates that as many as four million women and children fall victims to traffickers every year, most of whom are exploited for sexual purposes. According to the International Organisation of Migration, at least 500,000 women are sold annually to local prostitution markets in Europe. Traffickers are often highly organised, ruthless entrepreneurs who earn huge profits from the exploitation of women and children for sexual purposes. According to the Special Rapporteur of the UN Human Rights Commission who recently surveyed the situation of women trafficking, the main countries of origin and destination are as follows: (a) Countries of Origin: Afghanistan, Albania, Bangladeshi, Belarus, Bulgaria, Cambodia, China, Columbia, Croatia, Hungary, India, Indonesia, Jamaica, Kosovo, Latvia, Lithuania, Mexico, Myanmar, Nepal, Pakistan, the Philippines, Poland, Russia, Romania, Slovakia, Thailand,

Ukraine, former Soviet countries, Vietnam, etc; and (b) Countries of Destination: Austria, Australia, Belgium, Canada, China (including Hong Kong and Macau), Cyprus, Dubai, Federal Republic of Yugoslavia, Greece, Germany, Hungary, India, Israel, Italy, Japan, Malaysia, the Netherlands, Pakistan, Poland, Saudi Arabia, Singapore, Spain, Switzerland, Taiwan, Thailand, Turkey, United Kingdom, U.S., the United Arab Emirates, etc.[19]

Thailand has one of the most serious human trafficking problems in Asia and is a primary source, transit point, and final destination for untold numbers of women and children. Because of its relative affluence, Thailand is the biggest recipient of labor migration, both legal and illegal, in the Greater Mekong sub-region[20], which includes Cambodia, Laos, China's Yunnan Province, Myanmar, and Vietnam. While there are no official government's statistics on numbers trafficked into and out of Thailand, it is widely accepted that significant number of illegal migrant workers are actually victims of trafficking.[21] Large-scale child prostitution occurs in many countries. Thailand, Cambodia, and the Philippines are popular travel destinations for *"sex tourists,"* including pedophiles, from Europe, North America, Japan, and Australia. Japan is considered the largest market for Asian women trafficked for sex. Victims are believed to come mainly from Philippines and Thailand. Burma/Myanmar is regarded as both a country from which persons are trafficked into Thailand and as a transit country for trafficking of Chinese women and girls from Yunnan province into Thailand. There are also reports of traffickers bringing people from Burma/ Myanmar across the border into China. China's family planning policy has left its mark on the country's demography with more boys than girls being born. Vietnamese women and girls are trafficked for forced marriage into China. The brides are sometimes resold. South Asia may be the second highest source for trafficking victims according to the State Department. The low status of women in some societies as well as the growth of sex tourism contributes significantly to trafficking in this region. Sri Lanka and India are among the favoured destinations of sex tourists from other parts of the world. Bangladesh and Nepal, the poorest countries in the region, are the main source countries. India and Pakistan are key destination countries. Thousands of

Nepalese girls and young women are lured or abducted to India for sexual exploitation each year. Human trafficking is a major problem throughout the region surrounding Iraq.

In Africa, internal conflicts have provided fertile ground for the trafficking of child soldiers and women forced to serve as combatants or to provide sexual services for troops. Africa is not only the origin of trafficked persons, but also an important region of destination for traffickers.[22] Young women are also trafficked into prostitution and domestic servitude, both within the region and externally to Europe and the Middle East, and children are trafficked into forced labour in agriculture, fishing, mining, domestic service, and prostitution. Kenya and Tanzania serve as transit routes for Ethiopian women being trafficked to Europe and the Middle East and Somalis trafficked to South Africa. Internal trafficking for the domestic sex industry has been identified in Tanzania and Kenya. Trafficking in children for labour is a serious problem in Togo and Benin as well as Botswana, Zaire, Somalia, Ethiopia, Zambia, Nigeria, Algeria.

Trafficking in children occurs in nearly every European country, even if there are significant differences across sub-regions and countries in perceptions of the phenomenon and in the quantity and quality of information available. An analysis of the flows and patterns of cross-border trafficking indicates that European countries are important destination countries in the trafficking chain, but are also countries of origin and transit. Internal trafficking, which does not involve the crossing of international borders, is reported to occur in about half of the countries in Europe. In nearly all these countries, children are reported to be trafficked within their own borders. Reports of internal human trafficking in Western European countries, including trafficking in children, invite a reassessment of the traditional understanding of the root causes of trafficking. The instability of Eastern Europe after the fall of the Berlin Wall has led to an increase in trafficking from Eastern Europe and the former Soviet Union. The former Soviet Union and Central and Eastern Europe have replaced Asia as the main source of women trafficked to Western Europe. Victims come from Russia, Ukraine, and other East European countries. With the economic and political turmoil after the collapse of the Soviet Union, trafficking from the region has escalated from a minor problem before 1991 into a major crisis.

Australia is a destination country for human trafficking. Australian authorities believe that traffickers are primarily of individual operators or small crime groups that often rely on larger organised crime groups to procure fraudulent documentation. It is a destination country for victims trafficked who are from East Asia, South East Asia, and Eastern Europe, particularly the People's Republic of China, the Republic of Korea, and Thailand. Sex trafficking in Australia should not come as a surprise. Sex industry businesses find a burgeoning. Each week in Victoria, more than 60,000 men buy women in prostitution. Consumer Affairs licenses brothel and escort agency businesses. Prostitution was legalised in Victoriain 1984 to tackle three problems: illegal prostitution and police corruption harm to women and street prostitution. Prostitution was decriminalised in New Zealand in 2003. Despite firmly optimistic assessment that decriminalised prostitution was a success in New Zealand, buried inside the 177 pages of a 2008 Review of the NZ law are a number of disturbing facts about the consequences of both the theory and the practice of a law that defines prostitution as work. In the five years since legally defining prostitution as work, the NZ law was unable to alter the exploitive quasi-contractual arrangements that existed before prostitution was decriminalised.

Prostitution existed throughout the world long before the U.S. was formed. Before 1800, colonial America was composed of a disproportionately large number of men.[23] The result was a seller's market of men seeking the companionship of the available women.[24] In the late Eighteenth century, the industrialisation of many American cities created numerous factory jobs, which often employed single women.[25] The major ports of entry for women and children being trafficked into the United States over recent years have been the country's major commercial airports: Los Angeles International Airport, the John F. Kennedy Airport in New York, Miami International Airport, the O'Hare Airport in Chicago, and the San Francisco International Airport. Other significant entry ports have been in Atlanta, Georgia, Cleveland, Ohio, Houston, Texas, Orlando, Florida, and Washington's Dulles International Airport. Canada is a source, transit, and destination country for men, women, and children trafficked for the purposes of labor and sexual exploitation. Women and children are trafficked from Africa, Central and South America, Eastern Europe, and Asia for sexual exploitation. Most trafficking victims have been identified from source countries in Asia including South Korea, Thailand, Cambodia, Malaysia, and Vietnam. Canada plays a prominent role in the international arena as a supporter and promoter of women's human rights. Trafficking in persons in Mexico is a highly complex issue. Trafficking in Mexico occurs internally, from other countries into Mexico, and from Mexico into other countries, and is often a part of, or hidden within, larger migratory processes. For example, the majority of victims of commercial sexual exploitation in Mexico City are Mexicans from other states or the Federal District itself. However, there is also a specific sector that receives women from countries as diverse as Argentina, Brazil, Cuba, Venezuela, Russia, and Hungary. In addition, many Mexicans have been trafficked in the U.S., Spain, and other countries for forced labor in the domestic and agricultural sectors, and for prostitution.

Human Trafficking in India

India is a source, destination, and transit country for men, women, and children trafficked for the purposes of forced labor and commercial sexual exploitation. Internal forced labor may constitute India's largest trafficking problem; men, women, and children are held in debt bondage and face forced labor working in brick kilns, rice mills, agriculture, and embroidery factories. The trafficking from Nepal largely takes place thorough the adjoining border districts of Bihar and West Bengal, from where they make an entry into other places in India. The Nepal-Uttar Pradesh border is also another easy entry point. Major cities like Mumbai (Kamathipura), Delhi (G.B. Road), Calcutta (Sonargachi, Bahubazar, Toliganj, and Kalighat), Bangalore, Hyderabad and Chennai have the largest concentration of prostitutes. Children in India are trafficked from rural areas to cities into a variety of exploitative situations, including prostitution, and are trafficked to work in rural-based industries such as carpet making in Bihar and Uttar Pradesh. Similar cases occur in Pakistan. Indian brothels take girls from Nepal and Bangladesh. Boys from South Asian countries are taken west to work in the Gulf as camel jockeys. Women are very vulnerable to sex trafficking, Traffickers promise them good jobs and then force them into the sex trade. Every year, many Bangladeshi and Nepalese women are trafficked into India for this purpose. They may end up in the brothels of Kamathipura in Mumbai or Sonagachi in Kolkata. The most shocking fact is that in many cases, relatives of women including fathers, husbands, lovers, brothers, uncles or aunts collude with the traffickers.[26] Most of the woman trafficking is happening in Muslim-dominated districts like Murshidabad, Maldah, Nadia, South and North 24 Parganas. Due to lack of education, village girls are trapped by traffickers. Most of the trapped girls are living in rural areas and are under the poverty. According to the National Crime Bureau report (2005), more than 40.9 per cent women in trafficking are from West Bengal. Trafficking for marriage is an inter-country and intra-country phenomenon. Young girls from poor families are taken in marriage to another state or country. Adhikar, a human rights group based in Bhubaneswar, discovered that a number of girls were being taken as brides from the Nayagarh district of Orissa, after paying bride price, and married to young men in Jhansi.

The Constitution of India which is the highest law of the land and from which all laws emanate, guarantees equality as a fundamental right and prohibits traffic in human beings. Article 23(1) specifically prohibits traffic in human beings, beggar and other forms of forced labour. The Indian Government has laid down laws in the Constitution like the Suppression of Immoral Traffic in Women and Girls Act, 1956, The Immoral Traffic (Prevention) Act, and many others. In September 2006, the Indian Government responded to the trafficking issue by creating a central anti-trafficking law enforcement *"nodal cell."* The nodal cell is a federal two-person department responsible for collecting and performing analysis of data related to trafficking, identifying the causes of the problem, monitoring action taken by state Governments, and holding meetings with state-level law enforcement.

Causes of Human Trafficking

The dramatic growth in migration and trafficking flows results from both push and pulls factors. Push factors include uneven economic growth and rising inequality, war and armed conflict, environmental degradation, natural disasters, and high levels of gender discrimination and family violence. At the same time, economic growth, stability and relative prosperity in developed countries act as *'pull'* factors, creating increased demand for imported labour.[27] Various factors are increasing the supply of women trafficking, like as gender *inequality, poverty, political inequality and imbalance, increase in organised crimes, inadequate legal instruments.* Factors that increasing the demand of women trafficking are globalisation and new liberalist market economy, national development strategies based on the sex industry, growth of the sex industry and restructuring of the sex trade market.[28]

Effects of Trafficking

Trafficking leaves victims with an array of problems including major health issues. Victims of sex trafficking are at a higher risk for contracting HIV/AIDS and many victims suffer serious emotional and psychological trauma. The effects of trafficking do not simply end once a person is rescued, as the stigma associated with being a victim often leads to returned victims becoming outcasts in their own communities, and frequently, within their own families. Trafficking deprives child victims the priviledge to exerce their wide range of rights, including the right to belong/identity, the right freedom, education, healthcare, to rest and leisure as well as the right not to be subjected to torture, or cruel and inhuman degrading treatment. When children are first recruited to be trafficked, they may leave home peacefully or by deception or violence, as well as abduction and application of drugs to secure children's obedience. Sexual exploitation is particularly damaging to the health of children. They are even more likely than adults to lack accurate information about the transmission and prevention of sexually-transmitted infections, including HIV/AIDS. The trafficking of women and children for sexual exploitation is accompanied by potentially lifelong and/or life-threatening health consequences. It prevents victims from attaining the highest possible level of physical, mental and social wellbeing. Trafficking into the sex industry leads to stigmatisation of the victims and their families. This makes it hard for the victims to return to their families, who may not welcome them.

Legal and Human Rights Issues

The gravity of the issue of trafficking in human beings has been recognised far way back in the nineteenth century by the international community and efforts have been made to fight against this evil. The first international conference on the prevention of trafficking in women was held in 1895 in Paris, followed by one in 1899 in London and another one in Budapest. The trafficking in women is clearly recognised as a human rights violation. In 1981, the United Nations General Assembly ratified the Convention on the Elimination of All Forms of Discrimination against Women (CEDAW). The Vienna Declaration and Programme of Action adopted by the World Conference on Human Rights in June 1993 (A/CONF.157/23) affirmed that the human rights of women and the girl child are inalienable, integral and indivisible elements of universal human rights.

In 1995 and 1997, the United Nations passed resolutions that, inter alia, called upon Governments to address the problem of trafficking in women and girls. The *Protocol to Prevent, Suppress and Punish Trafficking in Persons, Especially Women and Children* also addresses the human rights dimensions necessary for the protection of victims of trafficking. The Protocol recognises the need for a combined approach that integrates the protection of human rights and assistance to victims with effective prevention, prosecution and judicial cooperation. In 1998 at the recommendation of the Commission on Crime Prevention and Criminal Justice and the Economic and Social Council, the General Assembly established an inter-Governmental ad hoc committee for the purpose of drafting a comprehensive international convention against transnational organised crime and three supplementary protocols (General Assembly Resolution 53/111, Dec. 9, 1998).[29]

International instruments specifically addressing the trafficking of children include the *ILO Convention 182 Concerning the Prohibition and Immediate Action for the*

Elimination of the Worst Forms of Child Labour (1999), and the UN *Convention on the Rights of the Child* (1989) and its *Optional Protocol on the Sale of Children, Child Prostitution and Child Pornography* (2000). Additional information regarding laws, treaties and conventions can be sought in the text and guidance notes of the Slavery Convention (1926); Refugee Convention (1951); International Covenant on Economic, Social and Cultural Rights (1966); International Covenant on Civil and Political Rights (1966); European Convention on the Legal Status of Migrant Workers (1977); the International Convention on the Protection of Migrant Workers and their Families (1990); Protocol to Prevent, Suppress and Punish Trafficking in Persons; especially Women and Children (Palermo Protocol); Palermo: United Nations (2000); and the Council of Europe Convention on Action against Trafficking in Human Beings (2005).[29]

Conclusion

Human trafficking is a modern-day form of slavery. The problem of human trafficking is one that has plagued the world for much of the modern era. Forms of trafficking vary from sexual exploitation, organised prostitution, forced labour and street begging, to sales of organs and petty theft. Trafficking in women flourishes in many less developed countries because the vulnerabilities arising from women's lack of access to resources, poverty and gender discrimination are maintained through the collusion of the market, the State, the community and the family unit. The trafficking of girls into prostitution has achieved the highest profile in South Asia. Condition of Nepal, Bangladesh and India are worst than the other countries in this region. Child victims of human trafficking have a special need for protection and assistance and they must be ensured appropriate follow-up. There is an urgent need for mechanisms for systematic data collection, analysis and dissemination on child trafficking. There must be an adequate penalty for engaging in the practice. An adequate penalty is one that discourages the practice, or creates a disincentive to engage in the practice. Trafficked persons are victims, not criminals. They should not undergo additional negative consequences as a result of their condition of being victims.

REFERENCES

1. *The hidden problem of human trafficking: Addressing modern day slavery in New Hampshire (2008)*, p.8, Retrieved from http://www.nhcadsv.org/uploads/Human%20Trafficking%20in%20NH%20Report%20-%20Nov%202008.pdf
2. *Thematic issue relating to irregular migration and trafficking,* Retrieved from http://www2.ohchr.org/english/issues/migration/taskforce/docs/trafficking-campeche.pdf
3. Georgina Vaz Cabral and Federica Marengo (2003), *Assisting Victims of Trafficking in Human Beings,* Retrieved from http://www.esclavagemoderne.org/media/traite_etres_humains_uk.pdf
4. Sylvain E. Dessy and Stephane Pallage (2003), *The Economics of Child Trafficking*, p.3, Retrieved from http://www.childtrafficking.com/Docs/dessy_pallage_2003__economi.pdf
5. Alison Phinney, *Trafficking of Women and Children for Sexual Exploitation in the Americas*, Retrieved from http://www.oas.org/en/cim/docs/Trafficking-Paper%5BEN%5D.pdf
6. Sonide Simon (2008), *Human Trafficking and Florida Law Enforcement*, p. 8, Retrieved from http://www.fdle.state.fl.us/Content/getdoc/e77c75b7-e66b-40cd-ad6e-c7f21953b67a/Human-Trafficking.aspx
7. The United States of America is a federal Constitutional republic consisting of fifty states and a federal district. Paleoindians migrated from Asia to what is now the United States mainland around 15,000 years ago.
8. Francis T. Miko (2006), *Trafficking in Persons: The U.S. and International Response*, Retrieved from http://digitalcommons.unl.edu/cgi/viewcontent.cgi?article=1033&context=humtraffdata
9. *Pastoral Letter on Human Trafficking,* p.1, Retrieved from http://www.ipjc.org/links/HumanTraffickingAndCST.pdf
10. *Domestic Violence & Human Trafficking (2004),* Retrieved from http://www.ncadv.org/files/HumanTrafficking.pdf
11. *Human trafficking into an within the United States: A review of the literature*, p. 8, Retrieved from https://www.ncjrs.gov/pdffiles1/nij/grants/221035.pdf

12. *Brenda Ola (May 9, 2009)*, p.1, Retrieved from http://www.nyu.edu/classes/keefer/joe/olab.pdf
13. *National Plan of Action against Trafficking in Human Beings Finland (2007),* p.16, Retrieved from http://www.ungift.org/doc/knowledgehub/resource-centre/Governments/Finland_Revised_National_Plan_of_Action_against_Trafficking_in_Human_Beings_en_2008.pdf
14. Karen Dunlop(2008), Human Security, Sex Trafficking and Deep Structural Explanations, *Human security journal,* Volume 6, p.56, Retrieved from http://crides.fondationscelles.org/login/index.php
15. Stephenie Foster and Cindy Dyer (2010), *Ending violence against women and human trafficking: A guide to new strategies*, Retrieved from http://www.vitalvoices.org/sites/default/files/uploads/VAW%20and%20trafficking%20toolkit.pdf
16. Alison Phinney, *Trafficking of Women and Children for Sexual Exploitation in the Americas*, Retrieved from http://www.oas.org/en/cim/docs/Trafficking-Paper%5BEN%5D.pdf
17. Mark P. Lagon, *Closing the Window of Vulnerability: Preventing Human Trafficking of Migrant Laborers,* Retrieved from http://2001-2009.state.gov/g/tip/rls/rm/2008/104454.htm
18. *Trafficking in Women: Contributing Factors and Trends*, Retrieved from http://www1.umn.edu/humanrts/svaw/trafficking/training/materials/FactorsandTrends.PDF
19. *Korean Government's Role in Preventing Transnational Trafficking in Persons - Focusing on Trafficking in Women(2003),* Retrieved from http://fpc.state.gov/documents/organization/139278.pdf
20. The Mekong River is the world's 13th-longest river and the 7th-longest in Asia. The river is a major trading route linking China's southwestern province of Yunnan to Laos, Burma (Myanmar) and Thailand to the south, an important trade route between western China and Southeast Asia.
21. *Combating trafficking of women and children in Thailand,* Retrieved from http://www.humantrafficking.org/uploads/publications/TH-trafficking.pdf
22. Joy Watson and Christine Silkstone (2006), *Human trafficking as a form of gender-based violence – protecting the victim*, p.111,

Retrieved from http://www.unodc.org/documents/human-trafficking/2011/UN_Commentary_EU_Trafficking_Directive_2011.pdf

23. Vern Bullough and Bonnie Bullough, *Women and Prostitution: A Social History,* 210-11 (1987).
24. Id. *Bullough calls these women "unattached females" and states that they were "always...willing to look with favor on the sexual approaches of unattached males."* Id.
25. Bullough, supra note 14, at 216. *Women often preferred working in factories to working as domestic servants because of the greater freedom that factories provided, even though conditions at the factory boarding houses were cramped and unpleasant.* Id.
26. *Essay on human trafficking,* Retrieved from http://www.shareyouressays.com/1773/568-words-essay-on-human-trafficking
27. Noeleen Heyzer (2007), *Labour Migration and Trafficking: A Gender and Human Rights Approach*, p.1, Retrieved from http://www2.ohchr.org/english/bodies/cmw/docs/HLMigration/MigrationDevelopmentHC%27spaper.pdf
28. *Korean Government's Role in Preventing Transnational Trafficking in Persons - Focusing on Trafficking in Women(2003),* Retrieved from http://sgdatabase.unwomen.org/uploads/Republic%20of%20Korea%20%20Korean%20Governments%20Role%20in%20 Preventing%20Transnational%20Trafficking%20in%20Persons%202003.pdf
29. Recommended principles and guidelines on human rights and human trafficking (2010), Retrieved from http://www.ohchr.org/Documents/Publications/Commentary_Human_Trafficking_en.pdf

12

Orphan Children

"All the laws and legislation in the world will never heal this world like the loving hearts and arms of mothers and fathers. If every child could drift to sleep feeling wrapped in the love of their family - and God's love - this world would be a far more gentle and better place."

- Mitt Romney

Introduction

Life is often described as a journey from birth to death. On each person's journey they may encounter certain opportunities or face certain challenges. Children are more attached to parents. For them the parents are their hope and love and everything. UNAIDS defines an orphan as a child under 15 years of age who has lost their mother (maternal orphan) or both parents (double orphan) to AIDS. Based on this definition, the figure of 13 million is projected to rise to 24.3 million in 2010 and to reach 40 million by 2020. The definitions used by UNAIDS, however, excludes the following categories of orphans and other children affected by AIDS: paternal orphans; orphans aged 15 to 18; and Non-AIDS and *'social'* orphans i.e., children orphaned or abandoned as a result of other causes.[1] An orphan is a child permanently bereaved of or abandoned by his or her parents. In common usage, only a child who has lost both parents is called an *orphan*.

UNICEF classifies any child that has lost one parent as an orphan and estimates that approximately 143 million children are currently orphans. For the purposes of this document, an orphan is a minor bereft of parental care due to death, disappearance, or abandonment by either the mother or the father, as well as situations where the parent voluntarily or involuntarily terminates the parental relationship.[2] Orphan and Other Vulnerable Children (OVC), described as those living a particularly hard or difficult life, are often missing many basic needs, mostly due to poverty in the household they are left in (e.g. with their mother) or are passed to (e.g., grandparents). Orphan children tend to manifest more depression, personality disorder, and anxiety/insomnia tendencies than do non-orphans. Such children may present psychosomatic symptoms and health worries that may impede positive mental health. Orphans may often encounter hopelessness, and frustrations owing to their new circumstance that may require them to not only fend for themselves but also for their younger ones, in some cases.[3]

Orphan Children in Africa

The AIDS epidemic in Africa puts children at risk physically, emotionally and economically. All children are indirectly affected when their communities, and the services these communities provide are strained by the consequences of the epidemic. In sub-Saharan Africa, AIDS is the leading cause of death among adults ages 15–59. Although the total number of orphans from all causes in Asia and in Latin America and the Caribbean since 1990 has been decreasing, the number of orphans from all causes has risen by more than 50 per cent in sub-Saharan Africa, where an estimated 12 million children age 0–17 have lost one or both parents to AIDS. In the past, vulnerable children comprised the internationally recognised categories of street children, children exposed to hazardous or strenuous labour, children involved in sexual or domestic trafficking, and children affected by armed conflict.

There are 48.3 million orphans in Africa. The continent of Africa is second, only to Asia in the number of orphans. The three main contributing factors to an increasing number of orphans in Africa are: *disease, poverty,* and *an increasing number of runaways*. Disease is the greatest cause of orphans. There are many diseases in Africa, but none of which compare to AIDS. The numbers are astounding with 24 million infected Africans. Most families in Africa suffer from severe poverty. Sub-Saharan

Africa accounts for 239 million of the925 million impoverished people in the world. Often, parents can hardly afford to survive themselves, let alone provide for their children. Sadly, parents will abandon their children leaving them to fend for themselves.

AIDS is responsible for leaving vast numbers of children across Africa without one or both parents. In some countries, a larger proportion of orphans have lost their parents to AIDS than to any other cause of death. In 2007, AIDS killed approximately 330,000 children under age fifteen, and an estimated 2.1 million additional children under age fifteen were living with HIV.[4] The percentage of orphans in sub-Saharan Africa whose parents died because of AIDS increased from 3.5 per cent in 1990 to 32 per cent in 2001.[5] And the problem is growing; by 2010, an estimated fifty million children in the region will be orphaned, and more than one-third of them will have lost parents due to AIDS.[6] Africa is not the only region affected. Because of AIDS, there are an estimated 1.8 million orphans living in South and Southeast Asia, 330,000 in Latin America, 250,000 in the Caribbean, and 85,000 in East Asia and the Pacific.[7]

The numbers of orphans in Africa has risen steeply in the last decade and will continue to raise as the number of adult AIDS deaths mounts. The orphaning of large numbers of children by AIDS is confirmed by household surveys, where countries with the highest prevalence of orphanhood tend to have the highest prevalence of HIV. The HIV epidemic has revealed broad range of vulnerabilities faced by children and their families. The consequences of losing a parent differ among children: some live in families with only one surviving parent, some live with grandparents (exacerbating the poverty of the elderly on the continent) and some with no support from any source whatsoever are forced to eke out living in the labour force or become street children. The growing population of children orphaned by HIV/AIDS is a concern, because had it not been for HIV/AIDS, the global percentage of orphans would have been declining instead of increasing.

Orphan Children in Asia

In Asia, the number of orphans is much larger than in Africa because Asia is simply much bigger and has more people.[8] In

Russia, over 700,000 orphans, four million orphans and homeless kids in Russia. One of the most distinctive characteristics about HIV/AIDS is the ripple effect it has on children and families. In East Asia, frequently injecting drug use and sex work overlap—a trend particularly noticeable in Indonesia and Vietnam. Young injecting drug users do not just risk contracting HIV by sharing injecting equipment; many of them are selling sex to support the addiction i.e. further exposing themselves and others to HIV infection. In Cambodia there have been limited government policies and programmes to mitigate the impact of HIV and AIDS on children in Cambodia.[9] An estimated 570,000 children live without parental care in Cambodia. Poverty, the years of conflict, migration and the rising number of people suffering from HIV/AIDS are the main reasons why children no longer can live with their families.

UNICEF estimates that around one million children live in vulnerable conditions in Thailand. These include those who live in poverty, have lost parental care, have a disability or are forced to live on the streets. An estimated 290,000 children have been left without parental care due to HIV/AIDS. There are around 26 million children living in Vietnam. Children who are at risk of losing parental care include those whose parents have migrated in search of work. Their children are often left behind with grandparents or family members. Many are abandoned and forced to live on the streets. There are approximately 2.8 million children living in Laos. Children in rural areas are particularly disadvantaged. Basic services such as education, health or other forms of assistance cannot reach those living in remote areas with no access to road or railway networks. Schools in rural areas have fewer resources, and a lower enrolment rate than those in urban areas.[10]

The People's Republic of Bangladesh is in Southern Asia. Poverty is also rife with the majority of people living on less than $1 per day, with the majority of these relying on agriculture to support their families. In Bangladesh more than 170,000 children under the age of five die each year from malnutrition, disease and poverty, that is the equivalent of a child dying every three minutes of treatable causes. Various individuals and social organisations have voluntarily set up orphanages in Nepal to protect these children by offering a homely environment, education and skill training opportunities. According to a UNICEF study, the most vulnerable children in Nepal include those with disabilities, those living in violent and abusive families, street children and those involved in child labour. There are around 79 million children living in Pakistan. The decades of political turmoil and the aftermath of natural disasters have affected the lives of millions of children. There are 4.2 million orphan children in Pakistan. There are multiple reasons behind it, some became orphans because they were illegitimately conceived, while some become orphans because their parents are unable to feed them out of poverty and give them over to charitable organisation to be looked after. An estimated 340,000 children in Sri Lanka grow up without either one or both of their parents. Very often, poverty is cited as the main reason why children end up without parental care. Infants are often abandoned because poor mothers are not able to care for their child. The civil war that affected Sri Lanka for many years did not spare the youngest segment of population: many young boys were recruited for combat in certain areas of the country.

There are 20.6 million children under the age of 18 living in Japan. The extended family plays an important role in many children's lives, and if children cannot be cared for by their parents, members of the wider family will often look after them.[11] Armenia became an officially recognised independent nation in 1991. As a result, the majority of children who are taken into care are the so-called *"social orphans"* who have one or two parents still alive. Around 39 per cent of the population of Uzbekistan are children under the age of 18. The recent social and economic changes have affected the lives of young people. There are around 4.5 million children under the age of 18 in Kazakhstan. The social, economic and political changes have affected their lives in different ways. The Kyrgyz Republic is one of the poorest countries in Central Asia. An estimated four per cent of children under the age of 14 are involved in forced labour. Most come from low-income families and work in a variety of settings which include manual labour and heavy industry.

Orphan Children in Europe

Orphanages in Eastern European countries that were under the old Soviet Union have the absolute worst conditions in Europe. Massive corruption is a huge problem for the Eastern European countries because government officials illegally demand bribe money from the parents. Also, when these children turn 18 years old, they are thrown out of the orphanage, usually with no money, job, bad health, psychological problems, etc.[12] Across Eastern Europe; children born to HIV-positive mothers have a much higher risk than others of being abandoned at or soon after birth. The largest contributor to HIV transmission in Eastern Europe is injecting drug use. Vulnerable children from deprived background are at risk of falling into the hands of organised crime. Girls in particular are susceptible of being trafficked to other areas of Europe and the Balkans.[13] The radical economic and political changes of the last 20 years have negatively affected children's rights in Bulgaria. Recent estimates report between 2,500 and 4,000 street children. Most of the children are from Roma background.

Orphan Children in North America

The number' of orphans in the United States has implications for two social security programmes-old age and survivors, insurance and aid to dependent children. A number of orphaned children are receiving payment under social insurance add related programmes and under aid to dependent children. The number of orphaned children living on July 1, 1953, was estimated by applying the appropriate parental death rates; each parent was counted once for each child. The loss of a parent or family member and the requirements of caring for the ill often result in OVCs and their caretakers experiencing diminished productive capacity and economic hardship. The U.S. President's Emergency Plan for AIDS Relief (Emergency Plan/PEPFAR) supports varied interventions to help families, communities and governments to care for children living with and affected by HIV/AIDS. Over 14 million children have lost one or both parents to HIV/AIDS.

In Canada, around 45,000 children are orphans. Orphans are deprived of their first line of protection i.e., their parents. Parental neglect, abuse or the complete absence of parental care has a strong impact on a child's life as an adult. Thousands of Canadian children run away from home each year. Sexual, physical and psychological mistreatment is cited as the most relevant factor in homelessness for young people. The UN has criticised that in Mexico neither relevant data concerning the number of children who grow up without parental care, nor information about their living situation in general is available. However, it is estimated that roughly 1,600,000 children in Mexico are orphans.

Orphan Children in Latin America

The HIV epidemics in South and Central America have changed little in recent years. 630,000 children in Argentina have lost their parents. Many of those without parental care are grow up in dysfunctional families or on the streets. Adolescent pregnancies remain a problem in Argentina. Like in many other Latin American countries, thousands of Ecuadorian children are confronted with the effects of poverty on a daily basis. Often it is the children who have to go out, make money and bring home food for the entire family. To survive and make a living on the street, a higher number of children engage in begging, petty trade and petty theft. In Ecuador, an estimated 210,000 children are orphans. The HIV/AIDS prevalence rate in Uruguay is roughly 0.5 per cent. Orphans who have lost their mother due to HIV/AIDS face high risk of ending up in poverty. They also frequently have to deal with discrimination, abuse and neglect by other members of society.

Around 150,000 children in Paraguay are orphans. Without parental care, many of them end up in the streets where they often resort to robbery, begging or prostitution in order to survive. In Colombia, 820,000 children under the age of seventeen are orphaned. Many of them grow up without a family. They are vulnerable to recruitment by street-gangs in which drug abuse and high levels of violence rapidly become part of their everyday lives. According to the United Nations Children Fund, 36,000 children in Costa Rica are orphans. Due to dysfunctional or non-existent family structures, many of them are at risk of ending up on one of the crime-ridden streets. More than anyone else, children in El Salvador suffer the cruel effects of poverty and its side effects. Growing up in the streets of San Salvador, many of them without their parents, young people often end up joining gangs where they are confronted with high levels of brutality. Due to the war, more than 35,000 women in Guatemala have been widowed and 200,000 children have been left orphaned. Often, young boys have to nourish an entire family with the money they bring home from work in the streets of the city. The government of Honduras ratified the UN Convention on the Rights of the Child in 1990. Approximately 150,000 children in the country are orphans as a result of political and economic instability.

Impact of Orphan Crisis

Studies of childhood parental loss suggest that orphans tend to experience social depression, personality disorders and anxiety/insomnia. Parents are arguably the most fundamental agent of social stabilisation in the lives of children. When a mother, father or both parents die, their children are denied the love, nurturing and protection of their biological parents that play such critical role in early life and development. In Malawi, households with more than one orphan were much more likely to report food insecurity with moderate to severe hunger than households with no orphans. HIV/AIDS is striking at the heart of family and community support structures for the old and young, and is leaving a whole generation of children to be brought up by their grandparents. HIV/AIDS has had a negative impact on the extended family system.

The powerful stigma and discrimination related to the disease can result in the isolation of infected family members. In many communities hard hit by HIV/AIDS, access to safe water and sanitation has been identified as a severe problem for orphans, other vulnerable children and their families. Children orphaned by HIV/AIDS face a higher risk of malnutrition and stunting, as seen through sub-national studies of the impact of an adult death on child nutrition. Children whose parents are ill because of HIV/AIDS or those who have been orphaned by the disease face stigma and discrimination. They may be rejected by friends and schoolmates, as well as at health centres.[14] Parental illness and death is traumatic, stressful and sad for children. Children are often encouraged to keep their emotions to themselves or may find it difficult to express their feelings. Children who have lost their parents or siblings may experience feelings of sadness, anger and guilt. Children who are distressed may show aggressive, difficult or disturbed behavior. Children caring for sick parents are often left to cope alone without social and emotional support.

Legal and Human Rights Perspectives

Rights are laws and guidelines that protect people so they can live safe, happy, productive, and healthy lives, and be treated with equality and respect, regardless of age, sex, religion, appearance, or ethnicity. Ethical principles for protecting the lives and rights of children, as they relate to adoption, have been set forth in a number of international declarations (which are legally non-binding) and conventions (which are binding). In the past five years the issue of care for orphaned and vulnerable children has been actively taken up by a number of international organisations. The United Nations Convention on the Rights of the Child (CRC) was signed in 1990 and has been ratified by 192 member countries of the United Nations. Children are entitled to standards of care and protection that guarantee their rights. It is the primary responsibility of states to establish policies, laws and services for the protection of children in accordance with CRC. The Convention on the Rights of the Child (UNCRC) provides the over-arching framework for children's rights.

The UNCRC recognizes that children are entitled to the full range of rights - *economic, social, cultural, civil* and *political*. In the context of HIV, protections comprise legal approaches that implement international human rights commitments as well as efforts to address harmful social and gender norms that put women, men, and children at increased risk of HIV infection and increase its impact. The Convention recognises the right of every person to a nationality. In June 2003, the African Union adopted a protocol on the Rights of Women in Africa to the African Charter on Human and Peoples' Rights. The draft protocol had been adopted at a 1999 meeting of African parliamentarians. The Convention on the Rights of the Child does not contain any standards specifically concerning foster care. However, in 1986 the UN General Assembly adopted a Declaration on Social and Legal Principles relating to the Protection and Welfare of

Children, with special reference to Foster Placement and Adoption Nationally and Internationally. Fighting HIV/AIDS is a top priority for UNICEF since the epidemic is depriving millions of children of their right to survive, to develop, to be protected and to have a say in decisions that affect them. In this and other areas of work, UNICEF is guided by the Convention on the Rights of the Child, the world's most widely embraced human rights treaty. Assistance specially tailored for orphans can take several forms. These include fostering, subsidies, tracing and reunification programmes and institutional care in orphanages and children's villages.

Conclusion

Orphan child is common in more or less in every country. In Africa AIDS is a important reason for high number of such children. Children and youth affected by AIDS typically face a wide range of stressful events and circumstances, including poverty, the loss of caregivers and loved ones, having to drop out of school, the burden of adult like responsibilities, and social isolation. Orphan children in developing or poor countries are more deprived than the children in developed countries. In supporting OVCs, the relevant governmental institutions and non-governmental organisations have developed effective supporting mechanisms such as outreach programmes, comprehensive care and protection, etc. A number of institutions (e.g., orphanages), non-governmental organisations, and community-based organisations are undertaking the care and support of orphans and OVC.

REFERENCES

1. Stanley Phiri and Douglas Webb, *The Impact of HIV/AIDS on Orphans and Programme and Policy Responses,* Retrieved from http://www.unicef-irc.org/publications/pdf/aids_book/chapter11_phiri.pdf
2. *Adoption and the Care of Orphan Children: Islam and the Best Interests of the Child (2011),* Retrieved from http://www.wisemuslimwomen.org/images/activism/Adoption_%28August_2011%29_Final.pdf

3. Francis N Onuoha, Tsunetsugu Munakata (2010), *Inverse association of natural mentoring relationship with distress mental health in children orphaned by AIDS*, Retrieved from http://www.biomedcentral.com/1471-244X/10/6
4. *UNAIDS & WHO, AIDS epidemic update 1 (2007).* Retrieved from http://www.unaids.org/en/dataanalysis/knowyourresponse/countryprogressreports/2012countries/ce_KE_Narrative_Report.pdf
5. See UNICEF; supra note 14, at 10. Today, more than 34 million orphans live in sub-Saharan Africa, 11 million due to HIV/AIDS. Id. at 8.
6. *Press Release, UNICEF, Children on the Brink 2004 ¯# Global Orphan Numbers Would Be Falling without AIDS*, available at http://www.unicef.org/media/media_22247.html.
7. *See All-Party Parliamentary Group on AIDS, April 2003: Responding to the Needs of Children Affected by HIV in Developing Countries (April 2003),* http://www.appgaids. Org.uk/Meetings Minutes/April_2003.htm (providing report of meeting of parliamentary group of U.K. Government).
8. *An exploration of orphanages and orphans in Taiwan: A case study*, Retrieved from http://www.drama-therapy.net/Documents/Masters%20in%20Dramatherapy%20-%20Brief%20Dramatherapy%20Exploring%20Roles%20with%20an%20Adult%20Orphan%20in%20Mourning.pdf
9. *National AIDS Authority, Cambodia HIV / AIDS Policy Assessment and Audit*, Draft Report, January 2007
10. *Some facts about Laos*, Retrieved from http://www.sos-usa.org/About-SOS/Where-we-help/Asia/Laos/Pages/default.aspx
11. *Some facts about Japan*, Retrieved from http://www.sos-usa.org/About-SOS/Where-we-help/Asia/Japan/Pages/default.aspx
12. *An exploration of orphanages and orphans in Taiwan: A case study*, Retrieved from http://www.drama-therapy.net/Documents/Masters%20in%20Dramatherapy%20-%20Brief%20Dramatherapy%20Exploring%20Roles%20with%20an%20Adult%20Orphan%20in%20Mourning.pdf

13. *Some facts about Albania*, Retrieved from http://www.soschildrensvillages.ca/Where-we-help/Europe/Albania/Pages/default.aspx
14. Save the Children (UK), *The role of stigma and discrimination in increasing the vulnerability of children and youth infected with and affected by HIV/AIDS,* Research Report, Save the Children (UK), Arcadia, South Africa, November 2001.

13

Caste System

"Buddhism arose in India as a spiritual force against social injustices, against degrading superstitious rites, ceremonies and sacrifices; it denounced the tyranny of the caste system and advocated the equality of all men; it emancipated woman and gave her complete spiritual freedom."

- Walpola Rahula

Introduction

Every society is stratified in one way or another and the possibility of absence of any stratification in any society is almost very remote. In India we find social stratification in the form of caste, based on the birth of the individual in a particular caste/ family.[1] Broadly speaking, a *caste system* is a process of placing people in occupational groups. It has pervaded several aspects of Indian society for centuries. Rooted in religion and based on division of labor, the caste system, among other things, dictates the type of occupation a person can pursue and the social interaction that s(he) may have. Castes are an aspect of Hindu religion. Other religions in India do not follow this system.[2] Several characteristics distinguish a caste system. The first is the tendency toward endogamy, meaning that people marry exclusively within the same caste. Caste mobility is also extremely rare; one cannot transform from a laborer to a scholar except in very rare circumstances. Higher castes traditionally hold all of the political power, and the castes may be divided further through language, culture, and economics. The roots of the Indian caste system can be found in the Hindu scriptures, although the caste system was adopted by other religions in India as well.[3]

What is Caste?

Caste is a form of social stratification characterised by endogamy, hereditary transmission of lifestyle, which often includes an occupation, ritual status in hierarchy and customary social interaction and exclusion based on cultural notions of purity and pollution. The paradigmatic ethnographic example of caste is the division of Indian society into social groups, with roots in India's Vedic history and persisting until today. The caste-system in India may have several origins, one of them being the *varna* system which dates from the later Vedic period. The later Vedic society of northern India, especially Kuru-Panchala, used four categories to classify the society:

1. *Brahmin*: priests, scholars and teachers
2. *Kshatriyas:* warriors, administrators and law enforcers
3. *Vaishyas*: agriculturists, cattle raisers and traders
4. *Sudras:* service providers and artisans; originally non-Aryans admitted to Vedic society.[4]

The Untouchables

Outside of the Varna system are the *'Untouchables'*. Toilet cleaning and garbage removal were some of the tasks considered untouchable. Those performing these tasks were considered polluted and were not to be touched. Untouchables had separate entrances to homes and also drank from separate wells. They were considered to be in a permanent state of impurity. The Untouchables, nevertheless, have their own traditional professions and their own sub-castes. Those professions involve too much pollution to be performed by caste Hindus:

1. Dealing with the bodies of dead animals (like the sacred cattle wandering Indian villages) or unclaimed dead humans.
2. Tanning leather, from such dead animals, and manufacturing leather goods.
3. Cleaning up human and animal waste for which there is no sewer system in traditional villages.[5]

Caste System: Historical Review

Ancient Hindu texts suggest caste system was not rigid. This flexibility permitted lower caste Valmiki to compose the

Ramayana, which was widely adopted and became a major Hindu scripture. Other ancient texts cite numerous examples of individuals moving from one caste to another within their lifetimes. For thousands of years on the Indian subcontinent, a person's social class was determined by birth. Historians later called this the *caste system*. Caste members lived, ate, married, and worked with their own group. A person born into one caste rarely changed castes or mixed with members of other castes.[6] Indian society consists of thousands of endogamous clans and groups called *Jatis*. The British listed the untouchable castes as *'The Scheduled Castes,'* – i.e., I under a list or schedule – just as the aboriginal or indigenous tribes are listed as *'The Scheduled Tribes'* of India and this nomenclature remains the official one to this date. Mahatma Gandhi in an attempt to remove the stigma of untouchability coined the phrase *'Harijans,'* – meaning the children of God, but this has been rejected now-a-days in favour of the term *'Dalits,'* which means the *'broken people,'* itself a denunciation of the system.[7]

In Ancient India (3200-2500 B.C.), the caste system was non-existent since even the most learned men were good householders and had varied occupations. The women of ancient India were just as superior as men in learning, education, and intellect. The choice for her mate was according to her own wishes and marriage was solemonished after coming of the age. She attended parties, competitions, and religious functions as she wished. The remarriage of young widows was also a common practice.[8] There is no universally accepted theory about the origin of the Indian caste system. The Indian classes and Iranian classes show similarity, wherein the priests are Brahmin, the warriors are Kshatriya, the merchants are Vaishya, and the artisans are Shudra. From the Bhakti school, the belief was that castes were originally created by Krishna. According to the three modes of material nature and the work associated with them, the four divisions of human society are created.[9]

The British had an ambivalent position with regard to untouchables. The British Empire was founded because its sepoy armies, mostly of low-caste or untouchable castes, fought with great courage and skill against rajahs to whom they owed no loyalty. In the East India Company's army of the British they gained the respect but were denied in civil society. However, by the middle of the nineteenth century, the British armies were mostly composed of upper-caste Hindus in a vain attempt by the rulers to win legitimacy in the eyes of Indians.[10]

Caste System in India

In South Asia, the caste system has been a dominating aspect of social organisation for thousands of years. In India virtually all nontribal Hindus and many adherents of other faiths (even Muslims, for whom caste is theoretically anathema) recognise their membership in one of this hereditary social communities.[11] The caste system in India is a system of social stratification, which is now used as a basis for affirmative action. Caste is commonly thought of as an ancient fact of Indian life, but various contemporary scholars have argued the caste system to have been constructed by the British colonial regime. The Indian government officially recognises historically discriminated communities of India such as the Untouchables under the designation of scheduled castes, and certain economically backward shudra castes as other backward castes. Independent India has witnessed caste-related violence. According to a UN report, approximately 110,000 cases of violent acts committed against Dalits were reported in 2005.[12]

Primarily Hindu society is divided into four *varnas* and many castes and sub-castes and thus totally stands not only segmented but fragmented vehemently based on the idea of high and low, superior and inferior, pure and impure, touchable and untouchable. The various restrictions were put on shudras and Ati-shudras in the matters of residence, marriage, feeding etc. and the social theory of social exclusion worked as its peak in Indian social context. Hore theory of pollution played its detrimental role. A person born in a caste remains for life and dies in it. The Shudras had to stick to menial only jobs prescribed and cannot even think of changing the same even though they might have interest and inclination for other occupation. In India, the Brahmins retained their supremacy over Sudras and others for two thousand years.[13] With the evangelical influx of Christian missionaries, several untouchables converted to Christianity, just as they had converted to Islam several centuries ago partly to escape the injustices of the caste system and partly out of devotion to new monotheistic inclusive religion. However, for most *'inclusion'* remained elusive, with separate pews and entrances for them at church, and the upper caste converts refusing to marry into their families. Such exclusion has regrettably remained in Christian, Muslim and Sikh congregations even to this day. The National president of the All India Catholic Union made the following representation to the Dalit Chief Justice of India: *"The economic exploitation, cultural suppression and political domination of the Dalits in the whole country for hundreds of years have their own repercussions on the Catholic Church dominated by an upper caste clergy".*[14]

One of the most significant functions of the Indian caste system, of course, is its hierarchical distribution of power. Yet, in this respect, the Indian caste system may be at the turning point at the dawn of the new millennium. Modern forces such as urban migration, mass communication, transportation, consumerism and education are influencing the power structures within village India in complex ways. At the time of India's independence when untouchability was Constitutionally outlawed (though not effectively abolished), social scientists attempted to understand the agrarian society that made up the bulk of India's 500 million people. M. N. Srinivas asserted that rural peasant society was organised and structured around single dominant caste, which exercised control over village.[15]

Since only a small percentage of the total population of Dalit women is educated, the fate of the majority is very grim. According to India's Ministry of Labour, 85 per cent of the Dalit women have the most formidable occupations and work as agricultural laborers, scavengers, sweepers, and disposers of human waste. Many of these women work for minimal wages under the upper caste landlords, since it is proposed that by the National Commission for SC/ST that 85 per cent of Dalits are landless. According to the National Commission for Scheduled Castes and Scheduled Tribes, the majority of educated people are of the upper caste, many of whom may practice caste-based discrimination. Therefore, Dalit girls feel discouraged to enter education and we see the lowest literacy rate for Dalit girls compared to the total population of educated upper caste girls. According to the National Commission for Scheduled Castes and Scheduled Tribes 2000, approximately 75 per cent of Dalit girls drop out of primary school despite strict laws of the Government of India, which hold reservations for Dalit children. The 1992-93 Annual report from the Ministry of Welfare shows 1,236 reported cases of rape on Dalit women and the National Commission for SC/ST shows that approximately 10,000 cases of human right violations on Dalits are reported every month. But, what is even more disturbing is that only one out of ten cases are reported annually whilst nine go unreported. In addition, according to the Human Right Watch Report, approximately 115 million children are in slavery and 2.6 million children are held as bonded labourers.[16]

Effects of Caste System

However, caste discrimination continues to be a social evil experienced everyday in several covert forms, and in periodic public acts of murder, rape, and arson. Poor people identified as Dalit are routinely refused housing in communities dominated by the upper castes, even in urban conglomerations where such distinctions are hard to identify. In rural areas, where everyone's social origins are well established, Dalits suffer the most. Marriage with higher caste person is absolutely taboo. If anyone breaks the taboo, lynching is a common tragic occurrence. Dalits are expected to be submissive. A demand for better treatment can be met with beatings or even murder.[17] Upper caste landlords occasionally exercise the *droit de seigneur* over attractive poor Dalit women in rural areas. Minimum wages established by law are rarely paid. Bonded labourers are more often Dalits.[18]

Caste System and Social Reformers

There have been challenges to the caste system from the time of Buddha, till then several thinkers discussed and opposed this *Jatis/Varna* system. We will discuss about three thinkers only-Jyotiba Phule, Mahatma Gandhi, Dr B.R. Ambedkar and Bhagat Singh. Jyotiba Phule was one of the prominent social reformers of the nineteenth century India. He led the movement against the prevailing caste-restrictions in India. He revolted against the domination of the Brahmins and for the rights of peasants and other low-caste fellow. It is critique of the caste system began with attack on the Vedas, the most fundamental texts of Hinduism. In 1873, Jyotiba Phule formed the *Satya Shodhak Samaj* (Society of Seekers of Truth). The purpose of the organisation was to liberate people of lower-castes from the suppression of Brahmins.

Mahatma Gandhi is one of the most fascinating personalities of the twentieth century. The way in which he stood up against discrimination in South Africa and in India using non-violence combined with the theory. He developed own methods make him as one of the important examples in the history of humanity. He has been the inspiration for many people including Martin Luther King. M.K Gandhi is widely portrayed in and outside India as the main champion of the cause of the Untouchables (Dalits). Mahatma Gandhi called them *"Harijans"* (children of God) although that term is now considered patronizing and the term Dalit (downtrodden) is the more commonly used. In Indian context, to fight against untouchablity and for equality of all was a very challenging task. The attitudes of disappointment amongst dalits were very deep rooted on their social, economical and political exploitation from the centuries together. These considerations, it was very challenging to motivate them stand up to fight against exploitation and for the self respect.

Dr Bhimrao Ambedkar spent his whole life in this challenging task relentlessly. Dalits as other part of Indian society were themselves divided into many castes and sub-castes because of ignorance, backwardness and given social structure. According to Ambedkar, the caste system in India has been a divisive instrument from the beginning. He had a firm view that till this caste system continues, the outcaste's liberation is not possible. This was the reason that he started a strong movement against caste system.

Bhagat Singh finds a place not only among India's but world's greatest revolutionaries. His life, work, struggle and the way he kissed and embraced death bring him in league of world's great revolutionaries such as Socrates, Bruno, Joan of Arc, Che Guevara etc. His martyrdom will continue to inspire many generations of revolutionaries to sacrifice lives in defence of truth, justice and freedom.[19] The person accredited with framing of the Indian Constitution was Dr B.R. Ambedkar, an *'untouchable'* himself, a great and enlightened founder of Independent India, who has written extensively on the subject of *'Caste,'* and who finally gave into Mahatma Gandhi's plea that untouchables should not break away from the rest of Hindus but remain united in the freedom struggle. Because of Dr Ambedkar's personal eminence, Mahatma Gandhi's moral indignation against the caste system and the modernising zeal of the founders of Independent India, discrimination on the basis of caste is illegal under law and a culpable offence.[20]

Government Initiatives

The person accredited with the framing of Indian Constitution was Dr B.R. Ambedkar, an untouchable himself, a great and enlightened founder of Independent India, who has extensively written on the subject of caste, and who finally gave into Mahatma Gandhi's plea that the untouchables should not break away from the rest of the Hindus but remain united in the freedom struggle.[21] The Britishers introduced Uniform Criminal Law in India which totally abolished caste-based discrimination in the matters of dispensation of justice and especially in the matters of punishment which was not based on gravity of crime, but was based on the caste of the victim or the perpetrator of crime. They introduced: (1) *The Widow Remarriage Act, 1856.* For the first time, Hindu women in history of India, got the right to re-marry which no authority had introduced prior to the advent of Britishers in India. They also introduced; (2) *The Caste Disabilities Removal Act, 1850* - This law blew the caste integrity. The Act facilitates conversion to another religion or admission into another caste without affecting the property rights of the person; and (3) *The Special Marriage Act, 1872* - Any person can marry in any caste or creed provided the marriage is registered. During British rule, Jotiba Phooley opened girls schools wherein girls belonging to the low castes Mahars, Mangs, Chamars and others were admitted by him.[22]

The caste system has no legality in India and discrimination against lower castes is illegal in India under Article 15 of its

Constitution. However, caste-related discrimination and violence continue to be reported. Since 1950, the country has enacted many laws and social initiatives to protect and improve the socio-economic conditions of lower caste population. The Mandal Commission covered more than 3,000 castes under Other Backward Class (OBC) category, regardless of affluence or economic status and stated that OBCs form around 52 per cent of the Indian population. However, the National Sample Survey puts the figure at 32 per cent. B.R. Ambedkar and Jawaharlal Nehru had radically different approaches to caste, especially concerning Constitutional politics and the status of untouchables.[23]

Countless reformers have attempted to abolish or reform the caste system. However, these reform movements have had little effect. Today, the caste system continues to be the main clause of government in villages throughout India. In large part, its continuity depends on two central concepts: *caste dharma* and *karma*. In Hindu society, caste dharma is considered to be a divine law. In the words of Mahatma Gandhi, caste dharma is *"the duty one has to perform"* and *"the law of one's being."* Many Hindus believe that this obligation tends to enhance the spiritual development of the individual. Because of it, each person learns from an early age to overcome selfish desires and instead focus on groups goals and ideals. The concept of karma helps to explain differences in status that might otherwise be considered unfair. Because one's caste membership is thought to be a result of actions in previous life, a person tends to accept this status rather than complain. In the modern cities of India, people daily come in contact with hundreds of strangers in public transportation and in the workplace. In this context, the traditional caste rules of the villages cannot be observed. But many city dwellers nevertheless retain a strong sense of caste identity.[24]

Human Rights Violations against Dalits in India

According to the Hindu religious belief, *"All human beings are not born equal."* This creates caste-based discrimination against Dalits, open to various forms of violence, which include public humiliation, torture, rape, beating, and killing, etcetera. The untouchability is the basis for atrocities and violence, denial of basic needs, land rights, legal discrimination, infringement of civil liberties, inferior or no people status, de-humanised living and working conditions, impoverishment, malnourishment, bad health conditions, higher levels of illiteracy and continued social ostracism as the reason for human rights violations against dalits. According to the National Commission of Human rights of India, more than 62,000 human rights violations are recorded annually. On an average, two Dalits are assaulted every hour, three Dalit women and children are raped, two Dalits are murdered, and at least two Dalits are tortured or burned every day. According to the National Commission for Scheduled Caste and Scheduled Tribes, there are an estimated 115 million children working under slavery, and amongst those, approximately 80-90 per cent are Dalit who work as bonded labour to pay off debts. According to government statistics, an estimated 800,000 Dalits are manual scavengers involved in clearing human faeces from public and private latrines and disposing of dead animals.[25]

Conclusion

The caste system in India is a system of social stratification, which is now used also as basis for affirmative action. Caste is commonly thought of as an ancient fact of Indian life. However, caste-related discrimination and violence continue to be reported. These caste classification for college admission quotas, job reservations and other affirmative action initiatives, according to India's Supreme Court, is based on heredity and is not changeable. The Indian government officially recognises historically discriminated communities of India such as the Untouchables under the designation of Scheduled Castes, and certain economically backward Shudra castes as Other Backward Castes. The Mandal Commission covered more than 3,000 castes under Other Backward Class category, regardless of their affluence or economic status and stated that OBCs form around 52 per cent of the Indian population.

REFERENCES

1. See http://shodhganga.inflibnet.ac.in:8080/jspui/bitstream/10603/5133/8/08_chapter%202.pdf

2. *India's Caste System,* Retrieved from http://www.dummies.com/how-to/content/indias-caste-system.html
3. See http://www.wisegeek.org/what-is-a-caste-system.htm
4. *Caste (2014).* Retrieved from http://en.wikipedia.org/wiki/Caste
5. Dr. Suninder Kaur, *Indian Anthropology: Indian village as a unity and extension, village and caste,* Retrieved from http://nsdl.niscair.res.in/dspace/handle/123456789/940
6. *The caste system*, Retrieved from http://www.mrdowling.com/612-caste.html
7. Vithal Rajan, *Dalits and the caste system in India*, Retrieved from http://www.transcend.org/tri/downloads/The_Caste_System_in_India.pdf
8. Sonia Mahey, *The Status of Dalit Women in India's Caste Based System,* Retrieved from
9. See http://positivephilosophy.webs.com/documents/Caste%20System% 20in%20India.pdf
10. Vithal Rajan, *Dalits and caste system in India: Some Explorations and Conjectures,* Retrieved from http://www.transcend.org/tri/downloads/The_ Caste_System_in_India.pdf
11. *Caste (2014)*. Retrieved from http://www.britannica.com/EBchecked/topic/285248/India/46404/Caste
12. *Caste system in India,* Retrieved from http://en.wikipedia.org/wiki/Caste_system_in_India
13. See http://shodhganga.inflibnet.ac.in:8080/jspui/bitstream/10603/5133/8/08_chapter%202.pdf
14. Vithal Rajan, *Dalits and caste system in India: Some Explorations and Conjectures*, Retrieved from http://www.transcend.org/tri/downloads/The_Caste_ System_in_India.pdf
15. Kirk Johnson and Michael Karlberg, *Rethinking power and caste in Rural India*, Retrieved from http://myweb.wwu.edu/karlberg/articles/Power&Caste.pdf
16. Sonia Mahey, *The Status of Dalit Women in India's Caste Based System,* Retrieved from http://www.dalits.nl/pdf/StatusDalit Women.pdf
17. Vithal Rajan, *Dalits and the caste system in India,* Retrieved from http://www.transcend.org/tri/downloads/The_Caste_System_in_India.pdf

18. Vithal Rajan, *Dalits and caste system in India: Some Explorations and Conjectures*, Retrieved from http://www.transcend.org/tri/downloads/The_ Caste_System_in_India.pdf
19. Dr Desh Raj Sirswal, *Caste System in India,* Retrieved from http://positivephilosophy.webs.com/documents/Caste%20System%20in%20India.pdf
20. Vithal Rajan, *Dalits and caste system in India: Some Explorations and Conjectures,* Retrieved from http://www.transcend.org/tri/downloads/The_ Caste_System_in_India.pdf
21. Vithal Rajan, *Dalits and the caste system in India,* Retrieved from http://www.transcend.org/tri/downloads/The_Caste_System_in_India.pdf
22. See http://shodhganga.inflibnet.ac.in:8080/jspui/bitstream/10603/5133/8/08_chapter%202.pdf
23. *Caste system in India,* Retrieved from http://en.wikipedia.org/wiki/Caste_system_in_India
24. *The caste system,* Retrieved from http://www.mrdowling.com/612-caste.html
25. Sonia Mahey, *The Status of Dalit Women in India's Caste Based System,* Retrieved from http://www.dalits.nl/pdf/StatusDalitWomen.pdf

14

Beggary

"It is not from your own goods that you give to the beggar; it is a portion of his own that you are restoring to him. The Earth belongs to all. So you are paying back a debt and think you are making a gift to which you are not bound."

- Saint Ambrose

Introduction

The meaning of life is in the philosophical and religious conception of existence, social ties, consciousness, and happiness, and borders on many other issues. According to existentialism, each man and each woman creates the essence (meaning) of his and her life; life is not determined by a supernatural god or an earthly authority. Per secular humanism, the human species came to be by reproducing successive generations in a progression of unguided evolution as an integral expression of nature, which is self-existing. People determine human purpose without supernatural influence. The religious perspectives on the meaning of life are those ideologies which explain life in terms of an implicit purpose not defined by humans.[1]

Personal life is the course of an individual's life, especially when viewed as the sum of personal choices contributing to one's personal identity. In the past, before modern technology largely alleviated the problem of economic scarcity in industrialised countries, most people spent large portion of their time attempting to provide their basic survival needs, including water, food, and protection from the weather.[2]

Who are Beggars?

According to the Oxford Dictionary, beggar is a person, typically a homeless one, who lives by asking for money or food.[3] Begging is the practice of imploring others to grant a favor, often a gift of money, with little or no expectation of reciprocation.[4] Begging which technically known as *"panhandling"* defines a situation wherein the needy ask for material benefits or money, often even basic amenities like food and clothing.[5]

Reasons of Beggary

Many religions have prescribed begging as the only acceptable means of support for certain classes of adherents, including Christianity, Hinduism, Sufi Islam, Buddhism, and Jainism, typically to provide a way for certain adherents to focus exclusively on spiritual development without the possibility of becoming caught up in worldly affairs. Beggars may be found in public places such as transport routes, urban parks, and near busy markets. Besides money, they may also ask for food, drink, cigarettes or other small items.[6] There are few justifiable cases of begging. Those who are paralysed, lame, deaf, dumb, and blind or disabled, are unable to earn their living. Some are in pathetic state that evoke pity and compassion. These poor beggars are well versed in the art of singing religious songs. Some beggars have very sonerous voice.[7] There are many reasons why begging still exists. Some think they cannot do anything some do not know whether they can do anything. Then there are some who think begging is an easy money. For some, it has become more of an art than an unwanted activity.[8]

The causes of begging are many. First of all, some people are physically incapable of doing any work. The only way of getting food open to them is begging. Secondly, some people take to begging due to religious sanction. In Hindus as well as in Muslims, some religious teachers encourage people to become beggars. Thirdly, there are organisations which train children in the art of begging. Orphans and kidnapped children are engaged in this profession from early childhood. Fourthly, some criminals when they return from jails are not treated sympathetically by society.

They are not given any chance to begin their life afresh. They become beggars and find shelter in this profession.[9]

Global Perspectives

Beggars have existed in human society before the dawn of history. Begging happened in most societies around the world, though its prevalence and exact form vary. In Buddhism, monks and nuns traditionally live by begging for alms, as did the historical Gautama Buddha himself.[10] *Nepal* child *beggars* beg on the streets of Kathmandu. Beggary is never a respectful profession. We can still accept when people beg due to extreme poverty or inexorable condition, such as inability to get proper job due to physical disabilities. However, recent tendency in Indonesian cities indicates that beggary is becoming a *'preferred'* job. Despite disrespect, there are people who consciously do it.[11] The authorities in Bangladesh are to carry out a survey of beggars in the capital, Dhaka. The aim is to find out the root cause of their problems and to offer them alternative livelihoods. There are some 40,000 beggars in Dhaka alone, a city of 12 million people. Despite the government's efforts to abolish begging, the practice remains widespread in the capital and other parts. Every day, hundreds of beggars can be seen on the roadside, at traffic signals and outside commercial buildings in Dhaka. Many of them are physically disabled.[12] Investigators say members of a criminal gang were trying to force the boys to become a beggars on the streets of Dhaka, Bangladesh's capital.[13]

Saudi Arabia is set to deport another batch of 46 Indian children, illegally staying in the oil-rich kingdom and begging on the streets near holy places there in. According to reports received by the Indian external affairs ministry from the Indian mission in Saudi Arabia, 40 boys and six girls are at present lodged at the deportation centre in Jeddah. The Indian consulate in Jeddah is arranging food, clothing and medical care for these children, most of whom hail from Murshidabad in West Bengal. Recently, 77 children, 76 of them females, were deported by the Saudi authorities. These children are at present lodged at the remand home in Mumbai, pending their restoration to their parents. The sources said the Indian government had started undertaking a stricter immigration check of Saudi Arabia-bound passengers in view of the deportation of these children. The sources said the Indian government has also asked the West Bengal government to closely monitor the situation in Murshidabad to which most of the children deported belong.[14] A 100-year-old woman in Saudi Arabia, who spent decades begging on the streets, has died leaving behind a secret fortune of gold coins, jewellery and a real estate portfolio worth a whopping $10,66,580. The blind woman had begged for 50 years on the streets of Jeddah, before she suddenly died at her home, leaving behind a sizable fortune.[15]

In an effort to sanitise the Nigerian city of Lagos, the state government is returning all beggars on the streets to their states of origin. They say they have already removed at least 3,000 beggars in the last year, but have now upped the commitment and banned giving alms to beggars as well. Violators will face two-year imprisonment without the option of paying a fine. Senegal attempted a similar project, but the number of beggars on the streets of Dakar remains high.[16] The increasing number of beggars and forms of begging has turned the phenomenon into a national concern. Senegalese novelists and film-makers, even Senegalese members of the parliament often engage in debates about that national plague and what to do about it.[17]

In the recent past, there has been increasing attention in many EU member states and other European countries to the phenomenon of child begging. Whilst a consensus exists among member states that child begging needs to be addressed, there is little evidence on what as the best policy approach. The phenomenon is considered to be linked to poverty, marginalisation, and that belonging to certain ethnic minorities but also to organised crime and trafficking in human beings.[18] Child begging is in a public park, outside a mosque or church, at traffic lights, along busy streets and bus-stops. In January 2011, the European Commission (EC) and DG Home Affairs commissioned the International Centre for Migration Policy Development (ICMPD) for a research project on child begging.[19] Beggars in Eastern Europe are quite common. While some travelers have become jaded by beggars in developed countries who beg by day only to drop the facade for a lunch break, beggars in Eastern Europe are often truly needy. The beggars in Eastern Europe may be Roma, who, because of their social standing, often have difficulty in getting education and finding jobs. They may be pensioners who get an income impossible to live on. Because begging is considered a social taboo, beggars are looked down upon by locals, even though their misfortune may be acknowledged.[20]

Beggary in India

Beggars are commonly found in India. They are seen in every town, city and village in India. The core areas of activities are the places of pilgrimage and worship. Some people give money or food to beggars in order to rid of them and not due to pity. Some beggars are so young and strong they do not justify charity at all. The number of beggars in India is increasing. These beggars are living on the earning of other people. It is a pity that even strong and fit people in India resort to begging. They further indulge themselves in drinking and gambling.[21] A recent survey in Delhi revealed that many beggars are able-bodied and educated, forced into beggary by unemployment. The findings underscore the absence of cohesive and humane national policy for beggars in India. Conducted across a swathe of geographical regions, the survey shows that a beggar's earning add up between Rs 50 and Rs 500 each day with most beggars opting to beg in the face of meagre earning capacity, poverty, infirmity, destitution, and age.[22]

According to a recent survey by Delhi School of Social Work, there has been a phenomenal increase in the numbers of beggars in India. In a decade since 1991 their number has gone up by 100,000. There are some 60,000 beggars in Delhi, over 3,00,000 in Mumbai according to a 2004 Action Aid report; nearly 75,000 in Kolkata says the Beggar Research Institute; 56,000 in Bangalore according to police records. In Hyderabad one in every 354 people is engaged in begging according to Council of Human Welfare in 2005. Mumbai is home to majority of beggars. According to the Maharashtra government they are worth Rs 180 crore each year with daily income ranging between Rs 20 and Rs 80 Almost every survey profiles beggars as a largely contented lot unwilling to take up honest labour. The biggest problem lies in the changing attitude towards beggars.[23]

In countries like India, it is considered a holy and religious duty to help the needy and religious men, *'sadhus'*, by giving them alms. In certain communities, there are sadhus who visit people of their caste residing in different states to get their *"entitled bhiksha"*. Encouraging begging means we are making them more dependent on us rather than themselves. Till the money keeps flowing they are happy; when it dries up, tactics are devised. If begging gets families through daily expenses, there is no incentive to improve the standard of living. Ultimately, generations after generations are stuck to begging only. Some in the beggary community have been known to be involved in crimes, minor and heinous.[24]

Despite India's rapid economic growth in recent years, poverty and begging in India are still big problems. While the poverty is real, begging is quite often carried out in organised gangs. For the privilege of begging in a certain territory, each beggar must hand over their earning to the ring leader, who keeps significant share for himself. The most common problem is that beggars are used begging that they actually prefer not to work. Mumbai, in particular, visitors are often approached by a child or woman wanting some powdered milk to feed a baby. Beggars also rent babies from their mothers each day, to give their begging more credibility. Begging is most prevalent anywhere there are tourists. This includes important monuments, railway stations, religious and spiritual sites, and shopping districts.[25]

Legal Mechanism

Begging has been restricted or prohibited at various times and for various reasons, typically revolving around a desire to preserve public order or to induce people to work rather than to beg for economic or moral reasons. Various European Poor Laws prohibited or regulated begging from the Renaissance to modern times with varying levels of effectiveness and enforcement. The province of Ontario introduced its Safe Streets Act in 1999 to restrict specific kinds of begging, particularly certain narrowly-defined cases of *"aggressive"* or abusive begging. In parts of San Francisco, California, aggressive panhandling is prohibited. In United Kingdom, begging is illegal under the Vagrancy Act of

1824. In Romania Law 61 of 1991 forbids the persistent call for the mercy of the public, by a person who is able to work. Begging has been legal in Finland since 1987 when the Poor Law was invalidated. In Portugal, panhandlers normally beg in front of Catholic churches, at traffic lights or on special places in Lisbon or Oporto downtowns. Begging is not illegal in Portugal. Begging in Luxembourg is legal except when indulged in as a group or the beggar as a part of an organised effort.[26]

Since 1961, Delhi has been administered by the antiquated Bombay Prevention of Begging Act, 1959, which makes begging in public places a crime and a punishable offence. Clause (d) of the Act describes beggars as people *"...having no visible means of subsistence and wandering about or remaining in any public place in such condition or manner (as) makes it likely that the person doing so exists by soliciting or receiving alms"*. Under this Act, officials from the social welfare department (assisted by the police) conduct raids to randomly pick up beggars who are then tried in a special beggars' court and, if convicted, sent to a certified institution. Unfortunately, however, the Begging Act lumps together an assortment of people (street performers, mendicants, small vendors, pavement-dwellers and migrants) who might solicit alms indirectly, as *'beggars'*. India's beggary laws are undoubtedly a throwback to the centuries-old European vagrancy laws that overlook the crucial difference between official text and practical reality. In other words, rather than address the socio-economic angle of beggary, beggary laws criminalise it. The Indian Penal Code (Section 363 A) deals with the kidnapping/maiming of a minor for purposes of begging. However, the police seem intriguingly unwilling to use this, preferring to book *'unwanted elements'* like homeless people/drug addicts in their area under the Bombay Act, as their responsibility then stops with the arrest. Thus, the current institutionalised approach to beggars merely serves to punish destitute people without aiming to help or reform them.[27]

Conclusion

Begging is the practice of imploring others to grant a favor, often a gift of money, with little or no expectation of reciprocation. Beggars may be found in public places such as transport routes, urban parks, and near busy markets. Besides money, they may also ask for food, drink, cigarettes or other small item. Begging has happened in most societies around the world, though its prevalence and exact form vary. Many religions have prescribed begging as the only acceptable means of support for certain classes of adherents, including Christianity, Hinduism, Sufi Islam, Buddhism, and Jainism. Begging has been restricted or prohibited at various times and for various reasons, typically revolving around a desire to preserve public order or to induce people to work rather than to beg for economic or moral reasons. The government should start its own institutions, where widows, orphans, and other helpless people may find shelter. This will prevent them from joining the profession. The government should also pass laws, which should make begging by persons below a certain age a crime. Many people with sound health and in their prime become beggars. The law should prevent such people from begging.[28]

REFERENCES

1. *Meaning of life,* Retrieved from http://en.wikipedia.org/wiki/Meaning_of_life
2. *Personal life*, Retrieved from http://en.wikipedia.org/wiki/Personal_life
3. Definition of *beggar* in English, Retrieved from http://dictionary.reference.com/browse/beggar
4. *Begging (2014),* Retrieved from http://en.wikipedia.org/wiki/Begging
5. Nirav Shah, *Beggary in India: Generously Putting Stop to It,* Retrieved from http://www.youthkiawaaz.com/2011/11/beggary-in-india-generously-putting-stop-to-it/
6. *Begging (2014),* Retrieved from http://en.wikipedia.org/wiki/Begging
7. *Essay on Beggars in India,* Retrieved from http://www.importantindia.com/6505/essay-on-beggars-in-india/
8. Nirav Shah, *Beggary in India: Generously Putting Stop to It,* Retrieved from http://www.youthkiawaaz.com/2011/11/beggary-in-india-generously-putting-stop-to-it/

9. *Essay on the Beggar Problem in India*, Retrieved from http://www.publishyourarticles.net/knowledge-hub/essay/an-essay-on-the-beggar-problem-in-india.html
10. *Begging (2014).* Retrieved from http://en.wikipedia.org/wiki/Begging
11. *Beggary in Indonesian Cities,* Retrieved from http://www.glbrain.com/index.php?r=tool/view&id=7137&toolType=4
12. Anbarasan Ethirajan (2011) *Bangladesh to survey beggars in the capital Dhaka,* Retrieved from http://www.bbc.co.uk/news/world-south-asia-15119854
13. See http://thecnnfreedomproject.blogs.cnn.com/2011/05/04/gang-profits-from-maimed-child-beggars/
14. *Saudi Arabia to deport 46 Indian beggar children,* Retrieved from http://m.rediff.com/news/jan/23child.htm
15. *The Times of India (March 20, 2014).* Saudi Arabia beggar dies leaving million-dollar fortune behind, Retrieved from http://timesofindia.indiatimes.com/world/middle-east/Saudi-Arabia-beggar-dies-leaving-million-dollar-fortune-behind/articleshow/32371696.cms
16. *How should we treat beggars?,* Retrieved from http://www.bbc.co.uk/blogs/legacy/africahaveyoursay/2011/05/how-should-we-treat-beggars.shtml
17. *Beggary in West Africa,* Retrieved from http://www.ncbi.nlm.nih.gov/pubmed/6725721
18. See http://tdh-childprotection.org/projects/child-begging-study/description
19. See http://tdh-childprotection.org/news/tdh-completes-eu-commissioned-study-in-albania-and-kosovo
20. *Before You Give: Beggars in Eastern Europe,* Retrieved from http://goeasteurope.about.com/od/introtoeasteuropetravel/bb/beggars.htm
21. *Essay on Beggars in India,* Retrieved from http://www.importantindia.com/6505/essay-on-beggars-in-india/
22. Neeta Lal, *Criminalising beggars instead of rehabilitating them,* Retrieved from http://infochangeindia.org/human-rights/features/criminalising-beggars-instead-of-rehabilitating-them.html

23. *Beggary in India,* Retrieved from http://www.azadindia.org/social-issues/beggary-in-india.html
24. Nirav Shah, *Beggary in India: Generously Putting Stop to It,* Retrieved from http://www.youthkiawaaz.com/2011/11/beggary-in-india-generously-putting-stop-to-it/
25. *India Beggars and Begging Scams: What You Should Know,* Retrieved from http://goindia.about.com/od/annoyances inconveniences/p/indiabegging.htm
26. *Begging (2014).* Retrieved from http://en.wikipedia.org/wiki/Begging
27. http://infochangeindia.org/human-rights/features/criminalising-beggars-instead-of-rehabilitating-them.html
28. *Essay on the Beggar Problem in India,* Retrieved from http://www.publishyourarticles.net/knowledge-hub/essay/an-essay-on-the-beggar-problem-in-india.html

15

Urban Slums

"The slum is the measure of civilization."

- Jacob Riis

Introduction

Urban area is characterised by higher population density and vast human features in comparison to the areas surrounding it. Urban areas may be cities, towns or conurbations, but the term is not commonly extended to rural settlements such as villages and hamlets. There are about 7.1 billion people living on the planet. In 2009, the number of people living in urban areas (3.42 billion) surpassed the number living in rural areas (3.41 billion) and since then the world has become more urban than rural.[1] When someone lives in an urban area, they have access to modern amenities, internet, public transportation, television, telephone, and satellites. They often have better housing, job opportunities, entertainment and a variety of social activities. Almost everything in an urban environment has more technological advances than that in other areas. The choice to stay in an urban or rural area is very crucial to the kind of lifestyle an individual wants to enjoy. The urban area is a great place to live with a lot of comfort that it offers but is not devoid of some challenges.[2]

Migration to urban areas is a regular phenomenon, but climate induced displacement forced to migrate to cities over the recent years is a matter of concern. Increased frequency and severity of natural disasters by climate change over the past recent years are not only displacing people physically but also exposing to enhanced poverty by Threatening their livelihoods temporarily and permanently. the rush of growing number of people to city's slums creates urban crisis.[3]

What is Slum?

A slum is a heavily populated urban informal settlement characterised by substandard housing and squalor. Slums were common in the 19th and early 20th centuries in the United States and Europe. More recently slums have been predominantly found in urban regions of developing and undeveloped parts of the world, but are also found in developed economies.[4] The census of India defines a slum as *"residential areas where dwellings are unfit for human habitation"* because they are dilapidated, cramped, poorly ventilated, unclean, or *"any combination of these factors which are detrimental to the safety and health"*. Slum Population simply refers to people living in slum areas below the poverty line.

Reasons of Slum

Slums come about because of a number of forces. Among these are rapid rural-to-urban migration, increasing urban poverty and inequality, insecure tenure, and globalisation. All contributes to the creation and continuation of slums. In many developing countries, squatters or informal settlers form close to the majority of urban dwellers and thus live in poverty without civic amenities, because urban development policies have not kept up with urban growth.[5] The formation of slums need not be inevitable with rapid urbanisation. Such an argument appears to be contradicted by evidence of large slum population in a large number of developing countries and particularly in rapidly urbanizing regions like Asia. The evidence discussed suggests that city authorities faced with rapid urban development lack the capacity to cope with the diverse demands for infrastructural provision to meet economic and social needs.[6]

Global Perspectives

According to UN-HABITAT, around 33 per cent of the urban population in the developing world in 2012, or about 863 million people, lived in slums. The proportion of urban population living in slums was highest in Sub-Saharan Africa (61.7 per cent), followed by South Asia (35 per cent), Southeast Asia (31 per cent), East Asia (28.2 per cent),West Asia (24.6 per cent), Oceania (24.1 per cent), Latin America and the Caribbean (23.5 per cent), and North Africa (13.3 per cent). Among individual countries, the proportion of urban residents living in slum areas in 2009 was highest in the Central African Republic (95.9 per cent). Between 1990 and 2010, the percentage of people living in slums dropped, even as the total urban population increased. The world's largest slum area is in Mexico City. Slums were common in the United States and Europe before the early twentieth century. New York City is believed to have created the world's first slum, named the points in 1825, as it evolved into a large urban settlement. Slums are often associated with Victorian Britain, particularly in industrial, northern English towns, lowland Scottish towns and Dublin City in Ireland. Engels described these British neighborhoods as *"cattle-sheds for human beings."* In France, slums were widespread in Paris and all urban areas in nineteenth century, many of which continued through first half of twentieth century. Rio de Janeiro documented its first slum in 1920 census. By the 1960s, over 33 per cent of population of Rio lived in slums, 45 per cent of Mexico City and Ankara, 65 per cent of Algiers, 35 per cent of Caracas, 25 per cent of Lima and Santiago, 15 per cent of Singapore. By 1980, in various cities and towns of Latin America alone, there were nearly 25,000 slums.[7]

Kibera is the largest slum in Nairobi, and the largest urban slum in Africa. Nairobi, where Kibera is located, is a city that was founded in 1899 when Uganda Railway line was built, thereby creating a need for its headquarters and British colonial offices. Asia's largest slum, Dharavi, lies on prime property right in the middle of India's financial capital, Mumbai (Bombay). It is home to more than a million people. Many are second-generation residents, whose parents moved in years ago. Dharavi also has a large number of thriving small-scale industries that produce embroidered garments, export quality leather goods, pottery and plastic. Most of these products are made in tiny manufacturing units spread across the slum and are sold in domestic as well as international markets. The annual turnover of business here is estimated to be more than $650m (£350m) a year. The state Government has plans to redevelop Dharavi and transform it into a modern township, complete with proper housing and shopping complexes, hospitals and schools.[8]

Slum Areas in India

Newly released census data shows families living in slums have a far better child sex ratio than the urban Indian average. Over a third of India's slum dwellers live in unrecognised slums. Over 65 million people live in slums, up from 52 million in 2001, but slum populations have grown slower than the average urban population over the last decade. The average household living in a slum is no larger than an average urban Indian household, with 4.7 family members. The child sex ratio (0-6 years) of an average slum household is 922 girls for every 1,000 boys, compared to 905 for urban India. Scheduled Castes (SCs) are over-represented in slums, with 1 out of every five slums residents belonging to SC, compared to just over one out of 10 for urban India as a whole. The proportion of SCs living in slums has risen over the last decade. Scheduled Castes in slums have far better sex ratios than other urban communities. Both men and women living in slums participate at a higher rate in the workforce than the urban average, even though fewer have employment through the year. The data shows that of the three types, identified slums have the largest sub-set of slum population, indicating that over a third of India's official slum population does not have official status as a slum, or access to legal protection and municipal services. With over 11 million of its residents in slums, Maharashtra has the highest slum population; 4.6 million of them in identified slums. Andhra Pradesh follows with over 10 million in slums, and West Bengal and Uttar Pradesh have over 6 million slum residents each. Over 1 million of Delhi's 1.7 million slum residents live in 'identified' slums.[9]

India's slum population will surge to 104 million by 2017 or around nine per cent of the total projected national population of 1.28 billion that year. According to data provided in Parliament, Maharashtra, Uttar Pradesh, Andhra Pradesh and Madhya Pradesh will host the largest chunks of India's slum population. The government offered a projection of the slum population on the basis of the Pranab Sen Committee report submitted in 2010. The committee's previous projection of slum population in 2011 was 93 million, or 7 percent of a total population of 1.21 billion. The census of 2011 recorded 1.3 crore urban slum households. So, if a household is estimated at five members, the urban slum population would be around 65 million. These 65 million figures are considerably lower than the Sen Committee's projection of 93 million slum dwellers in 2011 (based on the 2001 census). The 2011 census shows the problem is growing as it indicates the percentage of people living in slums in smaller cities with a population of less than a million is rising. While 62 per cent people in these cities are slum dwellers, it is 38 per cent in all million-plus cities that include mega metros like Delhi and Mumbai. Census data also shows how a large section of the urban population lives in slums in the four metropolitan cities as high as 41.3 per cent in Greater Mumbai, 29.6 per cent in Kolkata, 28 per cent in Chennai and about 15 per cent in Delhi.[10]

Over 70 per cent of slum households get their water from a tap but just half get water inside their homes. Over 90 per cent get electricity and most use LPG for cooking; 70 per cent have a TV and 10 per cent even a computer. The census data seems to indicate that the *"more cell phones than toilets"* line might be wrong for urban India: two out of three slum households have a toilet within the premises, while slightly fewer have a mobile phone. More than one in five urban households in Andhra Pradesh, Chhatisgarh, Madhya Pradesh, Odisha, West Bengal and Maharashtra are lives in a slum. In absolute terms, Maharashtra has the highest number of slum blocks of any state over 21,000 out of a total of just over one lakh for the whole country. Over a third of India's slum population lives in its 46 million-plus cities. Of the metros, Mumbai has the highest proportion of slum-dwelling households (41.3 per cent of its population). Kolkata is next at nearly 30 per cent with Chennai not far behind. Delhi has 14.6 per cent of its households living in slums while Bangalore is the best off of the five metros at less than 10 per cent. Among all million-plus cities, Vishakhapatnam has the highest proportion of slums (44.1 per cent of households). However, Census authorities were treating with skepticism the unexplained spurt in slum populations across cities in Andhra Pradesh.[11]

The NSSO report on urban slums doesn't swell to the Maharashtrian pride. The state, one of India's fastest growing historically is home to 7,723 of the country's 33,510 slums or 23 per cent of all slum habitations in the country, making it home to the largest number of slums in India. The number in percentage terms (29 per cent) is even higher if one accounts for non-notified slums. The state also has the distinction of having the highest number (38 per cent) of slum households of urban India. Ironically, Maharashtra has amongst the most progressive laws on slums which have become a reference point for many other acts being drafted in the rest of the country say experts. Eviction of slum dwellers is prohibited in the state, unless alternative accommodation is provided to the ousted. The state, has enacted at least a dozen policies and programmes to look into the issue of slum rehabilitation, but a lot of these have been hijacked by the corrupt nexus of builders-politicians and bureaucrats, rendering them ineffective.[12]

The financial capital of India known as Mumbai is home to estimate 6.5 million slum people. Nearly half of Mumbai's population lives in small shacks surrounded by open sewers. Nearly 55 per cent of Mumbai's population lives in Slum areas. After Mumbai, Delhi has the second largest slum population in India. Nearly 1.8 million people lives in slum areas in Delhi. These people are mostly unemployed or daily wage workers who cannot even afford basic necessities of life. According to recent estimates, Maharashtra, Uttar Pradesh, Andhra Pradesh and Madhya Pradesh will be having largest share of slum population in India by 2017. These states are already home to a large number of slum population which mostly lives in and around urban areas. By 2017, Maharashtra will be home to more than 20 million of slum population in India followed by Uttar Pradesh, Andhra Pradesh and Madhya Pradesh. It is estimated that by 2017, India's total slum population will be 104 million.[13]

Effects of Slum

The rapid urbanisation in conjugation with industrialisation has resulted in the growth of slums. Shortage of land for housing, the high prices of land beyond the reach of urban poor and a large influx of rural migrants to the cities fuelling the development of slums. As in slums, houses are crammed in a little space; they are often prone to dangerous hazards like floods, water logging, fire etc. Extent of hazard is increased because of high population density. The slum areas of Delhi especially Yamuna-Pushta are affected by flood-water of Yamuna every year. The Kutcha houses of slums frequently catch fire in summer. Slums are not planned hence they lack basic amenities. Slums have invariably extreme unhygienic conditions. There are no toilets and people defecate in open. The poor living condition in slums affects the health of people mentally and physically. Water contamination is cause disease, like blood dysentery, diarrhoea, malaria, typhoid, jaundice etc. Socially, slums remain isolated from rest of the urban society and exhibit pathological social symptoms like drug abuse, alcoholism, crime, vandalism and other deviant behavior.[14]

Homeless International supports slum dwellers to improve their lives and find lasting solutions to urban poverty. According to them slum affects society in various ways. From gender inequality to climate change, living in a slum significantly impacts upon many lives. Through the community-led projects that Homeless International supports, slum dwellers have a say in the issues that matter to them and receive support to find lasting solutions. Women and girls often bear the brunt of problems associated with living in slums. Women and girls are burdened with fetching and carrying water over long distances, and caring for sick family member. Hazardous conditions in slums lead to the spread of deadly illness and disease. Illnesses like cholera, malaria and diarrhoea are prevalent in many slums. Many children living in slums are denied the chance to go to school. Social and cultural barriers deny slum dwellers the opportunity to complete their basic education.

Without a reliable income, people living in slums are unable to invest in improving their homes and living conditions, making it very difficult to move out of poverty. People living in city slums are often unrecognised and ignored by Governments, excluding them from city development plans, voting and full protection through the law. Migration from rural areas and other countries is the main driving force of expanding city slums. As a result, slum communities are made up of varied age groups, ethnic origins and languages. The lack of toilets and overcrowding in slums leaves people with little or no privacy. This problem is particularly acute for women, adolescent girls, young couples, and large families. The majority of people at risk of sea-level rise in developing countries are those living in slums. Low elevation coastal zones are predominantly urban and where the highest population densities are found. Slum dwellers and their organisations are often dependent on grant aid from foreign countries for their projects and to improve their settlements, particularly when they start to address problems.[15]

Rural-Urban Migration

Rural-urban migration is one of the causes attributed to the formation and expansion of slums. Agriculture, meanwhile, has also become higher yielding, less disease prone, less physically harsh and more efficient with tractors and other equipment. The proportion of people working in agriculture has declined by 30 per cent over the last 50 years, while global population has increased by 250 per cent. Many people move to urban areas primarily because cities promise more jobs, better schools for poor's children, and diverse income opportunities than subsistence farming in rural areas. Many cities, on the other hand, do not provide enough low-cost housing for a large number of rural-urban migrant workers. Some rural-urban workers cannot afford housing in cities and eventually settle down in only affordable slums. The formation of slums is closely linked to urbanisation. Urbanisation might also force some people to live in slums when it influences land use by transforming agricultural land into urban areas and increases land value. Lack of affordable low cost housing and poor planning encourages the supply side of slums.[16]

Conclusion

Slum is a heavily populated urban informal settlement characterised by substandard housing and squalor. Slums sprout and continue for a combination of demographic, social, economic, and political reasons. Common causes include rapid rural-to-urban migration, poor planning, economic stagnation and depression, poverty, high unemployment, informal economy, colonialism and segregation, politics, natural disasters and social conflicts. The formation of slums is closely linked to urbanisation. Lack of affordable low cost housing and poor planning encourages the supply side of slums. Some of the slums in today's world are a product of urbanisation brought by colonialism. Many slums grow because of growing informal economy which creates demand for workers. Urban poverty encourages the formation and demand for slums. Major natural disasters in poor nations often lead to migration of disaster-affected families from areas crippled by the disaster to unaffected areas, the creation of temporary tent city and slums, or expansion of existing slums. Slum areas are characterised by sub-standard housing structures. Slum dwellers usually experience a high rate of disease. In some slums, gender inequality increases women's risk of HIV/AIDS. Violence in slums involves both males and females. It has various forms including domestic violence, armed violence and threats from gangs and other groups.

REFERENCES

1. *Urban area (2014)*, Retrieved from http://en.wikipedia.org/wiki/Urban_area
2. See http://www.lifepaths360.com/index.php/the-advantages-and-disadvantages-of-urban-living-2175/
3. Tahera Akter, *Migration and living conditions in urban slums: implications for food security*, Retrieved from http://www.bdresearch.org.bd/home/attachments/article/174/Migration.and.living.conditions.in.urban.slums.pdf
4. *Slum*, Retrieved from http://en.wikipedia.org/wiki/Slum
5. *Slums: the causes*, Retrieved from http://www.youthxchange.net/main/ffB237_slums-d.asp
6. Giok Ling Ooi and Kai Hong Phua, *Urbanization and Slum Formation*, Retrieved from http://www.ncbi.nlm.nih.gov/pmc/articles/PMC1891640/
7. *Slum*, Retrieved from http://en.wikipedia.org/wiki/Slum
8. See http://news.bbc.co.uk/2/shared/spl/hi/world/06/dharavi_slum/html/dharavi_slum_intro.stm
9. *The Hindu (Oct 1, 2013)*. 65 million people live in slums in India, says census data, Retrieved from http://www.thehindu.com/todays-paper/tp-national/tp-newdelhi/65-million-people-live-in-slums-in-india-says-census-data/article5188234.ece

10. *The Times of India (Aug 20, 2013).* By 2017, India's slum population will rise to 104 million, Retrieved from http://timesofindia.indiatimes.com/india/By-2017-Indias-slum-population-will-rise-to-104-million/articleshow/21927474.cms
11. *The Times of India (Mar 22, 2013).* 17% of urban India lives in slums: Census, Retrieved from http://timesofindia.indiatimes.com/india/17-of-urban-India-lives-in-slums-Census/articleshow/19118219.cms
12. *Business Standard (May 17, 2013).* Why is Maharashtra India's slum capital? Retrieved from http://www.business-standard.com/article/current-affairs/why-is-maharashtra-india-s-slum-capital-113122600642_1.html
13. *Slum Population in India,* Retrieved from http://www.indiaonlinepages.com/population/slum-population-in-india.html
14. *Harmful impacts of slums on society and people living in it, Social windows in India*, Retrieved from http://inindiaaa.blogspot.in/2013/08/harmful-impacts-of-slums-on-society-and.html
15. *The impacts of slums, Homeless international,* Retrieved from http://www.homeless-international.org/About-Slums/impacts-of-slums
16. *Slum,* Retrieved from http://en.wikipedia.org/wiki/Slum

16

Migration

"Electronic aids, particularly domestic computers, will help the inner migration, the opting out of reality. Reality is no longer going to be the stuff out there, but the stuff inside your head. It's going to be commercial and nasty at the same time."

- J. G. Ballard

Introduction

Migration is the barometer of changing socio-economic and political conditions at the national and international levels. It is a sign of wide disparities in economic and social conditions between the origin and destination. Rural migration is the phenomenon that describes the movement of people from their villages to urban areas, usually in search of a better livelihood.[1] It occurs when the place of utility in a few locations becomes better than that of the present location. Migration is infact, a boon for industrial advancement. It is a blessing for jobless persons who spend their valuable time uselessly.[2]

Migration is often temporary or circular, and many migrants maintain links with their home countries. While migrants make important contributions to the economic prosperity of their host countries, the flow of financial, technological, social and human capital back to their countries of origin also is having a significant impact on poverty reduction and economic development. Remittances from migrants are a major source of capital for developing countries.[3]

What is Migration?

Migration can be defined as the movement of people between countries. It is the movement of animals from one place to another to avoid bad weather food or reproduce. According to the Oxford dictionary migration means movement of people to a new area or country in order to find work or better living conditions.[4] Migrant can be understood as *"any person who lives temporarily or permanently in a country where he or she was not born, and has acquired some significant social ties to this country."* The UN Convention on the Rights of Migrants defines a migrant worker as a *"person who is to be engaged, is engaged or has been engaged in a remunerated activity in a State of which he or she is not a national."*[5] Migration in general may be in the form of internal and international. International migration in general has become an extensive global phenomenon. Within the last decade at least, the number of people crossing borders has increased around six millions annually.[6]

Reasons of Migration

Urbanisation has been one of the dramatic global social transformations of the twentieth century. The propensity of migration is usually influenced by a combination of push-pull factors. People migrated to cities and towns because they are attracted by livelihood opportunities. Studies on migration have established a positive association between levels of infrastructural development of a region and the magnitude of out-migration. Regardless of skill, the migrated population can find diversified livelihood opportunities with various incomes in the towns and cities. Thus, the poor rural population considers migration a livelihood coping strategy.[7]

Though subsistence economies of the past have been noted for incidence of high birth rates, death rates etc. have been equally high due to heavy incidence of epedemics like Cholera, Small pox and high infantile mortality. The population of such economies was practically stagnant. Under such circumstances normally there arise no urge for the people to migrate. The deep rooted socio-economic class structure of an agrarian society has been operating as a powerful constraint on the migration of population. Various factors such as language barrier, predominance of agriculture as a source of livelihood, caste system and cohesiveness of village life etc. have in past, operated as powerful constraints.[8]

Global Perspectives

In general, human migration has occurred throughout history and began with the movements of the first human groups out of their origins in East Africa. In 2010, some 214 million people (three per cent of the world's population) lived outside their country of origin. The magnitude and complexity of international migration makes it an important force in development and a high-priority issue for both developing and developed countries. Internal migration within countries is also on the rise, as people move in response to inequitable distribution of resources, services and opportunities, or to escape violence, natural disaster or the increasing number of extreme weather events. The majority of migrants cross borders in search of better economic and social opportunities. Economic migrants are the world's fastest growing group of migrants. Globalisation has increased the mobility of labour, and a decline in fertility and working-age populations in many developed countries is leading to a rising demand for workers from abroad to sustain national economies. One of the most significant changes in migration patterns in the last half century is that more women are migrating than ever before. Migration is increasingly being perceived as a force that can contribute to development, and an integral aspect of the global development process.[9]

A majority of Canadians believe immigrants who are in the country illegally or after their visas expire should be deported, even if they have family ties in the country, a newly released Government poll shows. The number of illegal immigrants in Canada generally ranges from 35,000 to 120,000, i.e. a relatively small percentage of the national population when compared to 13 million in the United States.[10] There isn't much that happens to illegal immigrants, who are residing in Canada. In Toronto alone, there are tens of thousands of illegal immigrants who are working in construction jobs and other hard labour type professions. The Canadian Government is more concerned with the removal of war criminals and regular criminals to become preoccupied with illegal immigrants. As of right now, there isn't any laws such as those of the USA that affect illegal's in Canadian territory.[11] The number of illegal immigrants in Canada is expected to rise by 2015, according to Canada's Immigration News

Source (CICS). Over 190,000 immigrants arrived in Canada last year. Many of them are on a four-year-work-permit that is set to expire by April 2015. The number of temporary foreign workers in Canada has sharply increased from around 100,000 in 2002, to over 300,000 in 2013, and the new rule was an attempt to reduce over-dependence of Canadian employers on the Temporary Foreign Worker Programme to meet their permanent labor needs.[12]

Bihar has been experiencing a large scale migration of rural population to different industrial towns and rural areas of Bengal, Maharashtra, Delhi, Punjab and Haryana. These rural labourers have also shifted to developing states of Assam, Orissa and Arunachal Pradesh. Unlike other states of Gujarat, Kerala, Tamil Nadu and Bengal the migration of rural labourers of Bihar are mostly confined to different urban centres inside the country. Migration of rural labourers of Bihar is both of permanent as well as seasonal in nature. The seasonal migration of Bihari labourers in Assam is mostly categorised as weavers, bricklin workers, rice godown workers, while permanent migration includes workers who get regular work throughout the year and acquire handsome income from the work. Such workers are washermen, shoemakers, hawkers, kerosene sellers, rickshawallas, thellawallas, bag carrier's railway porters.[13]

The number of immigrants in the US illegally edged up to 11.7 million in 2012 from 11.3 million in 2009, the Pew Research Center found. The number of illegal immigrants had declined over several years from a high of 12.2 million in 2007. The recent growth is largely driven by immigrants from outside of Mexico. Labour demand in the US is still slack and wages are eroding, whereas there are jobs in Mexico and wages are slowly rising as labour force growth there decelerates. Immigrants from Mexico now make up 52 per cent of illegal immigrants in the US, down from 57 per cent in 2007, Pew estimated. Meanwhile, illegal immigration from countries other than Mexico rose to a record 5.65 million in 2012, although that figure is preliminary. In the meantime, President Barack Obama has used his executive authority to grant provisional legal status to some undocumented immigrants brought to the US as children.[14]

Australia gradually became a promising land with the vastness of land in contrast to rareness of labour. Around 1970, there was a fundamental change in immigration policy. Millions of migrants and refugees came to Australia during the 1970s which resulted in the issue of a policy of multiculturalism. Australia and Switzerland, with about a quarter of their population born outside the country, are the two countries with the highest proportion of immigrants in the world. New South Wales has the largest population, and the largest foreign born population. Victoria, the second most populous state, also has the second largest number of overseas-born persons. Queensland had 695,525 overseas-born residents, and attracted the greatest proportion of persons born in Papua New Guinea (52.4 per cent) and New Zealand (38.2 per cent).[15]

Migration in South Asia

Internal migration has become both a major policy concern and a subject of a heated public debate in Bangladesh. It is undeniable that migration is major a feature of Bangladesh's recent history. Internal migration has generally been thought of as an urbanization phenomenon. However, most of the existing literature identifies economic forces as underpinning the strongest population movements, and especially in driving migration to the core urban centres of Dhaka and Chittagong. An equally significant development has been the growth of slum conditions in urban localities, even within the core cities, together with considerable levels of unemployment and under-employment. Clearly, the promise of opportunities and better lives has not been realised in full. Yet, in-urban flows have continued apace.[16] The issue of illegal immigration from Bangladesh is changing the demography of West Bengal and the earlier the country wakes up to the fact, the better for it. Compassion can never be an issue across borders unless persecution in the country of origin is decisively proved. Then, too, immigration may be allowed only on the merits of the case. Here, India is facing a situation where immigration is taking place unhindered and without reports of large scale persecution in Bangladesh.

Further, most of those who are entering India illegally are from the majority community in Bangladesh. They are escaping from lack of economic opportunity and India cannot allow her to bear the burden of such people.[17] Assam shares an international border with Bangladesh and has been plagued with the problem of illegal immigration by Bangladeshi Muslims for the past four decades. The Governor of Assam, in a secret communique to the central Government in 2005, revealed that *"upto 6,000 Bangladeshis enter Assam every day."* According to conservative estimates, India is host to around ten million illegal Bangladeshi immigrants. Assam itself is inhabited by around five million illegal immigrants. The Indian polity, with its penchant for encouraging illegal immigration for the sake of vote-bank politics, prefers the *'ostrich head in sand'* approach to this issue.[18]

Migration: Africa to Europe

There is significant migration from Africa to Europe. As of 2007, there were an estimated seven million African migrants living in OECD countries. Some of this migration is illegal. In Australia, the number of immigrants from Africa has grown substantially since the 1990s, mostly concentrated in Sydney, Melbourne, and Perth.[19] Southern Europe is all-too familiar with irregular migration from North African countries such as Morocco, Algeria, and Tunisia. Since the early 1990s, thousands of North Africans have attempted to cross the Mediterranean to reach Spain and Italy. These migrants come from an increasingly diverse array of countries and regions, such as Senegal, the Gambia, Sierra Leone, Liberia, Mali, Côte d'Ivoire, Ghana, and Nigeria as well as the Democratic Republic of Congo, Cameroon, Sudan, the Horn of Africa, and even Asia. According to different estimates, between 65,000 and 120,000 sub-Saharan Africans enter the Maghreb (Mauritania, Morocco, Tunisia, Algeria, and Libya) yearly, of which 70 to 80 per cent are believed to migrate through Libya and 20 to 30 per cent through Algeria and Morocco. Several tens of thousands (not hundreds of thousands, as media coverage might suggest) of sub-Saharan Africans try to cross the Mediterranean each year.[20]

Sub-Saharan Africans migrate to North Africa, Europe, North America, and beyond. The research offered here focuses generally on two aspects of sub-Saharan migration: the outcome for these migrants and their children once they have settled in their countries of destination, the United States among them, and the roles that diasporas and development policies can play in the economic improvement of these African nations.[21] The Africa Migration Project was undertaken jointly by the African Development Bank and the World Bank to improve understanding of migration and remittances in Sub-Saharan Africa, including their magnitude, causes, and impacts on poverty reduction, with a view to generating informed policy recommendations.[22]

Migration in India

Opportunities in urban areas for employment, education, have been a pull factor attracting migrants from rural to urban areas and from smaller towns and cities to larger urban areas. There is also migration in the opposite direction from urban to rural areas due to various reasons. Out of about 98 million, total intra-state and inter-state migrants in the country during last decade, 61 million have moved to rural areas and 36 million to urban areas. Migration stream out of rural areas (73 million) to another rural areas was quite high (53 million) in comparison to from rural to urban areas (20 million). About 6 million migrants went to rural areas from urban areas. On the basis of net migrants by last residence during the past decade, i.e., the difference between in-migration and out-migration, in each state, Maharashtra stands at the top of the list with 2.3 million net migrants, followed by Delhi (1.7 million), Gujarat (0.68 million) and Haryana (0.67 million) as per census. Uttar Pradesh (-2.6 million) and Bihar (-1.7 million) were the two states with largest number of net migrants migrating out of the state.[23]

People have been migrating from the northern Indian state of Bihar for decades. In the time of the Green Revolution in Punjab, Biharis left for seasonal labor in the high-yield variety agricultural areas of north India. The work was more consistent, the wages were higher, and the agricultural system in Bihar was meanwhile becoming less prosperous. More Biharis began to leave their rural homes, moving to major cities, such as Delhi and Mumbai. Children came too. Leaving behind their homes for a more promising future, they came alongside families, with friends, or even alone.[24] The rural poor from the downtrodden and backward communities and backward regions such as Bihar, Orissa, Uttar Pradesh travel to far distances seeking employment at the lowest rungs in construction of roads, irrigation projects, commercial and residential complexes etc. During the last ten years, it came into notice through different reports and statistics that the agricultural sector and rural inhabitants in many regions across the country have suffered from continuous neglect and even outright discrimination. Studies aptly indicate that the costs and risks of migration are heavy, including the risk of disease, injury and not being able to send children to school. Given a choice, migrants would not sacrifice their children's future or their own health, but they are compelled to do so because they cannot look after themselves or their children properly when they migrate.[25]

The phenomenon of migration is believed to have taken roots in the aftermath of severe drought of the 1960s. Today thousands of people across the length and breadth of the region leave their native villages in search of food and employment. Most end up as bonded labourers being paid minimal daily wages. Alienation of land, labour and produce is the driving force for migration.

Rural-Urban Migration

Rural-urban migration usually leads to a loss of necessary manpower in the rural areas to work on the farm lands. It also leads to congestion in the urban centres, thus higher unemployment level, poor housing situations and an increase in crime levels. On the other hand, increased man power in urban centres provides cheap labour to the industries in these areas.[26] Causes of rural to urban migration are generally rooted in social or economic situations. Many people will migrate from a rural area to an urban area in search of work or income. People will also migrate to urban areas from rural areas because of a lack of available farmland. This makes it impossible to continue living from the land in certain areas. People will move from rural to urban areas in search of better schools, medical care, or housing for their families.[27] Rural-urban migration has long been associated with economic development and growth in the economic literature. In particular, Todaro and Harris-Todaro-type probabilistic models that examine migration have concentrated on the expected wage disparities between rural and urban (formal) labor markets as a driving force behind migration decision. These models, which are static and partial equilibrium in nature, have virtually ignored the cost-of-living differentials across regions that arise from the presence of regional non-traded goods.[28]

One of the factors that are responsible for rural-urban migration is lack of or inadequate social amenities and facilities in the rural areas. These include pipe borne water, electricity, good roads, hospitals, schools, recreational centres (like Stadium, Zoo, Amusement park) among others. Inadequate jobs in the rural areas also make many youths to migrate to the urban areas that can provide better opportunities for them. Rural-urban migration has negative consequences. It leads to overpopulation of the urban areas thus encouraging crime in the society. Those who engage in crime prefer the urban areas being turgid with wealthy individuals.[29]

Effects of Migration

The villagers tend to migrate along with their families hoping that they might be able to employ their children in cities. This is not only exposing the children to the hazards of child labor but also leading to children dropping out of school during the academic year which shows how the migration was directly connected to lack of education for children.[30] The remittance from migrants is likely to raise rural incomes and consumption, which add to the productive investment for the development and diversification of agriculture activities and relieve the poverty of their family living behind. It is also used productively for conspicuous consumption or building an excessive degree capital intensity into an agriculture, with diverse effect on employment. It increases the resources without the need for any effort on the part of the recipient. In some cases, remittances can compensate for the negative impact of out-migration by allowing hired labour to replace the agricultural labour force lost. In others, remittances may reduce agricultural labour and production, for example by increasing non-farm activities and limiting people's willingness to take on low-paid agricultural activities. Migration has impact on farms' technical efficiency, and migrant households invest more in productivity-enhancing and time-saving farm technologies for crop production. Although migration has fostered the adoption of improved technology, migrant households do not show better agricultural performance than non-migrant households, because a reduction in the labour effort tends to offset any investment and improved technologies from remittance receipts.[31]

Remedial Measures

Food processing and value addition are other grey areas which can create a boom in the employment. Our country has not utilised this huge untapped potential. Food processing can reduce the huge losses of Rs 55,000 crores in food grains, fruits and vegetables. Value addition can be done in food grains, fruits, vegetables, dairy products, meat, poultry, fish and medicinal and aromatic plants. There are number of diversified ventures in agriculture which are suited to almost every region and economic strata of the population. Food processing Industry is employment intensive. The Central government has launched various schemes to engage the unemployed agricultural graduates. The scheme of agri-clinic and agri-business centres was launched in 2002 as a follow-up of finance minister's budget speech for 2001. The objective of the scheme is to provide fee-based extension and other services to the farming community and avail self-employment opportunities for agriculture graduates. Trained graduates are expected to set up agri-clinic and agri-business centres with the help of bank finance. The scheme is being implemented with the help of small farmers agri-business consortium and national bank for agriculture and rural development. The training is open for graduates in agriculture and any subject allied to agriculture like horticulture, sericulture, veterinary sciences, forestry, dairy, poultry farming, fisheries, etc.

The Ministry of Micro, Small and Medium enterprises supplements the efforts of state governments by implementing the prime minister's employment generation programme, a credit-linked subsidy programme since 2008-09, through khadi and village industries commission throughout the country for availing self-employment opportunities through establishment of micro enterprises including rural and agro industries by organising traditional artisans and unemployed youth, helping in preventing their migration besides increasing their earning capacity. There are number of examples in different states like Maharashtra, Kerala, Rajasthan, Jharkhand, Gujarat and Himachal Pradesh which are running successful ventures which are helping in augmenting the income of the people in rural areas. In Maharashtra, people in the rural areas have formed

Maharashtra state agri and rural tourism. There are 150 agri-tourism centres in the state and the centres are running without any government help. However, the state government has subsidised the agri-tourism activities.[32]

One of the significant objectives of the MGNERA is to arrest out-migration of unskilled, landless labour force from the rural areas to urban areas by ensuring up to 100 days of wage employment within their native jurisdiction so that the guaranteed wage employment can be judiciously and rationally utilised by the landless peasants during lean seasons. This will reduce the problems of excessive population pressures in Indian cities as surplus rural labour will find employment in their own villages. MGNERA will also have an impact on permanent migration trends. While it is difficult to ascertain what the exact impact will be, one can assume that the created infrastructure and the increased activity in the rural economy due to increased purchasing power will lead to higher rates of permanent job creation and thus mitigating the urgency to migrate. The MGNERA income in wages has two dimensions. The families owning small agricultural land insufficient to generate food security for the whole of the year or create additional surplus of cash to meet other basic needs, families are supplementing agricultural income with wage income of MGNERA.[33]

Conclusion

Migration primarily occurs due to disparities in regional development. The causes of migration are usually explained by using two broad categories, namely, push and pull factors. the lack of exact official data on migration is a matter that should be corrected as soon as possible as it is quite important to quantify this as accurately as possible as rural-urban migration can become quite a problem for both the source and the destination areas. Migration has continued under the form of both voluntary migration within one's region, country, or beyond and involuntary migration. People who migrate into a territory are called immigrants, while at the departure point they are called emigrants. According to the International Organisation for Migration's World Migration Report 2010, the number of international migrants was estimated at 220 million in 2013. Migration for work in the 21st century has become a popular way for individuals from impoverished developing countries to obtain sufficient income for survival.

REFERENCES

1. Dr Jamshed Nasir, Mahvish Anjum and Ullas T, *Migration of cottage industry workers (a Case Study of ambedkarnagar district), Kurukshetra,* February 2012, Retrieved from http://yojana.gov.in/cms(S(m2mzef55ipvmrc45ehppdef4))/pdf/Kurukshetra%5CEnglish%5C2012/February.pdf
2. Dr Kumar Amarendra Narain, *Impact of rural migration of agricultural labours of Bihar in Assam (a Case study of Cachar district), Kurukshetra*, February 2012, See http://yojana.gov.in/cms/(S(m2mzef55ipvmrc45ehppdef4))/pdf/Kurukshetra%5CEnglish%5C2012/February.pdf
3. See http://www.unfpa.org/pds/migration.html
4. See http:// www.oxforddictionaries.com/definition/english/migration
5. See http://www.unesco.org/most/migration/glossary_migrants.htm
6. K. S. Farid, L. Mozumdar, M. S. Kabir and K. B. Hossain, Trends in international migration and remittance flows: Case of Bangladesh, *J. Bangladesh Agril. Univ.* 7(2): 387–394, 2009, Retrieved from http://www.banglajol.info/index.php/JBAU/article/viewFile/4751/3785
7. M. Z. Hossain, *Rural-Urban Migration in Bangladesh: A Micro-Level Study,* Retrieved from http://archive.iussp.org/Brazil2001/s20/S28_P02 _Hossain.pdf
8. Dr Kumar Amarendra Narain, Impact of rural migration of agricultural labours of Bihar in Assam (a Case study of Cachar district), *Kurukshetra,* February 2012, See http://yojana.gov.in/cms/(S(m2mzef55ipvmrc45ehppdef4))/pdf/Kurukshetra%5CEnglish%5C2012/February.pdf
9. See http://www.unfpa.org/pds/migration.html
10. *Canadians want illegal immigrants deported: poll,* Retrieved from http://www.nationalpost.com/news/story.html?id=f86690ed-a2ed-447c-8be8-21ba5a3dd922

11. See http://www.ask.com/question/what-happens-to-illegal-immigrants-in-canada
12. *Illegal Immigration Is Expected To Rise in Canada By 2015*, Retrieved from http://ca.ibtimes.com/articles/430779/20130202/immigration-canada-new-rule.htm
13. Dr. Kumar Amarendra Narain, Impact of rural migration of agricultural labours of Bihar in Assam (a Case study of Cachar district), *Kurukshetra*, February 2012, See http://yojana.gov.in/cms/(S(m2mzef55ipvmrc45ehppdef4))/pdf/Kurukshetra%5CEnglish%5C2012/February.pdf
14. *Decline in illegal immigration to US ends amid recovery*, Retrieved from http://www.bbc.com/news/world-us-canada-24214980
15. *Immigration to Australia*, Retrieved from http://en.wikipedia.org/wiki/Immigration_to_Australia
16. Richard Marshall and Shibaab Rahman, *Internal Migration in Bangladesh: Character, Drivers and Policy Issues*, Retrieved from http://www.bd. undp.org/content/dam/bangladesh/docs/Publications/Pub-2013/Internal% 20Migration%20in%20Bangladesh%20UNDP%20Final.pdf
17. *Illegal Immigration from Bangladesh is Alive, Kicking and Hurting India,* See more at: http://www.theindianrepublic.com/tbp/illegal-immigration-bangladesh-alive-kicking-hurting-india-100034836.html#sthash.mJ RLVdE8.dpuf
18. *Illegal immigration from Bangladesh has turned Assam explosive*, Retrieved from http://www.niticentral.com/2012/10/31/illegal-immigration-from-bangladesh-has-turned-assam-explosive-16664.html
19. *Emigration from Africa*, Retrieved from http://en.wikipedia.org/wiki/Emigration_from_Africa
20. *Trans-Saharan Migration to North Africa and the EU: Historical Roots and Current Trends*, Retrieved from http://www.migrationpolicy.org/article/trans-saharan-migration-north-africa-and-eu-historical-roots-and-current-trends
21. See http://www.migrationpolicy.org/regions/africa-sub-saharan
22. *Africa Migration Project,* Retrieved from http://econ.worldbank.org/WBSITE/EXTERNAL/EXTDEC/EXTDECPROSPECTS0,,contentMDK:21681739~pagePK:64165401~piPK:64165026~theSitePK:476883,00.html

23. See http://censusindia.gov.in/Census_And_You/migrations.aspx
24. *Rural-Urban Migration and Agricultural Transformation in India: Observing the Impact on Childhood Migration from Bihar to New Delhi*, Retrieved from http://www.studentpulse.com/articles/769/rural-urban-migration-and-agricultural-transformation-in-india-observing-the-impact-on-childhood-migration-from-bihar-to-new-delhi
25. Anupam Hazra, Rural India: Still floating towards cities, *Kurukshetra,* February 2012, see http://yojana.gov.in/cms/(S(m2mzef55ipvmrc45 ehppdef4))/pdf/Kurukshetra%5CEnglish%5C2012/February.pdf
26. See http://www.ask.com/question/what-are-the-effects-of-rural-urban-migration
27. See http://www.ask.com/question/causes-of-rural-to-urban-migration
28. *Rural-urban Migration and Economic Growth in Developing Countries*, Retrieved from http://ideas.repec.org/p/red/sed004/241.html
29. See http://voices.yahoo.com/causes-effects-rural-urban-migration-4933406.html?cat=6\
30. Dr S.M Jawed Akthar and N.P. Abdul Azeez, Rural Employment Guarantee Programme and Migration, *Kurukshetra,* February 2012, Retrieved from http://yojana.gov.in/cms/(S(m2mzef55 ipvmrc45ehppdef4))/pdf/Kurukshetra%5CEnglish%5C2012/February.pdf
31. Gaurav Turkhade, Migration: Impact and Relevance of remittance on rural areas, *Kurukshetra*, February 2012, Retrieved from http://yojana.gov.in/cms/(S(m2mzef55ipvmrc45ehppdef4))/pdf/Kurukshetra%5CEnglish% 5C2012/February.pdf
32. Dr Harender Raj Gautam, Can we check migration from Rural India? *Kurukshetra,* February 2012, Retrieved from http://yojana.gov.in/cms/(S(m2mzef55ipvmrc45ehppdef4))/pdf/Kurukshetra%5CEnglish%5C2012/February.pdf
33. Dr S.M Jawed Akthar and N.P. Abdul Azeez, Rural Employment Guarantee Programme and Migration, *Kurukshetra,* February 2012, Retrieved from http://yojana.gov.in/cms/(S(m2mzef55 ipvmrc45ehppdef4))/pdf/Kurukshetra%5CEnglish%5C2012/February.pdf

17

Terrorism

"In many parts of the world, especially Pakistan and Afghanistan, terrorism, war and conflict stop children to go to their schools. We are really tired of these wars. Women and children are suffering."

- Malala Yousafzai

Introduction

Terrorism has been described variously as both a tactic and strategy; a crime and a holy duty; a justified reaction to oppression and an inexcusable abomination. Terrorism comes from the French word terrorisme, and originally referred specifically to state terrorism as practiced by the French government during the 1793–94 Reigns Of Terror. The United States Department of Defense defines terrorism as *"the calculated use of unlawful violence or threat of unlawful violence to inculcate fear; intended to coerce or to intimidate Governments or societies in the pursuit of goals that are generally political, religious, or ideological."*

Terrorism is a criminal act that influences an audience beyond the immediate victim. The strategy of terrorists is to commit acts of violence that draws the attention of the local populace, the government, and the world to their cause. The terrorists plan their attack to obtain greatest publicity, choosing targets that symbolise what they oppose[1] Terrorism is as old as the Roman Empire and it existed in some form or the other, be it the Zealots in Judea or the Assassins in the 11th to 13th century with religion being a strong motivating factor behind terrorist activities until the French Revolution. Following the Second World War, there was a shift in the nature and locale of terrorist activities around the world. The focus of terrorist activities shifted from Europe to the Middle East, Africa and Asia with the emergence of various nationalistic and anti-colonial groups in these regions, notably in Israel, Kenya, Cyprus, Algeria, Palestine and Malaya.

Terrorism carried out in the name of the faith has long been a feature of human affairs. The histories of people, civilisations, nations, and empires are replete with examples of extremist true believers who engage in violence to promote their belief system. Some religious terrorists are inspired by defensive motives, others seek to ensure the predominance of their faith, and others are motivated by an aggressive amalgam of these tendencies. Religious terrorism can be communal, genocidal, nihilistic, or revolutionary. It can be committed by lone wolves, clandestine cells, large dissident movements, or governments. And, depending on one's perspective, there is often debate about whether the perpetrators should be classified as terrorists or religious freedom fighters.[2] Terrorism is the principal threat to global and national security in the post-11 September world. The attacks on New York and Washington D.C. demonstrated that worldwide terrorist organisations are operating with increasing complexity, audacity and lethality. Terrorism is evolving into a significantly more menacing threat that uses technology to access financial reserves, disseminate instructions, and propagate its vitriol. Likewise, terrorist objectives have evolved from publicity ploys to deliberate attempts to inflict mass casualties.[3]

Types of Terrorism

Researchers in the United States began to distinguish different types of terrorism in the 1970s, following a decade in which both domestic and international groups flourished.

1. *State Terrorism:* It can be argued that states can be terrorists. States can use force or the threat of force, without declaring war, to terrorise citizens and achieve a political goal. Germany under Nazi rule has been described in this

way. It has also been argued that states participate in international terrorism, often by proxy.

2. *Bio-terrorism:* Bio-terrorism refers to the intentional release of toxic biological agents to harm and terrorise civilians, in the name of a political or other cause. The U.S. Center for Disease Control has classified the viruses, bacteria and toxins that could be used in an attack.
3. *Cyber terrorism:* Cyber terrorists use information technology to attack civilians and draw attention to their cause. This may mean that they use information technology, such as computer systems or telecommunications, as a tool to orchestrate a traditional attack.
4. *Eco terrorism:* It is a recently coined term describing violence in the interests of environmentalism. In general, environmental extremists sabotage property to inflict economic damage on industries or actors they see as harming animals or the natural environment.
5. *Nuclear terrorism:* It refers to a number of different ways nuclear materials might be exploited as a terrorist tactic. These include attacking nuclear facilities, purchasing nuclear weapons, or building nuclear weapons or otherwise finding ways to disperse radioactive materials
6. *Narco terrorism:* It has had several meanings since its coining in 1983. It once denoted violence used by drug traffickers to influence governments or prevent government efforts to stop the drug trade.[4]

Internet and Terrorism

The Internet and the advent of the World Wide Web in particular, have significantly increased the opportunities for terrorists to secure publicity. This can take the form of historical information, profiles of leaders, manifestos, etc. Until the advent of the Internet, terrorists' hopes of winning publicity for their causes and activities depended on attracting the attention of television, radio, or the print media. Numerous terrorist groups request funds directly from Web surfers who visit their sites. Such requests may take the form of general statements underlining the organisations need for money, more often than not however requests are more direct urging supporters to donate immediately and supplying either bank account details or an Internet payment option. The Internet facilitates terrorist financing in a number of other ways besides direct solicitation via terrorist Web sites. Terrorists have also infiltrated branches of existing charities to raise funds clandestinely. Many such organisations provide the humanitarian services advertised: feeding, clothing, and educating the poor and illiterate, and providing medical care for the sick. The Internet allows not only for intra-group communication, but also inter-group connections. The Internet has the ability to connect not only members of the same terrorist organisations but also members of different groups.

As terrorist groups come under increasing pressure from law enforcement, they have been forced to evolve and become more decentralised. Online recruitment by terrorist organisations is said to be widespread. Fritz, Harris, Kolb, Larich, and Stocker provide the example of an Iranian site that boasts an application for suicide bombers guaranteeing that the new 'martyr' will take seventy relatives with him into heaven. Terrorists can also use the Internet to learn about antiterrorism measures. Gabriel Weimann suggests that a simple strategy like conducting word searches of online newspapers and journals could allow a terrorist to study the means designed to counter attacks, or the vulnerabilities of these measures. Hackers also took to the Net in the aftermath of terror attacks, some to voice their rage, others to applaud the attackers.[5]

Global Perspectives

In recent times Asia has taken the lead in world incidences of terrorism. By 2000, Asia already accounted for 75 per cent of all terrorism casualties worldwide. With the world's fastest-growing markets, fastest-rising military expenditures, and most serious hot spots (including the epicenter of international terrorism), Asia holds the key to the future global order. Much of Asia's terrorist violence is concentrated in its southern belt, which in the past decade emerged as the international hub of terrorism. This southern part of Asia, encompassing Afghanistan, Pakistan, Uzbekistan, Tajikistan, Chinese- ruled Xinjiang and Tibet, India,

Nepal, Sri Lanka, Bangladesh, and Burma, is wrecked by terrorist, insurgent, and separatist violence in a manner unmatched elsewhere in the world.[6]

The Middle East remains a major center of global terrorism that involves every country in the region. Active violence in Israel, Gaza, Lebanon, West Bank, and Iraq over the past four years has had a major impact on the region. Al-Qa'ida and its offshoots have been highly active, as well as various Islamic groups in Gaza and Iraq including Hamas and the Islamic State of Iraq/Mujahideen Shura Council. The Kurdistan Workers Party (PKK) also remained active in southern Turkey. Terrorist activity in Gaza was dominated by Hamas. Gaza had the highest rate of hostages taken than any other Middle Eastern country. Terrorist activity in the Southern Gulf region was minimal compared to the rest of the Middle East. The majority of attacks occurred in Yemen with al-Qa'ida in the Arab Peninsula (AQAP) as the largest known operative.

The whole of South Asia- India, Nepal, Bangladesh, Sri Lanka, Maldives, and Pakistan, is going through internal unrest and upheavals due to insurgency movements, ethnic conflicts and religious fundamentalism. Such unrest have a history of crossing national boundaries and leading to inter-state tensions.[7] Pakistan is confronted with two broad categories of terrorism namely internal and external. The banned organisations like Tahreek-e-Taliban and Lashker-e-Jhangvi, Mehdi Militia etc., have the means to create instability in Pakistan. The communal/regional cards like Sindhi, Balochi, Pathan, Saraike and Mohajir etc. seem to be dominating over the concept of nationalism which could be the essence of their strength. Pakistan has experienced separatist terrorism in the past in Khyber Pakhtunkhwa and Balochistan and the same is still going on in Balochistan currently. The province of Balochistan has experienced intermittent gorilla war since many decades. Religious extremism is responsible for creating division on religious grounds and is responsible for violence against followers of other religions. The communal violence in Gojra in August 2009 is the example of religious extremism.[8]

Pakistani authorities have long had ties to domestic militant groups that help advance the country's core foreign policy interests, namely in connection with Afghanistan and India. Concerns about Pakistan's commitment to counterterrorism heightened in May 2011, when U.S. commandos killed al-Qaeda mastermind Osama bin Laden at a compound not far from Islamabad. Leadership elements of al-Qaeda and the Afghan Taliban have made Pakistan's semi-autonomous tribal areas their home, where they often work with a wide variety of Islamist insurgent groups like the Haqqani Network. Supporters of the Afghan Taliban who sought refuge in Pakistan's tribal areas morphed into a distinct entity following the Pakistani army's initial incursion into the semiautonomous region in 2002.[9] The relationship between Afghanistan and the opium poppy has existed for thousands of years. The loose relationship between terrorist organisations, violence, decentralised governance, and poverty that existed prior to the Global War on Terrorism (GWOT) in Afghanistan, has coalesced into a truly narco-terrorism-driven system.[10] The patterns in Sri Lanka were driven largely by an ethnic civil war, and again raise questions about counting terrorist acts by states versus non-state actors. The patterns in Bangladesh reflect the continuing patterns of terrorism common in many poor countries with divided political systems.[11]

Terrorism in India

For a country like India cross border linkages of terrorism have been rather a normal phenomenon because of the very construction and nature of border and also absence of any conscious border policies of both the border sharing nations. Entire South Asia region is India-centric. All the South Asian countries including Bangladesh, Bhutan, Nepal, Pakistan and Sri Lanka have common border with India, whereas no other countries in the region have common borders between them. India has 15,106.7 kms. of land border and a coastline of 7,516.6 kms. India's Home Ministry report very emphatically states *"the terrorists aided and abetted by Pak ISI have caused enormous damage to Kashmiri people and the economy of the state, even public and private properties have not been spared by them."* The 2003 army campaign against the militants (ULFA, NDFB and KLO) hiding in the jungles of southeastern Bhutan for the last 12 years has brought to the fore an array of sensitive issues. Of late, the quadrangular zone consisting of northern Bengal, eastern Nepal, southern Bhutan and mid-western Assam has emerged as a diabolical vortex of militant activities.[12]

India remained severely affected by and vulnerable to terrorism from Pakistan-based groups and their affiliates as well as left-wing violent extremists. In response, Government of India continued to undertake efforts to coordinate its counter-terrorism capabilities more effectively. In 2013, Indian sources continued to attribute violence and deaths in Jammu and Kashmir to transnational terrorist groups that India alleges are backed by Pakistan. Continued allegations of violations of the Line of Control between India and Pakistan (the border along Jammu and Kashmir), Pakistan's failure to bring the perpetrators of the 2008 Mumbai attacks to justice, and activities of Pakistan-based terrorist groups remained serious concerns for the Indian government.[13]

India's northeast region has been marred by terrorist violence for more than fifty years. New Delhi has employed many different policies to counter terrorism in the northeast including economic incentives, military intervention, amnesty programmes for *"reformed"* terrorists, and political concessions. Each state is currently experiencing varying levels of terrorist and insurgent violence. However, terrorism is most severe in Nagaland, Assam and Tripura. These three states are excellent examples of terrorism in India because the most organised; experienced and active terrorist groups routinely operate there. Foreign intervention encourages many terrorist groups in India's northeast. In the 1990s, the Pakistan's Inter-Services Intelligence agency (ISI) allegedly made contact with insurgent groups in the northeast. The ISI's links to Indian terrorism is further explored in subsequent chapters but the mere allegation of ISI activity in the northeast is enough to prompt some terrorist attacks. Border problems are another aspect of geographic challenges common in the region.

The United Liberation Front of Asom (ULFA) was founded and remains the most recognised and prolific terrorist organization in Assam. ULFA believes that Assam was historically independent from India. ULFA contends that Assam should be independent and self-governing, both being geographically separate and ethnically distinct from India. ULFA adopted an extreme version of Maoist-Marxist socialism, which served as the ideological foundation for its terrorist attacks. ULFA remained closely allied to various socialist groups and anti-immigration parties throughout most of the 1980s and 1990s. Though many organisations claim to be the legitimate voice of the Bodo people, the National Democratic Front of Bodoland (NDFB) emerged as the most prominent in 1988. Terrorist groups in Assam owe their survival to international connections. ULFA was the first group to set up training camps in Bhutan and reportedly has nearly 2,000 personnel encamped there. ULFA and the NDFB are only two of many terrorist groups operating in Assam. There are two principal terrorist groups in Tripura. The first and most significant is the National Liberation Front of Tripura (NLFT). The NLFT was established on 12 March 1989 after its predecessor, the TNV, agreed with the government to disband. Tripura's second major terrorist organisation is the All Tripura Tiger Force (ATTF). Some NLFT members see the ATTF as competition and the two groups are often in direct conflict. Seeking independence and sovereignty, the Nagas have used violence since the earliest days of British influence in the region. The NSCN continued the NNC's efforts to establish an independent Naga nation. In 1988 the NSCN split over tribal, political and economic differences. Violence in Nagaland is on the decline. The Indian government has tried numerous political and military tactics to end the violence in the northeast.[14]

Like other countries, India has responded enacting special anti-terrorism laws, part of a broader array of emergency and security laws that periodically have been enacted in India since the British colonial period. Most recently, in the aftermath of the terrorist attacks of September 11, 2001, and the attacks soon thereafter on the Jammu & Kashmir Assembly and the Indian Parliament buildings, India enacted the sweeping Prevention of Terrorism Act of 2002. POTA incorporated many of the provisions found in an earlier law, the Terrorist and Disruptive Activities (Prevention) Act of 1985, which remained in effect until 1995. Laws such as TADA and POTA have been used to target political opponents, human rights defenders, religious minorities, Dalits and other *"lower caste"* individuals, tribal communities, the landless, and other poor and disadvantaged people. POTA and other Indian anti-terrorism laws have raised a host of human rights issues.[15]

While introducing AFSPA in the Parliament, authorising martial law in the North-east region, the then Union Home Minster justified the Act as a temporary measure to contain the uprising in the Naga Hills. But five decades latter, large part of the Northeast is still declared 'disturbed' under the Act and the civilian population is still under grip of the military rule. Thousands of lives have been extinguished in enforced disappearance and extra-judicial execution. Torture, rape, arbitrary detention, forced migration and displacement has become part of life. Constitutional validity of AFSPA was challenged in the Supreme Court of India since1980. The people of Manipur have moved heaven and earth to do away with the Act. From sustained public protest to disrobing of elderly women in front of the Army head quarters, self-immolation of student leaders to the ongoing six years *satyagraha* of Miss. Iram Sharmila.[16]

Left-wing extremists in India, as elsewhere, are known for resorting to violence in pursuance of their ideology of peoples' revolutionary movement. In West Bengal, this movement was started in 1967 by an extremists' break-away faction of the CPM. The first flush of the Left Extremist movement in the Naxalbari region was effectively controlled without much bloodshed and within a relatively short span of time. Various splinter groups of Naxalites started resurfacing in various parts of India during the early 1980s. The Naxalites of Andhra Pradesh regrouped as the CPI-ML (Peoples' War Group/ PWG); likewise the Bihar Naxalites rechristened themselves as the Maoist Communist Centre (MCC). Meanwhile the Maoists developed some expertise in the use of landmines and IEDs which caused very significant casualties among police and other security personnel operating in Chhattisgarh. In West Bengal, the Naxalites seem to be repeating some of their tactics of the 1969-72 period of attacks on their political opponents in addition to the police. There have been several terrorist incidents in India, which were motivated by religious fundamentalism. Some of these activities overlap with political ambitions, like separatist elements in Jammu and Kashmir. In

2001, several Islamic terrorist attacks took place in New Delhi, the most important being the attack on the Parliament House in December 2001. It is important to take a look at the role played by the Students' Islamic Movement of India (SIMI) in the promotion of Islamist extremism in India. While terrorism was largely a local phenomenon until recently, in today's world terrorist networks have taken advantage of the communications revolution to develop transnational links, making terrorism a global threat.[17]

Terrorism in Jammu and Kashmir

The violent struggle in J&K was initially planned by the Jammu and Kashmir Liberation Front (JKLF) for destabilising the Government and mustering international support for the independence movement. Pro-Pakistan elements took advantage of the turbulence created by this movement to generate widespread anti-India sentiments. By the end of 1987, the self-determination the of the JKLF was sidelined and a pro-Pakistan movement emerged in the Valley mainly supported by Jamaat-e-Islami (Kashmir) [JEI-K] and militant cadres of Hizb-ul-Mujahideen. By 1988, Pakistan had trained a large number of Kashmiri youth from both sides of the LoC, for subversion and terrorism. Pakistan extensively used Pakistani and Kashmiri religious parties and their militant cadres as a front to mount armed attacks in J&K. The armed groups operating in J&K depended mainly on the Inter-Services Intelligence (ISI) for training, weapon systems, communications, safe havens and financial support. Kashmiri Pandits, became the worst victims of terrorism because they did not fit in with Pakistan's plans for Kashmir; they were therefore pushed out the Valley as a collective group.[18] Fanatic Islamic fundamentalists such as the LeT and the Jaish-e-Mohammed (JeM) want to move Kashmir into the folds of the *Sharia*, where the voice of the people and the institution of democracy have no place. The first casualties of this ideology have been Kashmiriyat and Sufism. Today, Kashmir is in conflict with itself and the Kashmiri *Awam* is at a crossroads, where one road leads to Talibanisation and the other to peace, prosperity and progressive development.[19]

The roots of insurgency in Jammu and Kashmir can be traced to the later part of the 1940s when Pakistan attacked India with a view to capture Jammu and Kashmir. These groups aided and abetted from across the border have often indulged in insurgent activities. The rise of Islamist fundamentalism and emergence of Al-Qaeda has added another dimension to the insurgency in Jammu and Kashmir. Other affiliates of Al-Qaeda which continue to pose a serious threat to peace and security in India are the Jaish-e-Mohammed (JeM), HUM, HUJI and Al-Badr. Government of India has been endeavouring to tackle the problems of the troubled State through a multi-pronged strategy with a holistic approach calculated to address areas of concern on the political, security, developmental and administrative fronts.[20]

Effects of Terrorism

Terrorism has a lot of effects in any given country, most of which are negative. Terrorism impacts the economy negatively, since it leads to a slowdown due to a damage of consumer confidence. It also impacts tourism, since countries issue restriction orders and travel advisories, which affect the tourism sector negatively. In the social scene, terrorism may lead to numerous deaths and injuries, thus affecting or breaking the societal linkages.[21] There is no doubt among economists that wars, terrorism and political instability have a significant negative effects on the economies in which they take place. Recent economic literature investigates the consequences of political violence and the mechanisms that transform this violence into economic damage. The economy of the country will drop rapidly.[22] Terrorism imposes significant economic effects on societies and will not only lead to direct material damage, but also to long term effects on the local economy. Terrorism is a major problem that is reoccurring over the globe in different forms. The US alone spends about $5 billion dollars a year combating terrorists. The treats of bio-chemical, Suicide or psychological warfare, and information warfare are on the rise in today's societies as more political argument and group's emerge.[23]

Conclusion

Terrorism has been practiced by a broad array of political organisations to further their objectives. It has been practiced by right-wing and left-wing political parties, nationalistic groups, religious groups, revolutionaries, and ruling Governments. Terrorist attacks are usually carried out in such a way as to maximise the severity and length of the psychological impact. Religious terrorism is terrorism performed by groups or individuals, the motivation of which is typically rooted in faith-based tenets. Terrorist attacks are often targeted to maximise fear and publicity, usually using explosives or poison.

The United States has assembled a superficially impressive international coalition against the threat of terrorism. Many countries in that coalition contribute little of significance to the fight. Even worse, the willingness of some members of the coalition to actually combat terrorism is doubtful. Before terrorists struck with a vengeance against the United States in September 2001, terrorism had not received serious international attention, with some analysts even claiming that its threat was being exaggerated. A global anti-terror campaign was long overdue, but just as a strong police and a strong military do not stop crime and aggression, this offensive does not mean that terrorism will cease to be a cost-effective political tool for those unable to deal directly with their perceived adversaries.

REFERENCES

1. *What is terrorism?* Retrieved from http://www.terrorism-research.com/
2. *Religious tourism,* Retrieved from http://www.ficci.com/spdocument/20207/Diverse-Beliefs-Tourism-of-Faith.pdf
3. William Scott Latimer (2004). *What can the United States Learn from India to counterterrorism?* Retrieved from http://csis.org/files/media/csis/pubs/090201_bsa_pardesi.pdf
4. Amy Zalman, *Types of Terrorism: A Guide to Different Types of Terrorism,* Retrieved from http://terrorism.about.com/od/whatisterroris1/tp/DefiningTerrorism.htm
5. Maura Conway, *Terrorist use of the internet and fighting back,* Retrieved from http://www.isn.ethz.ch/Digital-Library/Publications/Detail/?ots591=4888caa0-b3db-1461-98b9-e20e7b9c13d4&lng=en&id=20642

6. Brahma Chellaney, *Fighting Terrorism in Southern Asia: The Lessons of History*, Retrieved from http://muse.jhu.edu/login?auth=0&type=summary&url=/journals/international_security/v026/26.3chellaney.html
7. *India's internal security challenges: New frontiers,* Retrieved from http://www.academia.edu/3465491/Peace_Building_in_North-East_India
8. Muhammad Irshad, *Terrorism in Pakistan: Causes & Remedies,* Retrieved from http://www.qurtuba.edu.pk/thedialogue/The%20Dialogue/6_3/Dialogue_July_September2011_224-241.pdf
9. *Pakistan's New Generation of Terrorists, Retrieved from* http://www.cfr.org/pakistan/pakistans-new-generation-terrorists/p15422
10. *Narco-Terrorism in Afghanistan: Counternarcotics and Counterinsurgency*, Retrieved from http://www.iar-gwu.org/node/39
11. Andrew C. Gagel & Anthony H. Cordesman, *Patterns in Terrorism in North Africa, the Middle East, Central Asia and South Asia: 2007-2010*, Retrieved from http://csis.org/publication/patterns-terrorism-north-africa-middle-east-central-asia-and-south-asia-2007-2010
12. Mahendra P Lama, Terrorism and insurgency in India: Economic Costs and Consequences, *ICSSR Journal of Abstracts and Reviews,* Retrieved from http://www.inflibnet.ac.in/ojs/index.php/JARPS/article/view/275/268
13. *India Severely Affected by Terrorism from Pakistan: US report,* Retrieved from http://www.ndtv.com/article/india/india-severely-affected-by-terrorism-from-pakistan-us-report-516537
14. William Scott Latimer (2004). *What can the United States Learn from India to counterterrorism?* Retrieved from
15. *Colonial continuities: Human rights, terrorism and security laws in India,* Retrieved from http://www.hrw.org/sites/default/files/reports/india0211W.pdf http://www.nycbar.org/pdf/ABCNY_India_Report.pdf

16. Babloo Loitongbam (2007). *North-east India Experience*, Retrieved from http://www.humanrights.asia/resources/journals-magazines/article2/0105/fear-of-rape-the-experience-of-women-in-northeast-india
17. *Terrorism in India, 3,* Retrieved from http://fsss.in/agni-volume/Bala.pdf
18. Major General Afsir Karim, AVSM (12007). *An analysis of the turmoil in Jammu and Kashmir: Present Situation and Future Prospects*, Retrieved from http://fsss.in/occassional-papers/an-analysis-of-the-turmoil-in-jammu-and-kashmir.pdf
19. Narender Kumar (2010). *Jammu and Kashmir: The Emerging Contours and the Way Ahead*, Retrieved from http://www.claws.in/administrator/uploaded_files/1272944475MP%2021.pdf
20. *Terrorism in India, 3*, Retrieved from http://www.claws.in/administrator/uploaded_files/1272944475MP%2021.pdf
21. See http://www.ask.com/question/what-are-the-effects-of-terrorism
22. *Effects of Terrorism to a Country*, Retrieved from http://www.studymode.com/essays/Effect-Of-Terrorism-On-a-Country-152805.html
23. *The Effects of Terrorism,* Retrieved from http://www.peacekashmir.org/views-articles/2012/0905-the-effects-of-terrorism.htm

18

Unemployment

"The Great Depression, like most other periods of severe unemployment, was produced by government mismanagement rather than by any inherent instability of the private economy."

- Milton Friedman

Introduction

The meaning of life is a philosophical question concerning the significance of life or existence in general. It can be expressed in different forms, such as *"Why are we here?"*, *"What is life all about?"*, and *"What is the purpose of existence?"* Work is defined as engagement in economic activity i.e. any activity resulting in production of goods and services that add value to the national product. Given the possibility of an individual being engaged in a multiplicity of activities over a year-long reference period, a majority time criterion was put in a place to yield estimates of employment and unemployment on the Usual Principal Status.[1] A person's livelihood refers to their *"means of securing the basic necessities-food, water, shelter and clothing- of life"*. Livelihood is defined as a set of activities, involving securing water, food, fodder, medicine, shelter, clothing and the capacity to acquire above necessities working either individually or as a group by using endowments (both human and material) for meeting the requirements of the self and his/her household on a sustainable basis with dignity.[2]

What is Unemployment?

Though there have been several definitions of *"voluntary"* and *"involuntary unemployment"* in the economics literature, a simple distinction is often applied. Voluntary unemployment is attributed to the individual's decisions, whereas involuntary unemployment exists because of the socio-economic environment (including the market structure, Government intervention, and the level of aggregate demand) in which individuals operate. Unemployed person are those people who are want to work at the current wage rate in the market but unable to get job. Unemployment occurs when people are without work and actively seeking work. The unemployment rate is a measure of the prevalence of unemployment and it is calculated as a percentage by dividing the number of unemployed individuals by all individuals currently in the labor force. During periods of recession, an economy usually experiences a relatively high unemployment rate. According to International Labour Organisation report, more than 197 million people globally are out of work or six per cent of the world's workforce was without a job in 2012.[3]

Reasons of Unemployment

The major causes which have been responsible for the wide spread unemployment are rapid population growth, limited land, seasonal agriculture, fragmentation of land, backward method of agriculture, decline of cottage industries, defective education, lack of transport and communication, inadequate employment planning etc.[4]

Types of Unemployment

There are three primary categories of unemployment. They are structural, frictional, and cyclical unemployment.

1. *Structural Unemployment:* Structural Unemployment, one of the three types of unemployment, is associated with the mismatch of jobs and workers due to the lack of skills or simply the wrong area desired for work. Structural unemployment depends on the social needs of the economy and dynamic changes in the economy.
2. *Frictional Unemployment:* Frictional Unemployment is always present in the economy, resulting from temporary transitions made by workers and employers or from workers and employers having inconsistent or incomplete information. This type of unemployment is closely related to structural unemployment due to its dependence on the

dynamics of the economy. It is caused because unemployed workers may not always take the first job offer they receive because of the wages and necessary skills

3. *Cyclical unemployment:* Unemployment that is attributed to economic contraction is called cyclical unemployment. The economy has the capacity to create jobs which increases economic growth. Therefore, an expanding economy typically has lower levels of unemployment. On the other hand, according to cyclical unemployment an economy that is in a recession faces higher levels of unemployment.[5]
4. *Open unemployment:* Open unemployment is a condition in which people have no work to do. They are able to work and are also willing to work but there is no work for them. They are found partly in villages, but very largely in cities.
5. *Voluntary unemployment*: Voluntary unemployment occurs when a working persons willingly withdraws himself from work. This type of unemployment may be caused due to a number of reasons.
6. *Involuntary unemployment:* Involuntary unemployment occurs when at a particular time the number of worker is more than the number of jobs. Obviously this state of affairs arises because of the insufficiency or non availability of work.
7. *Disguised unemployment:* Disguised unemployment implies that many workers are engaged in productive work. It follows that all the workers are not needed to maintain the existing level of production. The contribution of such workers to production is nothing. It is found that the very large numbers of workers on Indian farms actually hinder agricultural works and thereby reduce production.[6]

Global Perspectives

Youth unemployment and underemployment is prevalent around the world because young people lack skills, work experience, job search abilities and the financial resources to find employment. In developing countries, this situation is exacerbated by poverty and the competitive pressures that result from a rapidly growing labour force. Different labour market indicators provide various insights into the overall situation facing young people in a country like India that, despite the strong economic growth rate, continues to be dominated by the unorganised sector. Compared to advanced economies, overall rates of unemployment in developing countries are generally lower than observed in developed economies because most individuals cannot support themselves and their families through social protection schemes.[7]

Fast growing East Asian economies have rapidly increased the numbers of students attending university in recent years. Of particular concern is whether high graduate unemployment is a temporary blip or reflects a chronic oversupply of graduates, even as many employers say they cannot find people with the right skills. In South Korea the number of *'economically inactive'* graduates has passed three million for the first time, up just over three per cent from the previous year. Even in booming Singapore, which is importing highly skilled workers to stem a talent shortage, graduate unemployment rose from 3.3 per cent to 3.6 per cent in the first half of 2013, higher than the average unemployment rate in Singapore of around two per cent. In China job vacancies available to a record number of graduates have seen a year on year decrease, with official media saying that the number of graduates is 'outrunning' economic growth. The 2013 Talent Shortage Survey by Manpower Group, US-based human resources multinational, found acute problems in recruiting talent in many Asian countries but particularly in Japan and India.[8]

The youth population in sub-Saharan Africa is increasing rapidly. Nearly one in three people living in the region, or about 297 million, is between the ages of 10 and 24. Youth unemployment remains a barrier to the region's development. Some of the highest rates on the continent are in southern Africa, where 51 per cent of young women and 43 per cent of young men are unemployed. This large unemployed population indicates lost potential since communities and nations fail to benefit from what the young people could theoretically contribute.[9] Nearly 300 million people in sub-Saharan Africa are aged between 10 and 24, and that number is expected to climb to about 561 million by the middle of this century. Africa has the highest concentration of young people anywhere on the planet.[10]

Unemployment in India

India, the world's largest democracy, attaining independence in 1947, was faced with the twin problems of unemployment and poverty. It adopted the socialist form of development to overcome these problems. In July 1991, by introducing the New Economic/ Industrial Policy India implemented a fundamental shift in its economic policy, adopting market-led economic development. By 2004, India had become to be known as information and communication technology hub with a huge stock of employable IT professionals.[11] One of the greatest challenges in India is the lack of decent work in the organised sector. Looking at the nature of employment, almost half of the rural youth are self-employed. Among rural females, self-employment in the age group 20-24 is higher than the all-age average figure. On the other hand, the proportion of workers in casual wage in the same age group is lower compared to the all-age average. Young women are engaged more in the agriculture sector compared to males in rural areas. In comparison, the share of the tertiary sector in urban areas is higher than that of the secondary sector.[12]

The dominant features of employment and unemployment in India reflect those in developing countries. There are low rates of unemployment but much higher levels of poverty. In the absence of formal social security protection, remaining unemployed is not a choice for the majority. The NSSO's 66th Round data showed that 51 per cent of Indian workers were self-employed: 54.2 per cent in rural areas; 41.1 per cent in urban areas. The Planning Commission of the Government of India, in its 11th Five Year Plan (2007–12), also concludes that the Indian economy has failed to create sufficient volume of additional high-quality employment to absorb the new entrants into the labour market. The unemployment of young people in the labour market is high, due to their lack of marketable education and skills. The unemployment rate for the youth labour force in India was as high as eight per cent, according to usual status, in 2004–05 and it shows an increasing trend.[13] Socially disadvantaged groups, viz., Scheduled Castes, Scheduled Tribes and Other Backward Classes are generally believed to have low participation in labour force and may be having high unemployment rate.[14]

Effects of Unemployment

Various effects of unemployment are loss of human resources, increase in poverty, social problems, political instability, exploitation of labour, more emphasis on capital intensive techniques, defective education system, slow growth of tertiary s etc. sector.[15] Unemployment affects us all. It affects people with work, business that are hiring and cities that have created jobs. It affects our culture, our families, and our friendships. The ripple effects of unemployment go beyond the headlines of job loss and job creation.[16] Where there is high unemployment, the employed feel less secure; the workers themselves become less willing to leave unsatisfactory jobs; the divisions in the society increase; and the prospect of equality of opportunity, greatly decreases.[17] The unemployed people are a burden on the economy and society. According to Lewis there exists heavy unemployment and disguised unemployment in the rural and urban areas of less developed countries.[18] The impacts of unemployment on families include poverty and hardship, strained relationships, poorer health (although the causal relationships are not always clear), and housing stress. Unemployment could also harm children's development and employment futures. Some policy issues are explored including the need to provide protection for the living standards for families affected by unemployment and taking a number of actions to reduce unemployment. The dilemmas posed by mutual obligation and the trend to precarious low-paid work are also raised.[19] Long-term unemployment produces a sharp loss of income.

Government Initiatives

Ever since the initiation of planning in India in 1950, the Government has stressed the goal of increasing employment opportunities and eventually eradicating unemployment from the country. Acceleration of the rate of savings and investment and rising of the level of productivity has been prime goals of the successive five year plans of the country. Awareness about the difficulties of eliminating unemployment has, over the past three decades, led the successive governments at the centre and in the states to formulate and implement several schemes for eradicating unemployment and promoting employment. Some of the special employment schemos have been aimed specifically at the youth to improve their training and skills and to promote self-employment and entrepreneurship. They included: an effort to reorient the Indian educational system in the direction of vocational education; an apprenticeship training scheme supported by legislation passed in 1961 and amended in 1973 and 1986; the centrally sponsored scheme of Training of Rural Youth for Self-Employment (TRYSEM); and a Self-Employment Scheme for Educated Unemployed Youth (SEEUY) in urban areas. These schemes were intended to address the problems of urban youth. Some of the schemes have been modified in the light of experience and the findings of evaluations undertaken by various agencies and institutions on behalf of the government.

National Employment Service, operated by the Directorate General of Employment and Training, Ministry of Labour, runs nearly 900 Employment Exchanges in order to bring about a better matching of the demand for and the supply of work opportunities. In 1950, India had aimed at providing for free and compulsory primary education for all children up to the age of 14, within a decade; but the actual progress has been far slower than expected. Since the late 1950s, there has been a widespread recognition of the need to reorient the Indian educational system towards various vocations to minimize the problem of mismatch between the demand for and the availability of white-collar job. In the 1950s, the Government attempted to link the young work-seekers with the industrial units in the country in the area of formal training. An Apprenticeship Act was enacted in 1961 to make it obligatory for the employers in specified industries to engage apprentices for training for between six months to four years. The Act came into force on March 1, 1963. Over the past four decades, there has been a steady expansion in the number of Industrial Training Institutes which train the youth aged 15-25 in 42 engineering and 22 non-engineering trades for a period of one or two years. Between 1983 and 1993-94, India also had a scheme for self-employment for educated urban youth, which has now been subsumed under a new scheme called the Prime Minister's Rozgar (Employment) Scheme (PMRY) since 1994-95.

TRYSEM was initiated on August 15, 1979, *"to provide basic technical and managerial skills to rural youth from families below the poverty line"* to enable them to take up *"self-employment and wage employment in the broad fields of agricultural and allied sectors, namely industries, services and business services."* Besides the national schemes listed above, several state governments have been operating self-employment schemes. The government of Andhra Pradesh has set up a Society for Employment and Training in the Twin Cities (SETWIN) to provide informal training and assistance in taking up self-employment. The unemployed youth are also eligible for benefits from other employment schemes of the Government of India and the states. These include the Scheme of Urban Micro Enterprises (SUME), under which the eligible beneficiaries in all urban areas are helped to secure technical training and to set up.[20]

Conclusion

Unemployment occurs when people are without work and actively seeking work. According to International Labour Organisation report, more than 197 million people globally are out of work or six per cent of the world's workforce was without a job in 2012. High and persistent unemployment, in which economic inequality increases, has a negative effect on subsequent long-run economic growth. Unemployment can harm growth not only because it is a waste of resources. Unemployed individuals are unable to earn money to meet financial obligations. Unemployment increases susceptibility to malnutrition, illness, mental stress, and loss of self-esteem, leading to depression. During a long period of unemployment, workers can lose their skills, causing a loss of human capital. High unemployment can also cause social problems such as crime; if people have less disposable income than before, it is very likely that crime levels within the economy will increase. High levels of unemployment can be causes of civil unrest, in some cases leading to revolution. Many countries aid the unemployed through social welfare programs. These unemployment benefits include unemployment insurance, unemployment compensation, welfare and subsidies to aid in retraining. The main goal of these programs is to alleviate short-term hardships and, more importantly, to allow workers more time to search for a job.

REFERENCES

1. K. Sundaram, *Measurement of employment and unemployment in India, some issues,* Retrieved from http://www.cdedse.org/pdf/work174.pdf
2. *Livelihood,* Retrieved from http://en.wikipedia.org/wiki/Livelihood
3. *Unemployment (2014),* Retrieved from http://en.wikipedia.org/wiki/Unemployment

4. *What are the causes of unemployment in India?* See http://www.preservearticles. com/201105096376/what-are-the-causes-of-unemployment-in-india.html
5. *Types of unemployment*, Retrieved from http://www.econport.org/content/handbook/Unemployment/Types.html
6. *Different types of unemployment found in rural India*, Retrieved from http://www.preservearticles.com/201105096386/different-types-of-unemployment-found-in-rural-india.html
7. Arup Mitra and Sher Verick (2013). *Youth employment and unemployment: an Indian perspective*, Retrieved from http://www.ilo.org/wcmsp5/groups/public/—asia/—ro-bangkok/—sro new Delhi/documents/publication/wcms_211552.pdf
8. *Rising unemployment – Are there too many graduates?* Retrieved from http://www.universityworldnews.com/article.php?story=20140213153927383
9. *Reducing Youth Unemployment in Sub-Saharan Africa*, Retrieved from http://www.prb.org/Publications/Articles/2013/youth-unemployment-africa.aspx
10. *Africa's rising population and youth unemployment challenge,* Retrieved from http://www.theguardian.com/global-development-professionals-network/2013/jul/11/africa-kenya-population-youth-unemployment
11. *Combating Youth Unemployment in India,* Retrieved from http://library.fes.de/pdf-files/iez/09728.pdf
12. Arup Mitra and Sher Verick (2013). *Youth employment and unemployment: an Indian perspective*, Retrieved from http://www.ilo.org/wcmsp5/groups/public/—asia/—ro-bangkok/—sro new_delhi/documents/publication/wcms_211552.pdf
13. *Combating Youth Unemployment in India*, Retrieved from http://library.fes.de/pdf-files/iez/09728.pdf
14. *Report on Second Annual Employment & Unemployment Survey (2011-13).* Retrieved from http://labourbureau.nic.in/rep_1.pdf
15. *What are the effects of unemployment on our society? (India),* Retrieved from http://www.preservearticles.com/201107189269/what-are-the-effects-of-unemployment-on-our-society-india.html

16. *The Breakdown: The Ripple Effects of Unemployment*, Retrieved from http://www.marketplace.org/topics/business/breakdown/breakdown-ripple-effects-unemployment
17. See http://www.ask.com/question/what-are-the-effects-of-unemployment
18. *Negative Effects of Unemployment and Underemployment*, Retrieved from http://economics-exposed.com/negative-effects-of-unemployment-and-underemployment/
19. *Effects of Unemployment on the Family,* Retrieved from http://elr.sagepub.com/content/11/2/198.short?rss=1&ssource=mfc
20. Pravin Visaria (1998). *Unemployment among youth in India: Level, nature and policy implications*, Retrieved from http://www.ilo.org/wcmsp5/groups/public/—ed_emp/documents/publication/wcms_120233.pdf

19

Corruption

Introduction

Corruption is the intentional non-compliance with the arm's-length principle aimed at deriving some advantage for oneself or for related individuals from this behavior.[1] It means the state of being bad and dishonest, especially in matters concerning money. It creates a very impact to the country's education, occupation, living style and mostly the humanity. Although many developing nations especially in Africa are endowed with priced natural resources, yet they continue to struggle and scramble for position in the lower rungs of the United Nations Development Index. Most developing countries continue to grapple with the ever changing trends in global politics, economic and technological advancements having little or nothing to do due to the debilitating effects of corruption on their very existence.

What is Corruption?

Corruption is spiritual or moral impurity or deviation from an ideal. Corruption may include many activities including bribery and embezzlement. Government, or political corruption occurs when an office-holder or other governmental employee acts in an official capacity for personal gain.[2] Corruption can occur on different scales, like as: (1) Petty corruption occurs at a smaller scale and within established social frameworks and governing norms; (2) Grand corruption is defined as corruption occurring at the highest levels of government in a way that requires significant subversion of the political, legal and economic systems; and (3) Systemic corruption is corruption which is primarily due to the weaknesses of an organisation or process. It can be contrasted with individual officials or agents who act corruptly within the system.[3]

Types of Corruption

Corruption became a sway all over the world now-a-days. It can be categorised in three types. First is Political corruption second is Administrative corruption and third one is Professional corruption.

1. *Political Corruption* includes kidnapping, murder, violence, injustice etc. To win in election, political leaders are using wine, women, wealth and everything among the people.
2. *Administrative Corruption* includes persons like higher authorities, officers, police officers, clerks, peons, etc.
3. *Professional Corruption* includes duplicating medicines, duplicating import items/theft items, duplicating hygienic, mixture in eatables etc. Mixture in spices, stones in cereals, animal fats in ghee, kerosene in petrol etc. are under corruption.[4]

Reasons of Corruption

The causes of corruption in India include excessive regulations, complicated taxes and licensing systems, numerous Government departments each with opaque bureaucracy and discretionary powers, monopoly by government controlled institutions on certain goods and services delivery, and the lack of transparent laws and processes.[5]

Global Perspectives

Corruption is a serious problem in many countries. Indeed, in many parts of the world, corruption has become a way of life with its own local version of the term and manifestations of various forms of corrupt practices. Scandals involving corruption have also been unearthed in other developed countries, including several European countries and Japan. The epidemic of corruption scandals in the developed countries has not only shattered the myth that only the developing countries are plagued by corruption, but has also encouraged more research on the dynamics of corrupt behaviour in the developed countries.[6]

The problem of corruption is rampant in many Asian countries. It seriously affects all aspects of people's lives, as almost nothing can be done without giving bribes. All the public institutions, which are supposed to provide services and protection to safeguard the human rights of people have become dysfunctional because of corruption. In this sense, corruption is a main obstacle for the protection and promotion of human rights, as it destroys the proper functioning of the public institutions. Corruption is the enemy of the rule of law. Under corruption, there is no respect for laws, because laws cannot be enforced or they are enforced arbitrarily in favour of people who have power or can afford to pay bribes. To tackle the problem of corruption, the Asian Legal Resource Centre held a Regional Consultation on Anti-Corruption Mechanisms in Asia, in Hong Kong on 11-15 January 2010. The aims of the consultation were to develop knowledge and critique existing mechanisms for the elimination of corruption in Asia and to introduce the participants to the Independent Commission Against Corruption in Hong Kong, so as to provide opportunities for comparative studies on corruption control.[7] As corruption is a serious problem in many Asian countries their governments have introduced many anti-corruption measures since the 1950s.[8]

South Asians regularly have to pay bribes when dealing with their public institutions, be it to speed up paperwork, avoid problems with authorities such as the police, or simply access basic services. A new survey of six South Asian countries published by Transparency International, the anti-corruption organisation, found that more than one in three people who deal with public services said they pay bribes. Political parties and the police are the most corrupt institutions in all six countries according to the survey, followed closely by the parliament and public officials. Officials entrusted to oversee deals related to buying, selling, inheriting and renting land were the next likely to demand a bribe. According to the survey, the country most plagued by bribery is Bangladesh where 66 per cent report paying bribes to public institutions, mostly just to gain access to services that people should already be entitled to. In Nepal, Pakistan, India and Sri Lanka, bribes were mostly paid to speed things up, highlighting how corruption can also be a barrier to business expansion. In Sri Lanka significantly more people paid bribes to tax authorities than other services, while in Nepal and the Maldives, customs services reportedly receive the most bribes.[9]

Corruption affects many Africans on a daily basis. According to Transparency International's (TI) 2012 Corruption Perception Index (CPI), 90 per cent of African countries scored below the symbolic 50 pass mark. This is roughly on a par with Eastern Europe and Central Asia. On average, Africa's CPI score in 2012 was 33, which means corruption hampers business and the provision of decent public services. TI's 2011 Global Corruption Barometer indicates that African citizens believe corruption had worsened in the previous three years. Rwanda was the only African country where more than 50 per cent of respondents believed corruption had declined in this time. In Kenya and Ethiopia more people believed corruption had improved than got worse. The majority of countries at the bottom of the CPI have emerged from prolonged crisis, which highlights the strong detrimental effect of conflict on political and administrative institutions. Somalia, Sudan, Chad, Burundi, Zimbabwe, Libya, Congo Republic, DRC and Angola have the lowest scores for the continent.[10]

The annual release of the global Corruption Perceptions Index is rarely good news for Latin America. Since 1995, Latin America's inclusion has risen from six nations to all mainland countries except Belize, as well as the most populated and some smaller Caribbean nations. Due to its geographical location, Central America, home to some of the CPI's worst performers in the region, is a hub of drug trafficking and beset by criminal groups. In the face of weak economies and state institutions, drug trafficking organisations have historically acted with impunity to transport contraband through the isthmus, buying the loyalty of underpaid officials along the way.[11] According to Berlin-based organisation, the Americas' most transparent nation is Canada (9th worldwide) while the least is Haiti (163rd worldwide). The US ties with Uruguay for 19th place, while Brazil and Mexico rank 72 and 106, respectively. The 177-nation ranking is based on 13 data sources, from the World Bank to the Economist

Intelligence Unit. In Latin America, Guatemala showed the greatest increase in corruption over the past year, falling 10 places in the index to 123rd as gang violence and drug trafficking continues to spill over from Mexico. Regional neighbors such as Costa Rica, which has also seen an uptick in violence, also fell one spot to 49th.[12]

Corruption remains one of the biggest challenges for all societies, including European societies. Although the nature and scope of corruption may differ from one EU State to another, it harms the EU as a whole by lowering investment levels, hampering the fair operation of the Internal Market and reducing public finances. The economic costs incurred by corruption in the EU possibly amount to EUR 120 billion per year. The Union has a general right to act in the field of anti-corruption policies, within the limits established by the Treaty on the Functioning of the European Union. In particular, the EU should ensure a high level of security, including through the prevention and combating of crime and the approximation of criminal laws. Corruption is one of the particularly serious crimes with a cross-border dimension. It is often linked to other forms of serious crime, such as trafficking in drugs and human beings, and cannot be adequately addressed by EU States alone. In June 2011, the Commission set up a mechanism for the periodic assessment of EU States' efforts in the fight against corruption. Within the EU, the 2003 Framework Decision on combating corruption in the private sector aims to criminalise both active and passive bribery. With the anti-corruption package, the Commission is pursuing a coherent approach for shaping EU policies on the fight against corruption.[13] Corruption continues to be a challenge for Europe. Affecting all EU Member States, corruption costs the European economy around 120 billion euros per year. Member States have taken many initiatives in recent years, but the results are uneven and more should be done to prevent and punish corruption.[14]

Corruption in India

Corruption in India is a major issue that adversely affects its economy. A study conducted by Transparency International in year 2005 found that more than 62 per cent of Indians had firsthand experience of paying bribes or influence peddling to get jobs done in public offices successfully. In 2012 India has ranked 94th out of 176 countries in Transparency International's Corruption Perceptions Index, tied with Benin, Colombia, Djibouti, Greece, Moldova, Mongolia, and Senegal. Indian media has widely published allegations of corrupt Indian citizens stashing trillions of dollars in Swiss banks. Swiss authorities, however, deny this allegations.[15] India was ranked among the world's highly corrupt nations at the 94th spot in a global list topped by Denmark and New Zealand as the cleanest, while Somalia emerged as the most corrupt in December 2013. According to the list, India has scored 36 points on a scale of 0-100, where 0 means that a country is perceived as highly corrupt and 100 means it is perceived as very clean. None of the countries have managed to get the perfect 100 score. Top-ranked Denmark and New Zealand have scored 91 points each to share the first place on the list. Somalia shares lowest rank with North Korea and Afghanistan with eight points each. Those scoring marginally better than these three countries include Sudan, Libya, Iraq, Uzbekistan, Syria, Haiti, Venezuela, Zimbabwe and Myanmar. The Corruption Perceptions Index 2013 demonstrates that all countries still face the threat of corruption at all levels of government, from the issuing of local permits to the enforcement of laws and regulations.[16]

Corruption in the Indian society has prevailed from time immemorial in one form or the other. The basic inception of corruption started with our opportunistic leaders who have already done greater damage to our nation. Corruption in India is a result of the connection between bureaucrats, politicians and criminals. Earlier, bribes were paid for getting wrong things done, but now bribe is paid for getting right things done at right time. Political corruption is worst in India. The major cause of concern is that corruption is weakening the political body and damaging the supreme importance of the law governing the society. Now-a-days politics is only for criminals and criminals are meant to be in politics.[17]

There is widespread corruption in India in all levels of the government including judiciary, said a US Congress-mandated report. Corruption was widespread. According to the report, though the law provides criminal penalties for official corruption, the Indian Government did not implement the law effectively, and officials frequently engaged in corrupt practices with impunity. Corruption was present at all levels of Government. The CBI registered 583 cases of corruption between the months of January and November. The Central Vigilance Commission (CVC) received 7,224 cases in 2012, of those, 5,528 were received in 2012 and an additional 1,696 remained from 2011. The commission recommended action on 5,720 cases. The CVC operated a toll-free hotline to lodge complaints and a web portal to share information. NGOs noted that bribes typically were paid to expedite services, such as police protection, school admission, water supply, or Government assistance. Many government-run programmes to alleviate poverty and provide employment suffered from poor implementation and corruption. The judicial system remained seriously overburdened and lacked modern case management systems, often delaying or denying justice. Vacancies in the subordinate judiciary were also alarming, with more than 3,700 positions to be filled in the states. The law minister attributed lengthening delays of cases in courts to the vacancies.[18] The 2005 survey showed that the five least corrupt states were Kerala, Himachal Pradesh, Gujarat, Andhra Pradesh, and Maharashtra. These states (with the possible exception of Kerala) have attracted a lot of investment in the last decade. This suggests that low corruption does indeed improve growth. The five most corrupt states, according to the survey, are Bihar (worst by far), Kashmir, Madhya Pradesh, Karnataka and Rajasthan. Investors certainly avoid the three worst states, but invest massively in Karnataka and Rajasthan, both of which are fast-growing. Tamil Nadu is also corrupt and fast-growing.[19]

Indian Money in Foreign Accounts

Black money refers to money that is not fully legitimately the property of the 'owner'. According to a 2010 The Hindu article, unofficial estimates indicate that Indians had over US$1456 billion in black money stored in Swiss banks (approximately USD 1.4 trillion). Another report said that Indian-owned Swiss bank account assets are worth 13 times the country's national debt. These allegations have been denied by Swiss Bankers Association. According to a third report, published in May 2012, Swiss National Bank estimates that the total amount of deposits in all Swiss banks, at the end of 2010, by citizens of India were CHF 1.95 billion (92.95 billion, US$2.1 billion). The Swiss Ministry of External Affairs has confirmed these figures upon request for information by the Indian Ministry of External Affairs.[20]

India has slipped to 70th position in terms of foreign money lying with Swiss banks and accounts for a meagre 0.10 per cent of total global wealth held in the country's banking system. Among the top-ten jurisdictions in terms of source of money with Swiss banks, the UK is now followed by the US, West Indies, Jersey, Guernsey, Germany, France, Bahamas, Cayman Islands and Hong Kong. The sharp decline in Indian money in Swiss banks during 2012 followed a significant increase in the previous year, when such funds had risen for the first time in five years. The quantum of funds held by Indians in Swiss banks stood at a record high level of 6.5 billion Swiss francs (over Rs 41,000 crore) at the end of 2006, but has declined by over five billion Swiss francs (over Rs 32,000 crore) since then.[21]

The total overseas funds in Switzerland's banking system stood at 1.53 trillion Swiss francs (about Rs 90 trillion) at the end of 2011, which included 2.18 billion Swiss francs (Rs 12,700 crore) belonging to Indian individuals and entities. India is ranked 55th in terms of only direct deposits as well, while it is placed much lower at 76th rank for fiduciary funds, where the top-ranked jurisdictions include West Indies, Panama, U.K., Saudi Arabia, Bahamas, Liberia, Cayman Islands, UAE, Turkey, Russia, Germany and the U.S. The quantum of funds held by Indians in Swiss banks had last increased in 2006 by about one billion Swiss francs to 6.5 billion Swiss francs (over Rs 40,000 crore), but fell to less than one-third by the end of 2010.[22]

The Supreme Court (SC) declined to entertain the Centre's plea seeking recall of its order for setting up of a Special Investigation Team (SIT) to probe the stashing away of black money in foreign banks and bringing it back to India. The court said this as Additional Solicitor General Siddharth Luthra sought the recall of the July 4, 2011, judgment of the apex court, and March 26 and May 1, 2014, orders of the court. The July 4, 2011, order was passed on a petition by Jethmalani seeking investigation into the flight of unaccounted money to tax havens and bringing it back. On March 26, the court turned down the Centre's plea seeking the recall of the court's July 4, 2011 order setting up a SIT headed by its two former judges to monitor investigations into stashing away of the black money in tax havens. On July 4, 2011, the apex court had set up an SIT under the chairmanship of former SC judge Justice B.P. Jeevan Reddy and Justice M.B. Shah. But, according to its March 26, 2014 order, the court, while declining the Centre's plea, said the SIT probe into flight of black money to tax havens would go on.[23]

Supreme Court of India

The Supreme Court struck down a single directive provision which barred CBI from investigating corruption charges against joint secretary and above rank officers without prior permission of the Centre. The court held as invalid and unconstitutional the provision in the law requiring government's approval to probe senior bureaucrats on corruption charges. All government officials have to be treated equally and have to face the same process of inquiry in graft cases, the SC said, adding, *"Status of top bureaucrats is of no relevance in the offence under the Prevention of Corruption Act"*. The apex court said such a classification of bureaucrats for investigation purposes violated Article 14 of the Constitution which mandated that law would treat everyone equally.[24] In a strong message against corruption in the subordinate judiciary, the Supreme Court observed incorrigible judges who were bringing the entire judiciary to disrepute should be thrown out. Incorrigible judges should be thrown out," the bench said, while dealing with a contempt petition against an additional district judge (ADJ). The bench directed the chief justice of the HC to conduct an inquiry into the matter and take such action as he deemed fit.[25]

In a bid to tackle the growing cases of corruption in the country, the Supreme Court today, in a major move, asked all trial courts in the country to dispose off such cases quickly. A Bench comprising Justice P Sathasivam and Justice B S Chouhan directed all High Courts to monitor the cases of graft. The apex court also said that all High Courts should seek quarterly reports from trial courts on the progress in the trial of the corruption cases. Recently, Chief Justice of India S H Kapadia had written to all the Chief Justices of High Courts in the country asking them to deal with corruption cases on a priority basis. Normally, such cases which are tried under the Prevention of Corruption Act, linger on for a long time. Hence, the latest directive from the Supreme Court will help speed up trial of corruption cases.[26]

A five-judge Constitution bench led by Chief Justice R M Lodha ruled that Section 6A of the Delhi Special Police Establishment Act (DSPEA), which shackles investigations without approvals, was *"discriminatory"*, and *"impedes tracking down the corrupt senior bureaucrats"*. The court said that *"the protection in Section 6A has propensity of shielding the corrupt"*. The provision *"suffers from the vice of classifying offenders differently for treatment there under for inquiry and investigation of offences, according to their status in life". "Every person accused of committing the same offence is to be dealt with in the same manner in accordance with law. The status or position of public servant does not qualify such public servant from exemption from equal treatment. The decision making power does not segregate corrupt officers into two classes as they are common crime doers and have to be tracked down by the same process of inquiry and investigation,"* the bench said. The bench expressed the opinion that this provision in the DSPE Act defeated the objectives of the Prevention of Corruption Act, framed to deal with corruption and to act against senior public servant. *"The result of the impugned legislation is that the very group of persons, namely, high ranking bureaucrats whose misdeeds and illegalities may have to be inquired into, would decide whether the CBI should even start an inquiry or investigation against them or not,"* the court said.[27]

The CBI and the Centre appeared heading for a confrontation in the coalgate case with the agency asserting in the Supreme Court that no prior sanction is required to prosecute bureaucrats in the scam, a stand contrary to that of government. In a six-page affidavit, the CBI contended that no sanction or approval of the Government is required in court monitored cases and referred to the apex court's judgement in 2G scam in which time period for government was stipulated in granting sanction in other cases.[28]

Anti-Corruption Effort

Public servants in India can be penalised for corruption under the Indian Penal Code, 1860; Prosecution section of Income Tax Act,1961; The Prevention of Corruption Act, 1988; The Benami Transactions (Prohibition) Act, 1988 to prohibit benami transactions; Prevention of Money Laundering Act, 2002. India is also a signatory to the UN Convention against Corruption since 2005 (ratified 2011). The Convention covers a wide range of acts of corruption and also proposes certain preventive policies. The Lokpal Bill, 2011 is a bill pending before the Rajya Sabha. India's lower house of parliament, the Lok Sabha voted to pass The Whistle Blowers Protection Bill, 2011. The bill is now pending in the Rajya Sabha, the upper house. A committee headed by the Chairman of Central Board of Direct Taxes (CBDT), has been constituted to examine ways to strengthen laws to curb generation of black money in India, its illegal transfer abroad and its recovery. The Directorate General of Income Tax Investigation, Central Vigilance Commission and Central Bureau of Investigation all deal with anti-corruption initiatives. Certain states such as Andhra Pradesh (Andhra Pradesh Anti-corruption Bureau) and Karnataka (Lokayukta) also have their own anti-corruption agencies and courts.[29]

People who expose corruption in Government or irregularities by public functionaries can now be free of any fear of victimisation. The Whistleblowers Protection Act, 2011, which provides a mechanism for protecting the identity of whistleblowers—a term given to people who expose corruption—got the assent of President Pranab Mukherjee. The Act also provides for a system to encourage people to disclose information about corruption or the willful misuse of power by public servants, including ministers. As per the law, a person can make a public interest disclosure on corruption before a competent authority which is at present the Central Vigilance Commission (CVC). The Government, by notification, can appoint any other body also for receiving such complaints about corruption, the Act says. The Act, however, lays down punishment of up to two years in prison and a fine of up to Rs 30,000 for false or frivolous complaints. Any person who makes a malafide disclosure, knowing that it was incorrect or false or misleading, shall be punishable with imprisonment for a term which may extend up to two years as well as a fine which may extend up to Rs 30,000. The Act says that every disclosure shall be made in good faith and the person making the disclosure shall provide a personal declaration stating that he reasonably believes that the information disclosed by him and the allegation contained therein is substantially true. Information related to national security has been kept out of the purview of the Act. The Act is not applicable to Jammu and Kashmir, the armed forces and the Special Protection Group mandated to provide security to the Prime Minister and former prime ministers, among others. The Whistleblowers Protection Bill was introduced on August 26, 2010. It was referred to a Parliamentary Standing Committee on September 16, 2010, which had given its report on June 9, 2011. The Bill was passed by Lok Sabha on December 11, 2011 and by Rajya Sabha on February 21, 2014.[30]

India against Corruption

India Against Corruption (IAC) was a populist anti-corruption movement in India. The official position of figureheads in the IAC movement was that it had no formal organisation beyond a 24-member core committee. In 2011, the mostly middle-class organisers of IAC determined to launch a campaign to mobilise the masses in support of a demand that they hoped would help to bring about a corruption-free India.[31]

Effects of Corruption

The effect of corruption has many dimensions related to political, economic, social and environmental effects. In political sphere, corruption impedes democracy and the rule of law. In a democratic system, public institutions and offices may lose their legitimacy when they misuse their power for private interest. Corruption may also result in negative consequences such as encoring cynicism and reducing interest of political participation, political instability, reducing political competition, reducing the transparency of political decision making, distorting political development and sustaining political activity based on patronage, clientelism and money, etc. In Social sphere, corruption discourages people to work together for the common good. Frustration and general apathy among the public result in a weak civil society. Demanding and paying bribes becomes the tradition.[32] Corruption destroys the economic and administrative back bone of a nation. The politicians, the bureaucrat's and the criminals gain at the cost of the common man.[33]

Corruption facilitates environmental destruction. Corrupt countries may formally have legislation to protect the environment; it cannot be enforced if officials can easily be bribed. The same applies to social rights worker protection, unionisation prevention, and child labour. Violation of these laws rights enables corrupt countries to gain illegitimate economic advantage in the international market. Corrupt officials often accept substandard quality of service because of kickbacks thus depriving the country of value added service from contractors and consequently resulting to the implementation of water washed roads or schools. Healthcare facilities remain inadequate and inaccessible because most times, drugs meant for especially children and women particularly in provincial clinics and hospitals could be easily seen on the shelves of private pharmacies. Corruption undermines economic development by generating considerable distortions and inefficiency. In the private sector, corruption increases the cost of business through the price of illicit payments themselves, the management cost of negotiating with officials, and the risk of breached agreements or detection. Corruption also generates economic distortions in the public sector by diverting public investment into capital projects where bribes and kickbacks are more plentiful. Officials may increase the technical complexity of public sector projects to conceal or pave the way for such dealings, thus further distorting investment. Corruption also lowers compliance with construction, environmental, or other regulations, reduces the quality of government services and infrastructure, and increases budgetary pressures on government.[34]

Conclusion

Corruption in India is a major issue that adversely affects its economy. Black money refers to money that is not fully legitimately the property of the 'owner'. The causes of corruption in India include excessive regulations, complicated taxes and licensing systems, numerous government departments each with opaque bureaucracy and discretionary powers, monopoly by government controlled institutions on certain goods and services delivery, and the lack of transparent laws and processes. In government hospitals, corruption is associated with non-availability/duplication of medicines, getting admission, consultations with doctors and availing diagnostic services. Public servants have very wide discretionary powers offering the opportunity to extort undue payments from companies and ordinary citizens. Public servants in India can be penalised for corruption under the Indian Penal Code, 1860; Prosecution section of Income Tax Act, 1961; The Prevention of Corruption Act, 1988; The Benami Transactions (Prohibition) Act, 1988 to prohibit benami transactions; Prevention of Money Laundering Act, 2002.

REFERENCES

1. Boris Begovic, *Corruption: Concepts, Types, Causes, and Consequences,* Retrieved from http://www.cipe.org/sites/default/files/publication-docs/032105.pdf
2. *Corruption (2014),* Retrieved from http://en.wikipedia.org/wiki/Corruption
3. Ibid
4. *The Different Types of Corruption (2011),* Retrieved from http://www.indiastudychannel.com/resources/138785-The-different-types-Corruption.aspx
5. *Corruption in India,* Retrieved from http://en.wikipedia.org/wiki/Corruption_in_India
6. Jon S.T. Quah, *Corruption in Asia with special reference to Singapore: Patterns and consequences,* Retrieved from http://www.jonstquah.com/images/Corruption%20in%20Singapore%20AJPA.pdf
7. *Introduction: Corruption and counter-corruption across Asia,* Retrieved from http://www.humanrights.asia/resources/journals-magazines/article2/0901/01introduction-corruption-and-counter-corruption-across-asia
8. Jon S. T. Quah (2011). *Curbing Corruption in Asian Countries: An Impossible Dream?* Retrieved from http://books.google.co.in/books/

about/Curbing_Corruption_in_Asian_Countries.html?id=qKnKM2HbbO8C&redir_esc=y

9. *South Asia: Corruption plagues daily life,* Retrieved from http://www.transparency.org/news/pressrelease/20120116_south_asia
10. *Corruption,* Retrieved from http://www.africaneconomicoutlook.org/en/outlook/governance/corruption/
11. *Why Is Latin America So Corrupt?* Retrieved from http://www.insightcrime.org/news-analysis/why-is-latin-america-so-corrupt
12. *Global corruption: How does Latin America stack up?* Retrieved from http://www.csmonitor.com/World/Americas/Latin-America-Monitor/2013/1203/Global-corruption-How-does-Latin-America-stack-up
13. *Corruption,* Retrieved from http://ec.europa.eu/dgs/home-affairs/what-we-do/policies/organized-crime-and-human-trafficking/corruption/index_en.htm
14. *Commission unveils first EU Anti-Corruption Report*, Retrieved from http://europa.eu/rapid/press-release_IP-14-86_en.htm
15. *Corruption in India,* Retrieved from http://en.wikipedia.org/wiki/Corruption_in_India
16. *The Indian Express (Dec 3, 2013).* India Ranks 94th on Global Corruption Perception Index, Retrieved from http://www.newindianexpress.com/nation/India-Ranks-94th-on-Global-Corruption-Perception-Index/2013/12/03/article1925682.ece
17. *Corruption in India*, Retrieved from http://www.civilserviceindia.com/subject/Essay/corruption-in-india1.html
18. *The Times of India (Feb 28, 2014).* Corruption widespread in India, US report says, Retrieved from http://timesofindia.indiatimes.com/india/Corruption-widespread-in-India-US-report-says/articleshow/31143604.cms
19. *Why does corrupt India grow fast?* Retrieved from http://swaminomics.org/why-does-corrupt-india-grow-fast/
20. *Corruption in India,* Retrieved from http://en.wikipedia.org/wiki/Corruption_in_India
21. *Money in Swiss banks: India slips to 70th position; UK on top, NDTV (June 23, 2013).* See http://www.ndtv.com/article/india/

money-in-swiss-banks-india-slips-to-70th-position-uk-on-top-383065

22. *The Hindu (June 17, 2012).* India ranks 55th on foreign money in Swiss banks, Retrieved from http://www.thehindu.com/business/Economy/india-ranks-55th-on-foreign-money-in-swiss-banks/article3539521.ece
23. *SC declines Centre's plea on revisiting order on black money,* Retrieved from http://www.daijiworld.com/news/news_disp.asp?n_id=235347
24. *The Times of India (May 6, 2014).* CBI can investigate corruption charges against top babus without govt nod: SC, Retrieved from http://timesofindia.indiatimes.com/india/CBI-can-investigate-corruption-charges-against-top-babus-without-govt-nod-SC/articleshow/34726114.cms
25. Gyanant Singh (2011). *Supreme Court wants corrupt judges thrown out,* Retrieved from http://indiatoday.intoday.in/story/corruption-in-judiciary—sc-wants-corrupt-judges-thrown-out/1/137730.html
26. *Supreme Court fast-tracks corruption cases, NDTV (Feb10, 2011).* Retrieved from http://www.ndtv.com/article/india/supreme-court-fast-tracks-corruption-cases-84632
27. *The Indian Express (May 7, 2014).* All officials equal, no govt sanction needed to probe, Retrieved from http://indianexpress.com/article/india/india-others/sc-gives-cbi-more-teeth-to-fight-corruption-says-need-no-permission-to-probe-corrupt-government-officials/
28. *The Indian Express (April 8, 2014).* Coalgate: Centre,CBI heading for collision in Supreme Court on sanction issue, Retrieved from http://indianexpress.com/article/india/india-others/coalgate-centre-cbi-heading-for-collision-in-supreme-court-on-sanction-issue/
29. *Corruption in India,* Retrieved from http://en.wikipedia.org/wiki/Corruption_in_India
30. *The Times of India (May 13, 2014).* Whistleblowers Protection Act gets President's nod, Retrieved from http://indianexpress.com/article/india/india-others/whistleblowers-protection-act-gets-presidents-nod/

31. *India Against Corruption,* Retrieved from http://en.wikipedia.org/wiki/India_Against_Corruption
32. *What are the effects of corruption?* See https://in.answers.yahoo.com/question/index?qid=20111126000923AACX1s6
33. *What effect does corruption have on nation? who gains and who suffers?* See https://in.answers.yahoo.com/question/index?qid=20090223075351AABcWf4
34. See http://gnpai.org/researchlibrary/corruption/THE%20EFFECTS% 20OF%20CORRUPTION.pdf

20

Drug Abuse

"Drug misuse is not a disease, it is a decision, like the decision to step out in front of a moving car. You would call that not a disease but an error of judgment."

- Philip K. Dick

Introduction

Drug is in the broadest of terms, a chemical substance that has known biological effects on humans or other animals. In pharmacology, a drug is *"a chemical substance used in the treatment, cure, prevention, or diagnosis of disease or used to otherwise enhance physical or mental well-being."* Drug addiction is a chronic, often relapsing brain disease that causes compulsive drug seeking and use, despite harmful consequences to the drug addict and those around them. Drug addiction is a brain disease because the abuse of drugs leads to changes in the structure and function of the brain. Drugs are chemicals that tap into the brain's communication system and disrupt the way nerve cells normally send, receive, and process information. Some drugs, such as marijuana and heroin, have a similar structure to chemical messengers, called *neurotransmitters,* which are naturally produced by the brain.[1]

Today, there is no part of the world that is free from the curse of drug trafficking and drug addiction. Millions of drug addicts, all over the world, are leading miserable lives, between life and death. India too is caught in this vicious circle of drug abuse, and the numbers of drug addicts are increasing day by day. Drugs have been used for medical purposes since time immemorial. But these days, drugs and narcotics are being used freely by the people all over the world. The abuse of narcotics has caused widespread concern to nations of the world. The number of people using opium, cocaine, charas, sedatives and other narcotics has surpassed all dimensions.[2]

Types of Drug

Drug abuse is a serious public health problem that affects almost every community and family in some way. Each year drug abuse causes millions of serious illnesses or injuries among Americans. Abused drugs include:

1. *Amphetamines:* It is a very addictive stimulant drug. It is a powder that can be made into a pill or a shiny rock. The powder can be eaten or snorted up the nose. It can also be mixed with liquid and injected into your body with a needle.
2. *Anabolic steroids:* Anabolic steroids are man-made substances related to male sex hormones. Doctors use anabolic steroids to treat some hormone problems in men, delayed puberty, and muscle loss from some diseases.
3. *Club drugs:* The term club drug refers to a wide variety of dangerous drugs. These drugs are often used by young adults at all-night dance parties, dance clubs, and bars. Club drugs are also sometimes used as date rape drugs, to make someone unable to say no to or fight back against sexual assault.
4. *Cocaine:* Cocaine is a white powder. It can be snorted up the nose or mixed with water and injected with needle. Cocaine can also be made into small white rocks, called crack. Crack is smoked in a small glass pipe.
5. *Heroin:* Heroin is a white or brown powder or black, sticky goo. It is made from morphine, a natural substance in the seedpod of the Asian poppy plant. It can be mixed with water and injected with needle. Heroin can also be smoked or snorted up the nose.
6. *Inhalants:* Household products such as glues, hair sprays, paints and lighter fluid can be drugs for kids in search of a quick high. Many young people inhale vapors from these, not knowing that it can cause serious health problems.

7. *Marijuana:* Marijuana is a green, brown, or gray mix of dried, crumbled leaves from the marijuana plant. It can be rolled up and smoked like a cigarette or cigar or smoked in a pipe. Sometimes, people mix it in food and eat it.
8. *Prescription drugs:* Abusing some prescription drugs can lead to addiction. These include narcotic painkillers, sedatives, tranquilizers, and stimulants. Every medicine has some risk of side effects. Doctors take this into account when prescribing medicines.[3]

Reasons of Drug Abuse

Drug abuse is a complex phenomenon, which has various social, cultural, biological, geographical, historical and economic aspects. The disintegration of the old joint family system, absence of parental love and care in modern families where both parents are working, decline of old religious and moral values etc lead to a rise in the number of drug addicts who take drugs to escape hard realities of life. Drug use, misuse or abuse is also primarily due to the nature of the abused drug, the personality of the individual and the addict's immediate environment.[4] In order to become modern, students with heavy purses take to drug habit. When their money is spent they spread its use among others, some youth take drugs to overcome frustration in life. Some children take to drugs whose parents often quarrel at home. There are scores of other factors which lead children to drug addiction. They try to ape the Western youth who have fallen prey to drug addiction.[5]

Drug Abuse and Afghanistan

The area of the *'Golden Crescent'* consists of Afghanistan, Pakistan and Iran. It has emerged as the leading heroin producing region in the world. In fact, the Taliban regime of Afghanistan had covertly encouraged opium production and collected 20 per cent tax from opium dealers and transporters, which went straight to the war chest. Over 80 per cent of opium is grown in Afghanistan's northern province of Nangarhar and in the Helmand valley in southern Afghanistan. The ethnic bonds between the Baluchi tribesmen on both sides of the Afghan /Iran border provide the transnational link which safeguards the traffic. It is important to note that Pakistan's ISI supported drug smuggling as a means to laundering huge amounts of money to meet the heavy expenses of war on various fronts, including Afghanistan and India's states of Punjab and Kashmir. The Mujahideen of Afghanistan accelerated production of heroin, which became a lucrative business for them. Besides, the land route to Central Europe via the Balkans, the Indo-Pak border is also being used extensively for transporting narcotics first to India and then to other countries.[6]

Al Qaeda, the Taliban and other terrorist organisations are receiving hundreds of millions of dollars from illegal drugs in Afghanistan. In insurgent-controlled territory, insurgents collect this income by taxing poppy farmers, running protection rackets, operating heroin labs and conducting kidnapping and other smuggling schemes.[7] In Afghanistan's poppy-rich south and southwest, known links exist between Taliban insurgents and the drug traffickers who operate along the Pakistan border. There was also historic precedence for insurgents in Afghanistan to support the opium trade. The opium poppy has flourished along the Golden Crescent throughout recorded history. If the mujahideen's involvement in the poppy trade was cause for concern, more worrisome still were the Pakistan military's links to heroin trafficking. Taliban insurgents tax farmers in their control zones.[8]

Issues related to illicit drugs are not limited to the direct consequences for its users. In regions with high concentration of drug fields, the economy is affected by production of such plants instead of crops necessary for nutrition and in some provinces of Afghanistan, the family income depends from as much as 40 per cent on opium. Afghanistan is the world's top producer of opium and its derivates which accounts for 82 per cent of world production. Seizures of opium, morphine or heroin have been rising in recent years; the reason may be either bigger production or more effective seizure actions, or both. People involved in organised crime are taking part in both licit and illicit economy and as a result the borders of black/white or grey economy are very wide. Problem of opium production is being tackled by reducing the cultivation of poppy. Afghanistan is an insecure country in turbulent region and its complex issues pose a threat to peace and development of the entire world. Perils, such as organised crime, insurgencies and conflicts, are closely related to illicit drug production and trade.[9]

Drug Abuse and South-East Asia

The Golden Triangle refers to a roughly triangular zone in the highlands of South East Asia that overlaps Burma, Thailand and Laos. Although divided among the three countries, it is a region that shares significant attributes i.e. opium production, remote upland terrain, mountain minority populations, extreme ethnic diversity, mass Christian conversion, and a long history of insurgency.[10] Drug trafficking in the so-called Golden Triangle region of Myanmar, Laos, and Thailand is an evolving threat. A China-led anti-drug campaign in the three countries has helped stem the surging drug activity, with more than 1,000 arrests and three tonnes of drugs seized since April. But for Thailand, the war against narcotics appears to be far from won.[11] Thailand's Narcotics Act specifies that a *"competent official"* has the right to question, detain, search the premises, search the person, and seize any drug or any "property used to commit an offence" when dealing with a drugs suspect. The law also stipulates the officer must act in *"good faith"*, give reasons for his suspicion and record the event.[12]

Around 300,000 households in Burma are currently engaged in poppy cultivation. The country produced 690 tonnes of opium worth some $359 million, according to official figures about a fifth of the amount produced in Afghanistan. But demand for the drug is rising, and the UNODC warned that rising prices combined with poor harvest and a U.S.-backed eradication campaign in Afghanistan could provide strong cash incentives for Asian drug warlords to plug the gap. Poppies are a crop of choice for both cultural and commercial reasons, but mainly out of necessity. Ethnic-insurgent groups are usually blamed for the majority of Burma's drug trade.[13] Upsurge in drug trafficking in Laos is fuelling the potential for drug abuse among the youth. Although, there is no evidence of domestic manufacturing of yabaa, Laos's proximity to known production centres in neighbouring countries, particularly Myanmar, coupled with a lack of law enforcement resources and 5,000 km of borders, have made the land-locked country a conveyor belt for moving the drug to other large Asian markets, such as Thailand, Vietnam and China.[14]

Drug Abuse and Latin America

The illegal drug trade in Latin America concerns primarily the production and sale of cocaine and cannabis, including the export of these banned substances to the United States and Europe. Coco cultivation is concentrated in the Andes of South America, particularly in Colombia, Peru and Bolivia. This is the world's only source region for coco. The major drug trafficking organisations are Mexican and Colombian, and said to generate a total of $18 to $39 bn in wholesale drug proceeds per year. For more than ten years, the US has been funding Plan Colombia, which aims to combat illegal drugs production in the country, especially the growing of coca, the plant from which cocaine is produced.[15] Mexico's largest and most powerful drug gangs are the Zetas and the Sinaloa cartel. The Zetas operate in more than half of Mexico's states. Mexico's cartels control much of the illegal drugs trade from South America to the United States. Government security forces are fighting the drug cartels in an attempt to re-establish law and order. Rival cartels are at war with each other in bitter territorial battles. According to a study by international think tank Institute for Economics and Peace, northern Mexico continues to be the region worst affected by drug-related violence due to its proximity to the United States, the region's most important market for illicit drugs.[16]

Costa Rica and El Salvador, two countries highly affected by drug-related violence in recent years, have urged the United Nations to help fight drug cartels and organised crime, and called on member states with high numbers of drug consumers to take the lead on the issue.[17] Major drug crops in Latin America include coco bush, used to produce cocaine, and opium poppy, used to produce opiates, including heroin. Source zones for coco bush cover the Andean region of South America, particularly Colombia, Peru, and Bolivia. Source zones for opium poppy include Mexico, Colombia, and to a lesser extent, Guatemala. Drug consumption in Latin America remains low, compared to the primary global consumption markets led by the United States, Canada, and

Western Europe. The primary pathway today for illegal drugs entering the United States from abroad is through the Central America-Mexico corridor. The Caribbean-South Florida route continues to be active, and although it is currently less utilised than the Central America-Mexico route, some observers have warned that activity along this route may surge once more in the near future. Besides going to the United States, Latin American drugs, particularly cocaine, are also shipped to Europe. Latin America's central role in the illicit drug market stems largely from the Andean region's unique position as the world's only source region for coca and cocaine. Latin American drug trafficking organisations control various aspects of the drug supply chain and vary in terms of capabilities, organisational structures, and levels of associated violence. In addition, by the late 1990s, left-wing insurgent groups and right-wing paramilitary groups in Colombia had become extensively involved in the drug trade. The Latin America and the Caribbean region have among the highest crime rates, including violent crime rates of any region in the world. For at least 30 years, combating drug production and trafficking in Latin America and the Caribbean has been a major focus of U.S. international drug control effort. The U.S. and Colombian governments are committed to locking in existing gains as the United States gradually transfers responsibility for security and counterdrug programmes to the Colombians. [18]

Drug Abuse in India

India has been a traditional consumer of opium and various cannabis derivatives. These narcotics were mostly consumed for medicinal purposes, for recreation or during religious and social ceremonies. The proximity of the India-Pakistan border to the *'Golden Crescent'*, the largest producer of opium and cannabis in the world, has made it vulnerable to the trafficking of heroin and hashish. Other factors also contributed towards the increased inflow of heroin through the borders. The India-Pakistan border has been witnessing increased trafficking of heroin from the *'Golden Crescent'* since 1983, which can be surmised from the quantity of heroin seized by various law enforcement agencies. Since 1989, however, the total seizure of both heroin and hashish started registering a sharp decline indicating a dip in the trafficking of heroin from the Afghanistan-Pakistan region. However, various reports like those of the United Nations, the US State Department, Australian Crime Commission, etc. indicate that India has become a hub for the transshipment of heroin originating from the Afghanistan-Pakistan region to the rest of the world.[19]

A nexus among Pakistan's Inter Services Intelligence (ISI), Maoists and insurgent groups of North-East is using money earned from drug trafficking to fund terror activities in India. Major drug seizures on the India-Nepal border have put a spotlight on this revenue generation strategy adopted by terror groups.[20] Over the past three decades, the tiny western Indian state of Goa has become a popular beach destination for Indians and foreigners alike, offering a mix of sun, sand, music festivals, Ayurvedic-healing resorts and businesses bearing names such as Karmic Cafe, Buddha Tattoo and Nirvana Bar. People in Goa are reacting in a mixed and confused manner to all the changes tourism has brought.[21]

Prescription drug abuse is growing in India and the problem is serious in South Asia, according to a UN report which said drugs enter the region's illicit markets through various channels, being diverted from India's pharmacy industry and smuggled from Afghanistan. Drugs enter South Asia's illicit drug markets through a number of different channels, including diversion from India's pharmaceutical industry, illicit cultivation and/or manufacture within the region, and smuggling from other countries, including Afghanistan (through Pakistan) and Myanmar. Pharmaceutical preparations containing narcotic drugs and psychotropic substances continue to be diverted from India's pharmaceutical industry and are trafficked domestically or at the international level, including through illegal internet pharmacies. India remained one of the five main source countries for illicit cannabis resin mentioned by governments worldwide in seizure reports in 2011. The quantity of opium seized in India has been increasing since 2009, when about 1.7 tonne were seized, to more than three tonne in 2012. India also continued to be a main source of illicit amphetamine-type stimulants manufactured and trafficked in South Asia.[22]

Addicts and former police officers have confirmed widespread ties between political activists and drug-peddling in the Punjab. The scale of drug abuse in the state became public in 2009 through a submission to the Punjab and Haryana High Court by Harjit Singh, secretary of the department of social security and women and child development in Chandigarh. Singh said more than two-thirds of the state's rural household has at least one drug addict. Drug abuse in Punjab owes much to the state's declining agricultural economy, growing unemployment, the travails of rural life and Punjabi machismo. According to the 2009 Punjab government affidavit, the use of alcohol and drugs has become a part of culture in the state. Most cases have revealed a similar *modus operandi* among smugglers in both Pakistan and India of supplying and receiving consignments through border villages. Police investigations have uncovered links between political leaders, businessmen and drug smugglers.[23]

Effects of Drug Abuse

Drug abuse has led to a detrimental impact on the society. It has led to increase in the crime rate. Addicts resort to crime to pay for their drugs. Drugs remove inhibition and impair judgment egging one on to commit offences. Incidences of teasing, group clashes, assault and impulsive murders increase with drug abuse. Apart from affecting the financial stability, addiction increases conflicts and causes untold emotional pain for every member of the family.[24] The side effects of drugs vary depending on the type. Someone high on stimulants may experience an increase in energy that is by the cause drugs speeding up the body's metabolism and heart rate. Since these drugs increase the heart beat, an increase in blood pressure can be a related side effect. Each drug affects body in different ways. In addition, the long-term effects of drugs are different than the short-term effects. According to the National Institute on Drug Abuse, addiction occurs when a chemical dependency to a drug is combined with an overwhelming urge to use the substance.[25] Some drugs (such as alcohol, heroin and tranquillisers) have a sedative effect which slows down the way the body and brain function. Sedative drugs like alcohol and heroin can lead to fatal overdose, if a lot is taken. Stimulant drugs can produce anxiety or panic attacks particularly, if taken in large quantities. Hallucinogenic drugs sometimes produce very disturbing experiences and may lead to erratic or dangerous behaviour by the user, especially if they are already unstable.[26]

Government Initiatives

India has introduced a comprehensive national policy to help curb narcotic drug trafficking. It also attempts to curb the menace of drug use and contains provisions for treatment and rehabilitation. The recent unveiling of a national policy in India to combat the drug menace that affects up to 272 million people in the working age group has thus come as a *"shot in the foot"* for law enforcement agencies and those working in rehabilitation.[27]

The Narcotic Drugs and Psychotropic Substances Act, commonly referred to as the NDPS Act, is an Act of the Parliament of India that was assented to by President Giani Zail Singh on September 16, 1985, and came into force on November 14, 1985. The Narcotic Drugs and Psychotropic Substances Bill, 1985 was introduced in the Lok Sabha on August 23, 1985. It was passed by both the Houses of Parliament and was assented by the President on September 16, 1985. The Act extends to whole of India and applies also to Indian citizens outside India and to persons on ships and aircraft registered in India. Under one of the provisions of the Act, the Narcotics Control Bureau was set up with effect from March 1986.[28] The NDPS Act divides the powers and responsibility of regulation of licit activities. Section 9 of the Act has listed various activities which the central government can, by rules, regulate while. Section 10 lists various activities which the state governments can, by rules, regulate. Thus, we have NDPS Rules of the central government and the state NDPS Rules framed by each state government under the same Act.

The NDPS Act has created statutory authorities such as the Narcotics Commissioner (Section 5), the Competent Authority (Section 68D) and the Administrator (Section 68G). The organisation headed by the Narcotics Commissioner is known as the *Central Bureau of Narcotics* (CBN). Another authority called the Narcotics Control Bureau was created through a notification under Section 4 of the Act. Each of these authorities has specified functions. The state governments have their own health departments and social welfare departments each of which has its own set of activities relating to drug demand reduction.[29]

Conclusion

Drug abuse is a serious public health problem that affects almost every community and family in some way. Each year drug abuse causes millions of serious illnesses or injuries among Americans. Drug abuse plays a role in many major social problems, such as drugged driving, violence, stress, and child abuse. Drug abuse can lead to homelessness, crime, and missed work or problems with keeping a job. People abuse substances such as drugs, alcohol, and tobacco for varied and complicated reasons, but it is clear that our society pays a significant cost. Many substances can bring on withdrawal, an effect caused by cessation or reduction in the amount of the substance used. Many substances, such as alcohol, tranquilisers, opiates, and stimulants, over time can produce a phenomenon known as tolerance, where used in larger amount to produce the same level of intoxication.

REFERENCES

1. Drug Abuse, *Addiction, and the Brain*, Retrieved from http://www.webmd.com/mental-health/addiction/drug-abuse-addiction
2. *Short essay on Drug Addiction in India*, Retrieved from http://www.preservearticles.com/201105116461/drug-addiction-essay.html
3. *Drug abuse: Also called: Substance abuse,* Retrieved from http://www.nlm.nih.gov/medlineplus/drugabuse.html
4. Ahmad Nadeem, Bano Rubeena, Agarwal V.K., Kalakoti Piyush, *Substance abuse in India,* Retrieved from http://www.pravara.com/pmr/pmr-1-4-2.pdf
5. Short essay on Drug Addiction in India, Retrieved from http://www.preservearticles.com/201105116461/drug-addiction-essay.html
6. Aparajita Biswas, *Small Arms and Drug Trafficking In the Indian Ocean Region*, Retrieved from http://www.mu.ac.in/arts/social_science/african_studies/biswaswp.pdf
7. *Terrorist organizations still profit from Afghan drug trade,* Retrieved from http://www.washingtontimes.com/news/2013/sep/20/terrorist-organizations-still-profit-afghan-drug-t/

8. Gretchen Peters, *How Opium Profits the Taliban,* Retrieved from http://www.usip.org/sites/default/files/resources/taliban_opium_1.pdf

9. *Issue of drug trafficking and drug cultivation in Afghanistan,* Retrieved from http://www.studentsummit.cz/data/1354903850354NATO_Issue-of-drug-trafficking-in-Afghanistan.pdf

10. Aparajita Biswas, *Small Arms and Drug Trafficking In the Indian Ocean Region*, Retrieved from http://www.mu.ac.in/arts/social_science/african_studies/biswaswp.pdf

11. *Thailand battles escalating drug trade*, Retrieved from http://english.cntv.cn/program/asiatoday/20130607/106557.shtml

12. See http://reallifethailand.blogspot.in/2007/10/drugs-in-thailand.html

13. *Obstacles Ahead in Burma's Opium War,* Retrieved from http://world.time.com/2013/03/19/obstacles-ahead-in-burmas-opium-war/

14. *Laos: "Unprecedented" drug trafficking heightens risk to youth,* Retrieved from http://www.irinnews.org/report/93232/laos-unprecedented-drug-trafficking-heightens-risk-to-youth

15. See http://en.wikipedia.org/wiki/Illegal_drug_trade_in_Latin_America

16. *Who is behind Mexico's drug-related violence?* See http://www.bbc.com/news/world-latin-america-10681249

17. Drug trafficking greatest threat to Latin American countries today, UN hears, *Retrieved from http://www.un.org/apps/news/story.asp?NewsID=39726#. U3hvQTtQHFw*

18. Clare Ribando Seelke, Liana Sun Wyler, June S. Beittel & Mark P. Sullivan (2011). *Latin America and the Caribbean: Illicit Drug Trafficking and U.S. Counterdrug Programs*, Retrieved from http://www.fas.org/sgp/crs/row/R41215.pdf

19. Pushpita Das (2012). *Drug trafficking in India: A case for border security,* Retrieved from http://www.idsa.in/system/files/OP_DrugTraffickinginIndia.pdf

20. Drug trafficking: *'Money funds terror acts in India',* Retrieved from http://www.dailymail.co.uk/indiahome/indianews/article-2201870/Drug-trafficking-Money-funds-terror-acts-India.html

21. *Tourism crisis on India's 'cocaine coast,* Retrieved from http://www.thestar.com/news/world/2014/02/15/tourism_crisis_on_indias_cocaine_coast.html
22. *Prescription drug abuse growing in India: UN report (Mar 5, 2014).* Retrieved from http://indianexpress.com/article/india/india-others/prescription-drug-abuse-growing-in-india-un-report/
23. *Drug hurricane' lashing India's Punjab,* Retrieved from http://www.aljazeera.com/indepth/features/2014/04/hurricane-lashing-india-punjab-201442982348612953.html
24. Ahmad Nadeem, Bano Rubeena, Agarwal V.K., Kalakoti Piyush, *Substance abuse in India,* Retrieved from http://www.pravara.com/pmr/pmr-1-4-2.pdf
25. See http://drugabuse.com/library/drug-abuse-effects/
26. See http://www.drugscope.org.uk/resources/faqs/faqpages/what-are-the-dangers-from-using-drugs
27. See http://www.dw.de/india-introduces-new-policy-to-curb-drug-trafficking/a-15735799
28. *Narcotic Drugs and Psychotropic Substances Act,* Retrieved from http://en.wikipedia.org/wiki/Narcotic_Drugs_and_Psychotropic_Substances_Act_(India)
29. See http://cbn.nic.in/html/NationalPolicyEnglish.pdf

21
Superstition

"Science can purify religion from error and superstition. Religion can purify science from idolatry and false absolutes."
- Pope John Paul II

Introduction

In Shakespeare's time ignorance and superstition held relentless sway over the popular mind. The woods were the haunts of fairies. Our modern enlightenment has driven away these gentle creatures from their accustomed playgrounds.[1] Over 800,000 people in the United Kingdom have confessed that they believe in the power of lucky underwear, while 2.7 million people admit to holding onto the childhood belief that if you blow out all of your birthday candles in one breath, your wish will come true. And it seems people are just as superstitious when it comes to bringing about good luck too. The number seven scored as the number the nation cited as their luckiest number, with David Beckham, who plays in a number seven shirt and even gave his daughter the middle name Seven, counted among them. People believed having a lucky number brought them good fortune. And despite popular thinking that the number 13 is the unluckiest of all, in the survey, it came out as the second luckiest. People also create their own superstitions and rituals in the belief it will change their fortunes.[2] Superstition, like religion, is detrimental to those who follow it, mostly because manipulative characters ably use it against them.

Different cultures have traditionally held differing superstitious beliefs, beliefs that are deemed *"irrational."* Such beliefs go back to ancient cultures such as the Greeks and Romans, who believed that natural occurrences were a result of actions of gods. Such fear of gods, *deisidaimonia,* was what the Romans meant by *superstition*. In Western cultures, some superstitions actually caused more bad luck such as the belief in England that cats were witches and they were the cause of the Plague. By killing off the cats, the English caused the rat population to flourish, and, thus increase diseases. Many superstitious beliefs are connected to religion. For instance, if one holds out a cross or wears one, the person can ward off evil. Certain talismans worn or hung in houses were to have warded off evil.[3] Women are far more superstitious than men. This has a lot to do with the lack of education among women.

What is Superstition?

Superstition is the belief in supernatural causality that one event leads to the cause of another without any natural process linking the two events—such as astrology, religion, omens, witchcraft, prophecies, etc., that contradicts natural science According to the Oxford dictionary, Superstition means *"A widely held but irrational belief in supernatural influences, especially as leading to good or bad luck, or a practice based on such a belief."* The word superstition comes from two Latin words: *"Super"* and *"Stare"*. Super means above and stare means to stand. It refers to the blind faith in an idea without giving any consideration to reason, logic and evidence. Many superstitions have originated in human society on account of ignorance and fear of the unknown and incomprehensible. They thrive mainly on the greed of human beings. Superstitions primarily represent the underlying inherent fear of mankind, caused by the uncertainties of this world. In a way, it is a sign of acceptance of our ignorance and limitations of our power. In another way, it is a sign of accepting the grandiose of this universe and its scheme of operation, which is still largely beyond our comprehension and understanding.[4]

Reasons of Superstition

Superstition, an outcome of human fears and imagination, is the strongest belief which a human being has ever kept.

Psychologists say that it is a human tendency to believe the bad than the good. It is so because, the good does not strike a caution, but the evil does and steps need to be taken to prevent it from happening.[5] There are many reasons of superstitions. Many of them are age-old and inherited as part of our cultural heritage. These are changing fast with time, and their death has been hastened by mixing of cultures, modern scientific education, urbanisation and changing life styles.

On the other hand, superstitions that have a basis in our own experiences and psyche are growing and will be more difficult to remove. Many a time, we know that a particular belief is superstitious, irrational and hence illogical, yet we hesitate to go against it, because of some past experience, our own or that of others, which tells us that there may be something in it.[6] Superstitions originated perhaps, when man was at the mercy of natural elements. He respected and worshipped the forces of nature like the sun, the moon, water etc. He worshipped fire because of its destructive ability. When man started falling prey to diseases, he started appeasing gods with offerings, penances and sacrifices to ward off evil spirits.[7]

Superstition in India

Superstition in India is considered a widespread social problem. Superstition refers to any belief or practice which is an explained by supernatural causality, and is in contradiction to modern science. Superstitions are usually attributed to the lack of education. In India, educated people have also been observed following beliefs that may be considered superstitious. Thousands of people believe in superstitions, although a lot of people think of them as nonsense and not based on reason. Most of the people, more or less, believe in them. Even though they deny superstitions, they cannot help believing in them. They are superstitious. Unfortunately, we have hundreds of superstitions. Superstitions are around the world. They change from culture to culture and have a big influence in our lives.

There are two types of superstitions. Good luck superstitions and bad luck superstitions.[8] In India too, people are confronted by a number of superstitions. A cat crossing one's path, the sight of a Brahmin or a sneeze means the purpose of the journey which was being undertaken would remain unaccomplished. Hooting of an owl, howling of a dog augurs an impending death or a doom. Contracting chicken pox is considered to be wrath of a goddess *'Durga'*. So, the goddess is appeased with offerings.[9]

Humans, when unable to rule out a theory, howsoever irrational it might appear, prefer to take the safer route and make sure that won't do something which can later lead to some adversity, harm or injury. This is why most superstitions are associated with a fear of some harm that may befall the person, if s(he) does or fails to do a particular thing.[10] The following list notes some common superstitions of India: (a) Adding one rupee to a gift sum is auspicious, i.e., sums like 21 or 101 rupees are considered more auspicious than say 20 or 100; (b) There are several methods of warding of an *"evil eye"*. Lemon-and-chilli totems are a common method; (c) In some parts of India, it is considered inauspicious to sweep the floor at night; (d) To see a peacock before a journey is considered auspicious; (e) Widows are considered inauspicious in many parts of India; (f) Saturdays are considered very inauspicious, as it is associated with the god Shani (Saturn); (g) It is believed that looking in a broken mirror may bring bad luck; (h) Peepul trees are believed to be the abode of ghosts and they are avoided at night; (i) Dogs howling in the night signal a death; (j) A crow cawing at your window means a guest is sure to arrive; (k) Don't cut your hair on Thursdays.[11]

In the Western societies, during the Middle Ages (about 1,100 to 1.500) thousands of innocent men and women were killed merely on the grounds that they practised witchcraft. In Medico, during Azetic regime, hundreds of men were brutally sacrificed every year to appease Gods. In India, till mid-nineteenth century, thousands of women were burnt alive in the funeral pyre of their husbands on the superstition that they would live in heaven with their husbands. During Puri Jegannath Temple's car festival, many devotees would voluntarily fall before the wheels of the chariot to get killed. They committed this suicide on the supposition that they would go to heaven. In Western societies, Friday is an unlucky day and thirteen is an unlucky number. Contrarily, Friday is an auspicious day to Muslims and Hindus. Similarly, crossing of black cat on one's path is bad omen in

Western countries and India. But, it is a good omen in Egypt. Thus, the kind of superstitions varies from country to country. In India, superstitions are numerous and varied in nature. In Indian societies, idol worship is one of the major superstitions that preclude the development of scientific bent of mind. In India, majority are under the impression that they can peep into their future with the help of astrology. Even the educated Indians believe the blabbering of the illiterate astrologers.[12]

Good Luck Superstitions

1. If your right hand itches, you will earn money.
2. If you find a four-leaf clover, you will have good luck.
3. If you see a horseshoe which was lost, you will have good luck.
4. If you throw rice on a new bride and groom, they will have so many children.
5. If you dream about a white cat, you will have good luck.
6. If you see a black cat walking towards you, it brings you good luck.
7. If your right ear itches, someone is speaking well of you.
8. You can hang up garlic in your house for good luck.
9. If you put a mirror just across the door, you will have good luck.
10. If you put the sugar into the cup first, before the tea, you will have good luck.
11. If you step on your shadow, it brings you good luck.
12. Right eye twitching is good for men
13. Left eye twitching is good for women
14. Eye twitching signifies that somebody is about to arrive
15. If you catch a falling leaf on the first day of autumn, you will have good luck all winter.
16. If you blow all the candles out on your birthday cake in one blow, you will get whatever you want.
17. If the first butterfly you see in the year is white, it brings you good luck all year.
18. If girl drinks salty water then goes to sleep, she will see her future husband in her dream.[13]

Bad Luck Superstitions

1. If you open an umbrella indoors, it brings you bad luck.
2. If you sleep with your feet towards the door, a nightwalker will steal your soul.
3. If you whistle at night, a nightwalker will come to your home.
4. When a cat sneezes three times indoors, it will rain in 24 hours.
5. If you dream about a dog, you will have a lot of enemies.
6. If you break a mirror, it will bring you seven years of bad luck.
7. If an owl hoots in your garden, it brings you bad luck.
8. If you walk under a ladder, you will have bad luck.
9. If you kill an albatross, it brings you bad luck.
10. If you sleep on a table, you will have bad luck.
11. If a dog howls at night, death is near.
12. If you see a bird that comes towards you, you will have bad luck.
13. If you drop a dishcloth, you will have bad luck.
14. If you eat from the pot, it will rain at your wedding ceremony.
15. If you start a trip on Friday, you will meet misfortune.
16. Right eye twitching is a bad omen/ Left eye twitching is a bad omen.
17. Menstruating women are considered impure and unclean.
18. Pregnant women, especially, must stay indoors in order to ensure their babies are not born with any deformities.
19. If your left hand itches, you will lose money.[14]

Effects of Superstition

Superstition is widespread effect. Superstition is a belief in supernatural causality: that one event leads to the cause of another without any physical process linking the two events, such as astrology, omens, witchcraft, etc. that contradicts natural science. Superstitions have long been one of the strange phenomena, which are commonly observed, well accepted and yet hardly understood. To some, they are just crazy beliefs, to others, matters of faith and tradition. It affects the working ability and productivity of people. Some time it also waste money when people spend on religious activity for their safety. It increases dependent of people on their luck or other persons. It exploited people.

Science and Superstition

When we talk of science and superstition together it appears as though we are trying to put two opposites together, and, in doing so, putting forth an obviously awkward act. Science appeals to reason, logic and can be explained, Superstition relates to none of these three qualities. It appears very illogical to believe in any superstition, because it cannot be explained to any reasoning. Thus both science and superstition are obviously two opposites. Even the most advanced modern educated Indians still seem to believe that we can get rid of the effect of our sins by taking a dip in the Ganges.[15]

Conclusion

Superstitions are deep rooted and irrational beliefs, which have no profanity. It is common in both developed and developing countries. Superstitions are the legacy of every civilisation and are inherited by the following generations. There are so many superstitions. Friday the thirteenth is a scary day. Black cats are bad luck. Don't walk under a ladder. Breaking a mirror brings you seven years bad luck. There are examples from every culture, and they are somewhat similar. All civilisations have their respective superstitions. But some like beliefs in ghosts, sorcery, witchcraft and spirits are universal. Superstitions are deep rooted and irrational beliefs, which have no profanity.

REFERENCES

1. Superstition, *Alchemy and Astrology in Shakespeare's Day,* Retrieved from http://www.shakespeare-online.com/biography/superstition.html
2. See http://www.dailymail.co.uk/femail/article-2230328/Britons-superstitions-Walking-ladders-breaking-mirrors-opening-umbrellas-indoors.html
3. See http://www.enotes.com/homework-help/what-some-examples-superstitious-beliefs-391017

4. *Reasons why people believe on superstations,* Retrieved from http://vkumar.expertscolumn.com/article/reasons-why-people-believe-superstitions
5. *Superstitions And Their Reasons,* Retrieved from http://www.boldsky.com/insync/pulse/2010/reasons-superstition-130810.html
6. *Reasons why people believe on superstations*, Retrieved from http://vkumar.expertscolumn.com/article/reasons-why-people-believe-superstitions
7. See http://aman.hubpages.com/hub/Common-Superstitions-and-Superstitious-beliefs-in-India
8. *Good luck superstitions and bad luck superstitions (2008),* Retrieved from http://www.atakos.com/good-luck-bad-luck-superstitions-81/
9. See http://aman.hubpages.com/hub/Common-Superstitions-and-Superstitious-beliefs-in-India
10. *Reasons why people believe on superstations,* Retrieved from http://vkumar.expertscolumn.com/article/reasons-why-people-believe-superstitions
11. *List of superstations in India*, Retrieved from http://en.wikipedia.org/wiki/List_of_superstitions_in_India
12. *Superstitions and Indians-N.Anandan,* Retrieved from http://www.modernrationalist.com/2011/july/page08.html
13. *Good luck superstitions and bad luck superstitions (2008),* Retrieved from http://www.atakos.com/good-luck-bad-luck-superstitions-81/
14. What are Superstitious Beliefs? - Why do People Believe in Superstitions?, Hub Pages, Retrieved from http://valeed.hubpages.com/hub/What-are-Superstitions
15. What are Superstitious Beliefs? - Why do People Believe in Superstitions?, Hub Pages, Retrieved from http://valeed.hubpages.com/hub/What-are-Superstitions

Bibliography

- A. Kumar (2006). *Women and Crime: Dimensions and Remedial Measures,* Anmol Publications Pvt., Limited.
- A. S. Garg (1990). *Bride burning: crime against women,* Sandeep Publication.
- A. S. Srinivasar Aiyar (1930). *The Child Marriage Restraint Act, 1929*, Universal Law Publishing.
- Abdul Matin (1992). *The Law on Dowry Prohibition and Child Marriage* Restraint, Palak Publishers.
- Adam Hibbert (2004). *Children's Rights*, Sea-To-Sea Publisher

- Adam Hibbert (2004). *Children's Rights*, Sea-To-Sea Publisher.

- Alessandro Cigno and Furio Camillo Rosati (2005). *The Economics of Child Labour*, Oxford University Press.
- Alexandra Stiglmayer (1994). *Mass Rape: The War Against Women in Bosnia-Herzegovina,* U of Nebraska Press.
- Anaclaudia Gastal Fassa, David L. Parker, and Thomas J. Scanlon (2010). *Child Labour: A Public Health Perspective*, Oxford University Press.
- Andrea Dworkin (1981). *Pornography: Men Possessing Women,* Women's Press.
- Andrea Dworkin (1989). *Pornography: men possessing women*, Dutton.
- Andrea Warren (1998). *Orphan Train Rider: One Boy's True Story,* Houghton Mifflin Harcourt.
- Andrea Warren (2004), *We Rode the Orphan Trains*, Houghton Mifflin Harcourt.
- Andrea Warren (2011). *Charles Dickens and the Street Children of London*, Houghton Mifflin Harcourt.

- Arjun Prakash Aggarwal (1992). *Sexual Harassment in the Workplace*, Edition 2, Butterworth Pub Limited.
- Arvind Ganesan, and Patricia Gossman (1996). *Police Abuse and Killings of Street Children in India*, Human Rights Watch Children's Rights Project.
- Asha Bajpai (2003). *Child Rights in India: Law, Policy, and Practice,* Oxford University Press.
- Asha Bajpai (2003). *Child Rights in India: Law, Policy, and Practice,* 1st edition, Oxford University Press
- Assefa Bekele, and Jo Boyden (1988). *Combating Child Labour*. International Labour Organisation.
- Assefa Bekele, and William E. Myers (1995). *First Things First in Child Labour: Eliminating Work Detrimental to Children*, International Labour Organisation.
- B. S. Nagi (1993). *Child Marriage in India: A Study of Its Differential Patterns in Rajasthan*, Mittal Publications.
- Bella Chagall (1988). *Burning Lights: A Unique Double Portrait of Russia*, Knopf Doubleday Publishing Group.
- Bernie Anderson (2007). *Breaking the Silence: A Pastor Goes Public about His Battle with Pornography,* Autumn House Publishing.
- Beryl Rawson (1996). *Marriage, Divorce, and Children in Ancient Rome,* Humanities Research Centre.
- Bibek Bhandari (Aug 15, 2013), *No life for a child: The grim reality of Nepal's child laborers,* Retrieved from http://edition.cnn.com/2013/08/14/world/asia/nepal-child-labor/
- *Bhutan Child labour,* Retrieved from http://www.refworld.org/docid/4e8c397319.html
- *Bonded labour*, Retrieved from http://www.un.org.np/oneun/bondedlabour
- *Bonded Labour in South Asia,* Retrieved from http://weeklybolshevik.com/2013/06/10/bonded-labor-in-south-asia/
- C. P. Rai (2002). *Child labour: a reality*, Volume 2, Laxmi Shikshan Sansthan.
- Carol J. Adams (2004). *The Pornography of Meat*, Continuum.
- Carol Neel (2004). *Medieval Families: Perspectives on Marriage, Household, and Children,* University of Toronto Press.
- Catharine A. MacKinnon (1979). *Sexual Harassment of Working Women: A Case of Sex Discrimination,* Yale University Press.

- Catharine A. MacKinnon, and Andrea Dworkin (1997). *In Harm's Way: The Pornography Civil Rights Hearings*, Harvard University Press.
- Catharine A. MacKinnon, and Reva B. Siegel (2004). *Directions in Sexual Harassment Law,* Yale University Press.
- Cathryne L. Schmitz, Elizabeth KimJin Traver, and Desi Larson (2004). *Child Labor: A Global View,* Greenwood Publishing Group.
- Chitra Banerjee Divakaruni (2000). *Black Candle: Poems about Women from India,* Pakistan, and Bangaladesh, CALYX Books.
- Chapter I, *S7ntroduction and Review of Literature,* Retrieved from http://ietd.inflibnet.ac.in/bitstream/10603/648/6/06_chapter1.pdf
- *Child labour in Bangladesh,* UNICEF, Retrieved from http://www.unicef.org/bangladesh/Child_labour.pdf
- *Child labour in Nepal*, Retrieve from http://www.darvag.com/jamiat/bultan/wc-nepal.pdf
- Claire M. Renzetti, Jeffery L. Edleson, and Raquel Kennedy Bergen (2001). *Sourcebook on Violence Against Women*, SAGE.
- Clive Gifford (2009). *Child Labour,* Evans Brothers.
- Colin Wringe (1981). *Children's rights: a philosophical study,* Routledge and Kegan Paul.
- Colin Wringe (1991). *Children's rights: a philosophical study*, Routledge and Kegan Paul.
- Courtney Farrell (2010). *Children's Rights*, ABDO.
- Courtney Farrell (2010). *Children's Rights*, ABDO.
- D.C. Nanjunda (2008). *Child Labour and Human Rights: A Prospective,* New Delhi: Gyan Publishing House.
- David Archard (1993). *Children: Rights and Childhood,* 1st edition, Taylor & Francis.
- David Archard (1993). *Children: Rights and Childhood*, Routledge.
- David Archard (2004). *Children: Rights & Childhood,* 1st edition, Psychology Press.
- David Archard (2004). *Children: Rights and Childhood,* Routledge.
- David Finkelhor, Kersti Yllö (1987). *License to Rape: Sexual Abuse of Wives,* Free Press.

- Debarati Halder, and K. Jaishankar (2011). *Cyber Crime and the Victimization of Women: Laws, Rights and Regulations,* Idea Group Inc (IGI).
- Deborah M. Merrill (2011). *When Your Children Marry: How Marriage Changes Relationships with Sons and Daughters,* Rowman & Littlefield Publishers.
- Dennis Frederick (2007). *Conquering Pornography: Overcoming the Addiction: A Practical*, WinePress Publishing.
- Diana E. H. Russell (1990). *Rape in Marriage*, Indiana University Press.
- Dr. Sukanta Sarkar and Dr. Md. Alam (2014), *Microfinance and Women Empowerment*, New Delhi: Global Vision Publishing House.
- Eleanor Flexner, and Ellen Frances Fitzpatrick (1996). *Century of Struggle: The Woman's Rights Movement in the United States,* Harvard University Press.
- Elizabeth Podnieks, Jordan I. Kosberg, and Ariela Lowenstein (2005). *Elder Abuse: Selected Papers from the Prague World Congress on Family Violence,* Haworth Maltreatment & Trauma Press.
- Elizabeth Russell Connelly (2000). *Child Abuse and Neglect: Examining the Psychological Components,* Chelsea House.
- Ellen Carol DuBois (1998). *Woman Suffrage and Women's Rights,* NYU Press
- Ellen Lynn Hall, & Jennifer Kofkin Rudkin (2011). *Seen and Heard: Children's Rights in Early Childhood Education,* Teachers College Press.
- Ellen Lynn Hall, and Jennifer Kofkin Rudkin (2011). *Seen and Heard: Children's Rights in Early Childhood Education,* Teachers College Press.
- Ellen Murray (2010). *Children Matter: Exploring child and human rights issues in Canada,* MRU Book Store.
- Emma Guest (2003). *Children of AIDS: Africa's orphan crisis,* Pluto Press.
- Eugeen Verhellen (1996). *Monitoring Children's Rights*, Martinus Nijhoff Publishers.
- Eugeen Verhellen (1996). *Monitoring Children's Rights,* Martinus Nijhoff Publishers.
- F. M. Christensen (1990). *Pornography: The Other Side,* Greenwood Publishing Group.

- Facts On File, and Incorporated (2002). *Crimes Against Women*, Infobase Publishing.
- *Fighting Bonded labour in Nepal*, Retrieved from http://www.ilo.org/global country/bangladesh/
- Francis Achampong (1999). *Workplace Sexual Harassment Law: Principles, Landmark Developments, and Framework for Effective Risk Management,* Greenwood Publishing Group.
- Gail Dines, Robert Jensen, and Ann Russo (1998). *Pornography: The Production and Consumption of Inequality*, Psychology Press.
- Gamini Herath, and Kishor Sharma (2007). *Child Labour in South Asia,* Ashgate Publishing, Ltd.
- Geoffrey Steven Kyeyune (1996). *Street children: why are they out?,* Fountain Publishers.
- Georges Kristoffel Lieten (2005). *Child Labour: Burning Questions : Inaugural Lecture,* Amsterdam University Press.
- Garance Genicot, *Child Bonded Labor,* Retrieved from http://faculty.georgetown.edu/gg58/CBL.pdf
- Geraldine Terry (2007). *Women's Rights,* Copenhagen: Oxfam GB and Pluto Press.
- Geraldine Terry (2008). *Sex Trafficking: Inside the Business of Modern Slavery.* Columbia University Press.
- Geraldine Van Bueren (1998). *The International Law on the Rights of the Child*, Martinus Nijhoff Publishers.
- Geraldine Van Bueren (1998). *The International Law on the Rights of the Child, Martinus* Nijhoff Publishers
- Geraldine Van Bueren (2007). *Child Rights in Europe: Convergence andDivergence in Judicial Protection*, Council of Europe.
- Geraldine Van Bueren (2007). *Child Rights in Europe: Convergence andDivergence in Judicial Protection*, Council of Europe
- Gopal Bhargava (2003). *Child Labour*, Volume 2, New Delhi: Gyan Publishing House.
- Gopal Bhargava (2003). *Child labour,* Volume 2, New Delhi: Kalpaz Publications.
- Herma Silverstein (1994). *Date Abuse*, Enslow Pub Incorporated.

- Holly Johnson, Natalia Ollus, & Sami Nevala (2007). *Violence Against Women: An International Perspective*, Springer.
- Holly Littlefield (2001). *Children of the Orphan Trains,* Lerner Publications.
- Hugh D. Hindman (2002). *Child Labor: An American History,* M.E. Sharpe.
- Hugh D. Hindman (2011). *The World of Child Labor: An Historical and Regional Survey,* M.E. Sharpe.
- Human Rights Watch (Organisation), Women's Rights Project (Human Rights Watch) (1991). *Criminal Injustice: Violence Against Women in Brazil,* Human Rights Watch.
- Jane Fortin (1998). *Children's Rights and the Developing Law, Butterworth,* (Publishers) Limited.
- Jane Fortin (1998). *Children's Rights and the Developing Law,* Butterworth, (Publishers) Limited
- Jane Fortin (2003). *Children's Rights and the Developing Law,* 1st edition, Cambridge University Press
- Jane Fortin (2003). *Children's Rights and the Developing Law,* Cambridge University Press.
- Jane Fortin (2009). *Children's Rights and the Developing Law,* Cambridge University Press
- Jane Gallop (1997). *Feminist Accused of Sexual Harassment,* Duke University Press.
- Jane Humphries (2010). *Childhood and Child Labour in the British Industrial Revolution,* Cambridge University Press.
- Jaya Sagade (2005). *Child Marriage In India: Socio-legal And Human Rights Dimensions*, Oxford University Press
- Jessica Spector (2006). *Prostitution and Pornography: Philosophical Debate about the Sex Industry,* Stanford University Press.
- Joan Nordquist (1986). *Domestic violence: spouse abuse / marital rape*, Reference and Research Services.
- Joanne Belknap (2007). *The invisible woman: gender, crime, and justice*, Thomson/Wadsworth.
- Joanne Mariner (2001). *No Escape: Male Rape in U.S. Prisons*, Human Rights Watch.
- Joe Lugalla, and Colleta G. Kibassa (2002). *Poverty, AIDS, and street children in East Africa,* Edwin Mellen Press.

- John Kabutha Mugo (2004). *Rehabilitation of Street Children in Kenya: Approaches, Quality and Challenges, IKO,* Verlag für Kulturelle Kommunikation.
- John T. Pardeck (2006). *Children's Rights: Policy and Practice,* 1st edition, Psychology Press
- John T. Pardeck (2006). *Children's Rights: Policy and Practice,* Psychology Press.
- Joseph W. Slade (2001). *Pornography and Sexual Representation: A Reference Guide,* Volume 2, Greenwood Publishing Group.
- Joyce Hart (2009). *Human Trafficking*, The Rosen Publishing Group.
- Judy Westwater, and Wanda Carter (2006). *Street Kid: One Child's Desperate Fight for Survival*, HarperElement.
- Julia Sloth-Nielsen (2008). *Children's Rights in Africa: A Legal Perspective*, Ashgate Publishing, Ltd.
- Julie K. Ehrhart, and Bernice Resnick Sandler (1985). *Campus gang rape: party games?, Project on the Status and Education of Women,* Association of American Colleges.
- Julie Nelson, Julie Nelson, illustrated by Mary Gallagher (2006). *Families Change: A Book for Children Experiencing Termination of Parental Rights*, Free Spirit Publishing
- Julie Peters, and Andrea Wolper (1995). *Women's Rights, Human Rights: International Feminist Perspectives,* Psychology Press.
- Karla Fitzhugh (2005). *Prescription Drug Abuse,* Crabtree Publishing Company
- Kate Douglas Smith Wiggin (1892). Children's Rights: A Book of Nursery Logic, Houghton
- Kate Douglas Smith Wiggin, and Nora Archibald Smith (2007). *Children's Rights: A Book of Nursery Logic*, Houghton, Mifflin.
- Kate Walker (2009). *Cordero's Forced Bride,* Harlequin.
- Kathleen Barry (1984). *Female Sexual Slavery*, NYU Press.
- Kathryn Farr (2004). *Sex Trafficking: The Global Market in Women and Children,* Worth Publishers.
- Kaye Stearman (2004). *Child Labor,* Raintree.
- Keith Burgess-Jackson (1999). *A Most Detestable Crime: New Philosophical Essays on Rape,* Oxford University Press.

- Kelly Dawn Askin (1997). *War Crimes Against Women: Prosecution in International War Crimes Tribunals*, Martinus Nijhoff Publishers.
- Kevin Bales and Ron Soodalter (2010). *The Slave Next Door: Human Trafficking and Slavery in America Today, New Preface edition,* University of California Press.
- Kishore Kumar Chhetri (2011), *Child Labour in Bhutan: The Challenges of Implementing Child Rights in Bhutan*, Retrieved from http://munin.uit.no/bitstream/handle/10037/3501/thesis.pdf?sequence=1
- Kristoffel Lieten, and Benjamin White (2001). *Child labour: policy options*, Aksant Academic Publishers.
- Laxmi Devi (1998). *Crime Atrocities and Violence against Women and Related Laws and Justice,* Anmol Publications Pvt. Limited.
- Library Binding (2000). *Child Slavery in Modern Times*, Scholastic Library Publishing.
- Lisa M. Cuklanz (1996). *Rape on Trial: How the Mass Media Construct Legal Reform and Social Change,* University of Pennsylvania Press.
- Louise Shelley (2010). *Human Trafficking: A Global Perspective,* Cambridge University Press.
- Lynn Hunt (1996). *The Invention of pornography: obscenity and the origins of modernity, 1500-1800,* Zone Books.
- Lynn Walter (2001). *Women's Rights: A Global View*. Greenwood Publishing Group.
- Lynne Eisaguirre (1997). *Sexual harassment: a reference handbook*, ABC-CLIO.
- Mamta Rajawat (2004). *Child Labour: The Indian Perspective,* Kilaso Books.
- *Maldives: 2012 Findings on the Worst Forms of Child Labour*, Retrieved from http://www.dol.gov/ilab/reports/child-labor/maldives.htm
- Margaret Moberly (1999). *Fire Bride,* Charisma Media.
- Marian Meyers (1997). *News Coverage of Violence Against Women: Engendering Blame,* SAGE.
- Marietta Holley (2008). *Samantha on Children's Rights,* Kessinger Publishing

- Mark S. Fleisher, and Jessie L. Krienert (2009). T*he Myth of Prison Rape: Sexual Culture in American Prisons*, Rowman & Littlefield Publishers.
- Marlene Webber (1991). *Street Kids: The Tragedy of Canada's Runaways*, University of Toronto Press.
- Martin Guggenheim (2005). *What's Wrong with Children's Rights?*, Harvard University Press.
- Martin Guggenheim (2005).What's Wrong with Children's Rights?,1st edition, Harvard University Press
- Mary Ellen Richmond, and Fred Smith Hall (2007). *Child Marriages*, Russell Sage Foundation.
- Mary L. Boland (2005). *Sexual Harassment in the Workplace*, SphinxLegal.
- Matt Bernstein Sycamore (2000). *Tricks and Treats: Sex Workers Write about Their Clients*, Harrington Park Press.
- Maxwell Taylor, and Ethel Quayle (2003). *Child Pornography: An Internet Crime*, Psychology Press.
- Michael D. A. Freeman, and Michael Freeman (2011). *Children's Rights: Progress and Perspectives: Essays from the International Journal of Children's Rights*, Martinus Nijhoff Publishers.
- Michael D. A. Freeman, and Philip E. Veerman (1992). *The Ideologies of Children's Rights*, Brill Academic Pub.
- Michael Freeman and Michael David Alan Freeman (2006). *Children's Health And Children's Rights, M*artinus Nijhoff Publishers
- Michael Freeman, and Michael David Alan Freeman (2006). *Children's Health And Children's Rights*, Martinus Nijhoff Publishers.
- Michele Antoinette Paludi, Richard B. Barickman, and Richard Barickman (1991). *Academic and Workplace Sexual Harassment: A Resource Manual*, SUNY Press.
- Mohd Umar (2005). *Bride Burning in India: A Socio Legal Study*, APH Publishing.
- Nab Kishore Behura, Ramesh P. Mohanty (2005). *Urbanization, Street Children, and Their Problems*, New Delhi: Discovery Publishing House.
- Nazir Ahmad Shah (1992). *Child Labour in India*, New Delhi: Anmol Publications Pvt. Limited.

- Neera Burra (1997). *Born to work: child labour in India,* Oxford University Press.
- Neera Burra(1994). *Child labour: impact assessment*, Cornell University.
- Nelien Haspels, and Michele Jankanish (2000). *Action Against Child Labour*, International Labour Organisation.
- Orient Blackswan (2005). *Trafficking in Women and Children in India,* Orient Blackswan.
- *Pakistan's labour laws 'ignore abuse of children' (January 10, 2014),* BBC News, Retrieved from http://www.bbc.com/news/world-asia-25678508
- Pamela Paul (2007). Pornified: *How Pornography Is Transforming Our Lives, Our Relationships, and Our Families*, Macmillan.
- Paras Diwan, and Peeyushi Diwan (1997). *Law relating to dowry, dowry deaths, bride burning, rape, and related offences,* Universal Law Pub. Co.
- Parveen Nangia (1987). *Child labour: cause-effect syndrome*, Janak Publishers.
- Patricia Nieuwenhuizen (2006). *Street Children in Bangalore (India): Their Dreams and Their Future,* Het Spinhuis.
- Peggy Reeves Sanday (1992). Fraternity Gang Rape: Sex, Brotherhood, and Privilege on Campus, NYU Press.
- Phil Jones, Sue Welch, and Susan Welch (2010). *Rethinking Children's Rights: Attitudes in Contemporary Society,* Continuum.
- Philip Alston, and Stephen Parker (1992). *Children, Rights, and the Law,* Oxford University Press.
- Philip Alston, Stephen Parker, and John A. Seymour (1992). *Children, Rights, and the Law*, Oxford University Press
- Philip Jenkins (2003). *Beyond Tolerance: Child Pornography on the Interne,* NYU Press.
- Philip Leroy Kilbride, Collette A. Suda, & Enos Hudson Nthia Njeru (2000). *Street Children in Kenya: Voices of Children in Search of a Childhood,* Greenwood Publishing Group.
- Prabhat Chandra Tripathy (1998). *Crime against working women,* New Delhi: APH Publication.
- Prachi Jaiswal (2000). *Child labour: a sociological study*, New Delhi: Shipra Publications.
- Pramila H Bhargava (2003). *The Elimination of Child Labour: Whose Responsibility?,* New Delhi: SAGE Publisher.

- Premacanda, and Danid Rubin (1998). Widows, wives, and other herines: twelve short stories, Oxford University Press.
- Priscilla Alderson (2008). *Young Children's Rights: Exploring Beliefs, Principles and Practice,* Jessica Kingsley Publishers.
- Priscilla Alderson (2008). *Young Children's Rights: Exploring Beliefs, Principles and Practice,* Jessica Kingsley Publishers.
- Professor Julia Sloth-Nielsen (2013). *Children's Rights in Africa: A Legal Perspective,* 1st edition, Ashgate Publishing, Ltd.
- Raghbirlal Bhagatram Sethi (2007). *The Child marriage restraint act, as amended up to date,* Edition: 2, Law Book Co.
- Ram Ahuja (1987). *Crime against Women*, Rawat Publications.
- Ranjana Kumari (1989). *Brides Are Not for Burning: Dowry Victims in India,* Radiant Publisher.
- Rashmi Agrawal (1999). *Street children: a socio-psychological study*, Shipra Publications.
- Raymond Chandler (2002). *The High Window: A Novel*, Knopf Doubleday Publishing Group.
- Rebecca J. Cook (1994). *Human Rights of Women: National and International Perspectives,* University of Pennsylvania Press.
- Richard C.W. Miller (2014), *Work or Starve: Child Labour in Pakistan's Brick Kilns,* Retrieved from http:// www.huffingtonpost. co.uk/richard-cw-miller/child-labour-pakistan_b_4694541.html
- Richard Procida, and Rita James Simon (2007). *Global Perspectives on Social Issues: Pornography,* Lexington Books.
- Richard Wortley, and Stephen Smallbone (2012). *Internet Child Pornography: Causes, Investigation, and Prevention,* ABC-CLIO.
- Robert V. Makaramba (2008). *Children rights in Tanzania*, Friedrich Ebert Stiftung
- Robin Warshaw (1994). *I Never Called It Rape,* Harper Collins.
- Rory C. Reid, and Dan Gray (2006). *Confronting Your Spouse's Pornography Problem*, Silverleaf Press.
- Sambodh Goswami (2007). *Female Infanticide and Child Marriage,* Rawat Publications.
- Samya Burney (1999). *Crime Or Custom?: Violence Against Women in Pakitan,* Human Rights Watch.
- Sandy Hobbs, Jim McKechnie, and Michael Lavalette (1999). *Child Labor:A World History Companion,* ABC-CLIO.

- Selda Altun, Tom Burke, and Jabran Ali (2001). *Stand Up Speak Out: A Book about Children's Rights*, Cooper Square Pub.
- Shane Mountjoy, and Tim McNeese (2009). *The Women's Rights Movement: Moving Toward Equality,* Infobase Publishing.
- Sharon Detrick (1999). *A Commentary on the United Nations Convention on the Rights of the Child,* Martinus Nijhoff Publisher
- Shasta Gaughen (2003). *Women Rights*, Pennsylvania State University: Greenhaven Press.
- Shobha Saxena (1995). *Crimes against Women and Protective Laws,* Deep and Deep Publications.
- Shobhan Bantwal (2007). *The Dowry Bride,* Kensington Books.
- Siddharth Kara (2010). *Sex Trafficking: Inside the Business of Modern Slavery,* Columbia University Press.
- Simon Watney (1987). *Policing Desire: Pornography, AIDS, And the Media*, University of Minnesota Press.
- Simon Watney (1996). *Policing Desire: Pornography, AIDS, and the Media,* U of Minnesota Press.
- Smiljana Simeunovic Frick (2011). *Children's Rights: Experienced and Claimed : Children's Reports to the UN Committee on the Rights of the Child,* LIT Verlag Münster.
- *Sri Lanka: 2012 Findings on the Worst Forms of Child Labour,* Retrieved from http://www.dol.gov/ilab/reports/child-labor/sri_lanka.htm
- Stanley G. French, Wanda Teays, Laura Martha Purdy (1998). *Violence against women: philosophical perspectives,* Cornell University Press.
- Stuart N. Hart (2001). *Children's Rights in Education,* Jessica Kingsley Publishers.
- Stuart N. Hart (2001). *Children's Rights in Education,* Jessica Kingsley Publishers
- Susan Griffin (1981). *Pornography and silence: culture's revenge against nature*, Harper & Row.
- Susanna Paasonen (2011). *Carnal Resonance: Affect and Online Pornography,* MIT Press,
- Sydney Newton, and Julie Gerrits (2010). *Child Abuse,* Crabtree Publishing Company.

- *The Hindu (March 6, 2013),* Sloppy loan waiver edges out deserving farmers: CAG, Retrieved from http://www.thehindu.com/news/national/sloppy-loan-waiver-edges-out-deserving-farmers-cag/article4478433.ece
- Thoko Kaime (2011). *The Convention on the Rights of the Child: A Cultural Legitimacy Critique*, Sussex Academic Press.
- Thoko Kaime (2011). *The Convention on the Rights of the Child: A Cultural Legitimacy Critique*, Sussex Academic Press
- Tobias Hecht (1998). *At Home in the Street: Street Children of Northeast Brazil,* Cambridge University Press.
- *Types of Slavery in Africa,* Retrieved from http://africanhistory.about.com/od/slavery/p/SlaveryTypes.htm
- United Nations Children's Fund (UNICEF) (2005). *Early Marriage: A Harmful Traditional Practice, a Statistical Exploration,* UNICEF.
- Usha Sharma (2006). *Child Labour in India,* New Delhi: Mittal Publications.
- Veena Talwar Oldenburg (2002). *Dowry Murder: The Imperial Origins of a Cultural Crime*, Oxford University Press.
- Walter M. Kendrick (1987). *The Secret Museum: Pornography in Modern Culture,* University of California Press.
- Werner Menski (1998). *South Asians and the Dowry Problem,* Trentham Books.
- William M. Struthers (2009). *Wired for Intimacy: How Pornography Hijacks the Male Brain*, InterVarsity Press.
- William Petrocelli, and Barbara Kate Repa (1998). *Sexual harassment on the job: what it is & how to stop it,* Nolo Press.
- William Pinar (2001). *The Gender of Racial Politics and Violence in America: Lynching, Prison Rape, & the Crisis of Masculinity,* Lang.

Index